Leadership Symposia Series

James G. Hunt and Lars L. Larson, *General Editors*

Previously Published Titles in the Series

Current Developments in the Study of Leadership.
Edited by Edwin A. Fleishman and James G. Hunt. 1973. ISBN: 0-8093-0635-2. $6.95. *Out of print.*

Contingency Approaches to Leadership.
Edited by James G. Hunt and Lars L. Larson. 1974. ISBN: 0-8093-0689-1. $10.00. *Out of print.*

Leadership Frontiers.
Edited by James G. Hunt and Lars L. Larson. 1975. ISBN: 0-8093-9998-9. $12.50.

Leadership: The Cutting Edge.
Edited by James G. Hunt and Lars L. Larson. 1977. ISBN: 0-8093-0840-1. $15.00.

Crosscurrents in Leadership

Edited by
James G. Hunt and
Lars L. Larson

SOUTHERN ILLINOIS UNIVERSITY PRESS
Carbondale and Edwardsville
Feffer & Simons, Inc.
London and Amsterdam

To Donna and Doris

Library of Congress Cataloging in Publication Data

Main entry under title:

Crosscurrents in leadership.

(Leadership symposia series; v. 5)
Papers presented at a symposium held at Southern
Illinois University, Carbondale, Oct. 4–6, 1978.
Bibliography: p.
Includes indexes.
1. Leadership—Congresses.   I. Hunt, James G.
II. Larson, Lars L.   III. Series.
HM141.C76   301.15′53   79-13576
ISBN 0-8093-0932-7

$35, 104$

Contents

Tables

Figures

Preface

This book examines the kaleidoscopic variety of leadership approaches that are characteristic of the field today. It is volume 5 in the Leadership Symposia Series originating in 1971. This series covers the content of biennial symposia held at the Carbondale campus of Southern Illinois University. This volume, which covers the symposium held October 4–6, 1978, joins the earlier ones: *Current Developments in the Study of Leadership* (1973), *Contingency Approaches to Leadership* (1974), *Leadership Frontiers* (1975), and *Leadership: The Cutting Edge* (1977) in charting the state of the field.

These symposia were established to provide in-depth consideration of current and future leadership directions and to provide an interdisciplinary perspective for the scholarly study of leadership. Taken as a whole, they were established to build on one another, show the evolution of the field over time and be at the forefront of new developments.

The format of these symposia has encouraged the achievement of these objectives in a number of ways. First, a mix of work from well-known scholars, widely recognized for many years, and younger scholars, whose work has recently received attention, has been utilized. Second, expert discussants/discussion leaders have prepared commentaries on each of the presentations. Third, audience interchange has been encouraged and cryptic summaries of key issues raised by the audience have been provided. Fourth, an outstanding scholar has provided an overview to put the book contents into perspective. Typically that perspective has ranged far afield from the content of the chapters themselves. Finally, in more recent volumes, the editors have provided a considerable amount of additional commentary to help balance the content of the volumes in terms of current thrusts. Present in all of these have been the many controversies that accompany a rapidly changing field. The symposia have attempted to highlight these as well as points of agreement.

To further encourage scholarship in the leadership area, the Ralph M. Stogdill Distinguished Scholarship Award was established in 1976. That award is given to a leadership scholar "in recognition of his/her outstanding contribution to the advancement of leadership research and for devotion to the development of a new generation of leadership scholars." Thus, the award is intended not only for the scholarly contribution of the person himself but, equally important, for the contribution to the development of other scholars. The first award was presented to Stogdill himself and the award at this symposium was presented to Fred E. Fiedler.

This fifth symposium was sponsored by the Southern Illinois University at Carbondale Department of Administrative Sciences and the College of Business and Administration. We thank Robert Bussom, former chairman; John Sutherland, current chairman; and John Darling, the dean, for the continuing sponsorship of their units and for their encouragement and support.

Planning and arrangements for this undertaking were extensive and involved a number of people. First, there was a symposium executive committee from within the department for planning and decision making. In addition to the editors, that committee consisted of Thomas N. Martin, Richard N. Osborn, Uma Sekaran and William M. Vicars.

Second, to host the symposium and implement travel and lodging arrangements, the M.B.A. Association and especially David Davis and Larry Buchamon, M.B.A. graduate assistants, provided invaluable help.

Third, the departmental secretaries, Sharon Pinkerton and Kimberly Stover, ably assisted by a number of student workers, handled a host of symposium-related duties too numerous to mention.

Finally, the leadership symposium advisory board assisted in advice and planning and helped with paper reviewing. Members of the board are:

CHRIS ARGYRIS
Harvard University

BERNARD BASS
State University of New York-Binghamton

DAVID BOWERS
University of Michigan

ELMER BURACK
University of Illinois-Chicago Circle

JOHN CAMPBELL
University of Minnesota

MARTIN CHEMERS
University of Utah

JOHN CHILD
University of Aston

LARRY CUMMINGS
University of Wisconsin-Madison

MARTIN EVANS
University of Toronto

GEORGE FARRIS
York University

FRED FIEDLER
University of Washington

EDWIN FLEISHMAN
Advanced Research Resources Organization

WILLIAM FOX
University of Florida

GEORGE GRAEN
University of Cincinnati

CHARLES GREENE
Indiana University

EDWIN HOLLANDER
State University of New York-Buffalo

ROBERT HOUSE
University of Toronto

T. OWEN JACOBS
Army Research Institute

STEVEN KERR
University of Southern California

ABRAHAM KORMAN
City University of New York

CHARLES LEVINE
University of Maryland

RENSIS LIKERT
Rensis Likert Associates

JAMES PRICE
University of Iowa

MARSHALL SASHKIN
University Associates

CHESTER SCHRIESHEIM
University of Southern California

HENRY SIMS, JR.
The Pennsylvania State University

JOHN SLOCUM, JR.
The Pennsylvania State University

JOHN STINSON
Ohio University

PETER WEISSENBERG
State University of New York-Binghamton

The paper review process was also aided by a number of *ad hoc* reviewers. Those who provided such assistance were:

PATRICK CONNOR
Oregon State University

PAUL DUFFY
Army Research Institute

HOWARD FROMKIN
York University

ROBERT LORD
University of Akron

RICHARD MOWDAY
University of Oregon

SAMUEL SHIFLETT
New York University

ANDREW SZILAGYI
University of Houston

The above individuals have been most helpful in providing an all-important outside perspective to supplement the inside one of the executive committee.

This symposium could not have been provided without the planning and moral support of those above. Neither could it have been conducted without financial support. The bulk of such support came from the United States Army Research Institute for the Behavioral and Social Sciences.

This was supplemented by external support from the Smithsonian Institution and the Office of Naval Research, and internal support from the department and college.

Finally, once again, our wives Donna and Doris and children, Holly Hunt and Gregory and Wendy Larson, assisted with proofreading and various other manuscript preparation details. To them and to all who helped, we express our heartiest thanks!

Carbondale, Illinois   J. G. HUNT
April 1979   L. L. LARSON

Notes on Contributors

Chris Argyris is James Bryant Conant Professor of Education and Organizational Behavior, Harvard University, Cambridge, Massachusetts.

Elmer H. Burack is Professor of Management, University of Illinois at Chicago Circle.

David Campbell is Vice-President, Center for Creative Leadership, Greensboro, North Carolina.

John Child is Professor of Organizational Behavior and Head of Organizational Sociology and Psychology Group, University of Aston, Birmingham, England.

Stephen H. Cooley is a doctoral candidate in psychology, University of Illinois at Chicago Circle.

Robert Dubin is Professor of Administration, University of California at Irvine.

Fred E. Fiedler is Professor of Psychology and of Management and Organization and Director of the Organizational Research Group, University of Washington, Seattle.

Howard Garland is Associate Professor of Management and Organizational Behavior and of Psychology, The University of Texas at Arlington.

L. Richard Hoffman is Professor of Psychology in the Graduate School of Business and Professor in the Department of Behavioral Sciences, University of Chicago.

Edwin P. Hollander is Professor of Psychology, State University of New York at Buffalo.

Dian-Marie Hosking is Lecturer, Organizational Sociology and Psychology Group, University of Aston, Birmingham, England.

James G. (Jerry) Hunt is Professor of Administrative Sciences, Southern Illinois University at Carbondale.

Steven Kerr is Professor of Management, University of Southern California, Los Angeles.

Lars L. Larson is Associate Professor of Administrative Sciences, Southern Illinois University at Carbondale.

Robert G. Lord is Assistant Professor of Industrial/Organizational Psychology, University of Akron.

Fred Luthans is Regents Professor of Management, University of Nebraska-Lincoln.

Joseph L. Moses is Personnel Manager-Research, American Telephone and Telegraph Company, New York.

Richard T. Mowday is Assistant Professor of Management, University of Oregon, Eugene.

Wayne F. Nemeroff is Assistant Professor of Management, State University of New York at Albany.

Paul J. Patinka is Manager of Human Resources, Motorola, Inc., Chicago.

Richard W. Pearse is a doctoral student in behavioral sciences, University of Chicago.

Marshall Sashkin is Senior Editorial Associate, University Associates, La Jolla, California.

Chester A. Schriesheim is Assistant Professor of Management, University of Southern California, Los Angeles.

Henry P. Sims, Jr., is Associate Professor of Organizational Behavior, The Pennsylvania State University, University Park.

Blanchard B. Smith is Senior Research Associate, Kepner-Tregoe, Inc.

R. Timothy Stein is Assistant Professor of Psychology, University of Illinois at Chicago Circle.

Ralph M. Stogdill is late Professor Emeritus of Management Sciences and Psychology, The Ohio State University, Columbus.

Karl E. Weick is Nicholas H. Noyes Professor of Organizational Behavior and Professor of Psychology, Cornell University, Ithaca, New York.

Gary A. Yukl is Professor of Management, State University of New York at Albany.

Crosscurrents in Leadership

1

Crosscurrents in Leadership: An Introduction

JAMES G. HUNT AND LARS L. LARSON

To us, the conflicting tendencies implied in the meaning of the word *cross-currents* serves to highlight the state of the leadership field as it lies poised between the concerns of earlier volumes and those yet to come. Let's elaborate.

The two most recent volumes in this series, *Leadership Frontiers* and *Leadership: The Cutting Edge* tended to leave those interested in leadership in a depressed state. Much was written about the fact that current studies did not build upon past studies, that sound research instruments were not available, and that even our most advanced models were flawed. It was suggested by some that the leadership concept be abandoned while others took leadership researchers to task for being fair-weather friends who, in tough times, left practitioners to cope for themselves with day-to-day leadership problems.

This volume appears to be different. The problems raised in past volumes are still there waiting to be solved but there seems to be more of a willingness to tackle these problems that was not apparent in the past. Perhaps the beginning stages of a renewal are developing. Several major crosscurrents evident in the leadership field are reflected in this book. Most of these crosscurrents are not new. A cursory review of the field reveals that they have been in existence for some time. What is new is that now these conflicting tendencies seem to be particularly relevant and we appear to be at the point where they need to be resolved if the field is to continue to develop in a meaningful way.

Daniel Levinson's (1978) theory of adult development presented in *The Seasons of a Man's Life* provides an interesting, and we think helpful, analogy to the growth and development of the leadership field. Levinson suggests a theory of developmental periods that one's life structure evolves through in an alternating sequence. The sequence consists of two periods:

> A relatively stable structure building period . . . followed by a transitional, structure changing period. The major developmental tasks of a structure building period are to make crucial choices, to create a structure around them, to enrich the structure and pursue one's goals within it. . . . In a transitional period the major tasks are to reappraise the existing structure, explore new possibilities . . . and work toward choices that provide a basis for a new structure. [P. 317]

Levinson suggests that one of the major tasks of a transitional period is the reintegration of basic polarities in a man's life into a form appropriate for the next structure building period. These polarities are present throughout adult life but become particularly acute at certain stages of adult development. If these polarities are not successfully integrated the next developmental stage will be flawed.

We would like to suggest that the leadership field is in a stage similar to one of Levinson's transitional periods. For several years we have been reappraising the past and attempting to work toward a new structure. During this transitional period researchers in the field must reintegrate several polarities, which we label crosscurrents, if the field is to build a structure for the next stage of development. We feel that a failure to confront these crosscurrents will result in continued stagnation and will block any meaningful advance of the leadership field.

To help focus the crosscurrents revealed in the chapters of this volume, it is divided into five parts. The first of these centers on the Stogdill Award contribution by Fred E. Fiedler. The next three parts, each consisting of several chapters, comprise the heart of the crosscurrents emphasis. That heart is built around three pertinent questions for the leadership researcher: What is the purpose of a particular research study? What is to be studied? How is it to be studied? The last part consists of an overview and an epilog which together are designed to help move the field toward a new stage of development.

We will discuss in this chapter each of these questions and the crosscurrents which emerge in the chapters. That discussion is supplemented with more specific commentary preceding each of the parts. Included at the beginning of each part are editorial comments based on our own insights reinforced by concerns expressed by those at the symposium. These are in addition to concluding commentary chapters which contain discussants' reactions to the contributions for which each has been asked to react.

As will soon be evident, our emphasis on these questions and crosscurrents broadens the focus of this volume as compared with previous ones in the series. Those concentrated almost exclusively on issues of concern to academicians. This volume, on the other hand, focuses not only on these kinds of concerns but looks at issues of concern to the practitioner as well. Let's now consider each of the three leadership research questions and the crosscurrents we see emanating from them.

What Is the Purpose of Research?

Two crosscurrents, Action/Discovery and Practitioner/Researcher, emerge around the purpose of research question. The Action/Discovery crosscurrent appears throughout the volume but is highlighted in part 2. The basic question to be resolved in the Action/Discovery crosscurrent is what is the purpose of the research we conduct? J. P. Campbell in his overview chapter in *Leadership: The Cutting Edge* raised the question of why do we study leadership, which Sashkin and Garland pick up on in this volume. Campbell noted that most research ignores the question of the purpose for which leadership concepts are to be used. Karmel (1978) also reiterates this point.

The theme for the Action/Discovery crosscurrent is set in chapter 3, "Leadership Findings and Applications: The Viewpoints of Four from the Real World," where it takes the form of a Practitioner/Researcher crosscurrent. The practitioner focuses on two major purposes—selection of individuals with leadership potential, and leadership problem solving and skill training. It is clear that for the practitioners the purpose of research is to develop and refine the selection and training process. We did not poll the academicians present on the purpose of their research and we hesitate to speculate on what the results would show but our guess is that there would not be the clarity of purpose that is evident in the concerns of the practitioners.

Argyris in the General Discussion (chapter 6) expands on the purpose of research question and provides a label for the Action/Discovery crosscurrent when he suggests the following sequence for problem solving. Discovery, invention, production (action) and evaluation. He suggests that the majority of research on leadership is for the purpose of discovery while the practitioner is concerned with production or application. The concept of production or application has most recently taken the rubric "action research" which connotes research for the purpose of bringing about a change in the situation being studied.

Argyris's contribution (chapter 4) "How Normal Science Methodology Makes Leadership Research Less Additive and Less Applicable" uses his familiar Model I and Model II concept in an attempt to show that the reasons researchers have not been more successful in advancing the field is that the "normal science" approach does not allow one to get at the "theories-in-use" of leaders. Instead, researchers obtain information on "espoused theory." He suggests that we need to study the behaviors that result from an individual's "theory-in-use" if we are to advance our understanding and we need to develop ways of helping individuals discover and change their "theories-in-use" from Model I to Model II if we are to make any further contribution to the field of leadership.

In chapter 6 Karl Weick suggests that the issue of application (action) does not have to mean organizational development and change. He suggests some new ways of looking at the issue. These new ways range from complicating the individual to match a complicated environment to concentrating on leadership activities that have ill-defined forms. He concludes: "The best we can do right now is to try to counteract our natural tendency to overvalue that which we can count and to undervalue that which we cannot."

Sashkin and Garland in chapter 5 suggest a possible solution to the Action/Discovery crosscurrent when they present a research and diffusion model. They argue that a linking agent who spans the gap between research and practice or "between science and life" provides for a possible reintegration of the Action/Discovery crosscurrent.

The issue of research for the purpose of discovery versus research for the purpose of application in "real world" settings has been kicked around for some time. However, at this juncture in the development of the leadership field it needs to be resolved to allow for the next structure building developmental period to be successful. The heart of the Action/Discovery crosscurrent is the answer each researcher gives to the question: Why am I doing this study? If we wear our cynical hat we suspect the answer is: to get another publication and the rewards that publication brings. If we wear our altruistic hat the answer is, as Sashkin and Garland in this volume suggest: "to help organizations function more effectively and at the same time result in more 'humane' organizations." If the latter answer is really our goal we, as researchers, need to work seriously to resolve the Action/Discovery crosscurrent.

What Should Be Studied?

A second group of crosscurrents emerges around the question of what should be studied. Three crosscurrents Leader/Manager, Leader/Non-Leader, and Leader/Group deserve comment.

The Leader/Manager and the Leader/Non-Leader crosscurrents are highlighted in chapter 3. The practitioners make little effort to separate management activities from leadership activities in their discussion of the real-world problems of organizations. Dubin, in his overview chapter picks up on this crosscurrent and suggests that there is an important distinction between management and leadership. He feels that this distinction should be articulated by researchers. Others do not seem to be concerned with such a distinction between the two terms and tend to use them interchangeably. The reader should pause a moment to consider this crosscurrent as his view of the following chapters will be influenced by his resolution of the Leader/Manager question.

The Leader/Non-Leader crosscurrent is, perhaps, the more important of the two and is elaborated by Joseph Moses in chapter 3. Moses points out that out of the thousands of individuals tested in A.T.&T. assessment centers only 25 percent score at the high end of the scale on leadership skills and abilities. He suggests that if researchers want to advance the field they must be careful to study the 25 percent who are leaders and not assume that all individuals in leadership positions are effective leaders.

Stein, Hoffman, Cooley, and Pearse present, in chapter 8, a model of emergent leadership and describe a method for determining the stages of the emergence process. Their model and Lord's excellent critique (chapter 9) provide one possibility of resolving the Leader/Non-Leader crosscurrent by focusing attention on the "leaders" in a problem solving situation.

Schriesheim, Mowday, and Stogdill present a model in chapter 7 that brings focus to the third crosscurrent—Leader/Group. Their model, in an early stage, attempts to highlight the important interactions between the leader and the group. This model brings together in one place the somewhat divergent literatures that tend to focus only on the group (cohesiveness, process, task-goal accomplishment) or only on the leader.

Finally Dubin in his overview (chapter 13) underscores the Leader/ Manager, Leader/Non-Leader, and Leader/Group crosscurrents when he points out that leadership is typically used as a synonym for management and supervision, that leadership is a rare phenomenon in organizations (most of what we observe are acts of managing and supervising), and—of secondary importance to researchers—leadership in informal, natural, and temporary groups. In addressing the basic question of what should be studied Dubin points out that the majority of leadership research has been focused on face to face relationships between leader and follower but in the "real world" the most frequent leadership situations do not involve face to face relationships with followers. He goes on to stress the study of "leadership of organizations" and suggests a number of leadership metaphors worthy of study. Dubin suggests some different directions for research in the leadership field. They are not all new directions, but they do provide interesting alternatives to be considered as we work toward choices that will hopefully provide the basis for a new structure in the next stage of development.

How Should It Be Studied?

This third question and the crosscurrents that develop around it are perhaps the most difficult to resolve. They are the most difficult to resolve because, we suspect, they occur in an area where researchers' values are most strongly held. Dubin in his book on theory building (1978) says "The behavioral scientist tends to accumulate belief systems and call this the *theory* of his field" (p. 229). These belief systems apparently include the method of research that is best! Three crosscurrents emerge around the issue of how to study leadership. They are Lab/Field, Questionnaire/Observation, and Model/Empirical.

The Lab/Field crosscurrent is most evident in chapter 5 where Sashkin and Garland in their research and diffusion model argue for the use of both laboratory and field methods of research in a preferred sequence of laboratory research first and field research second. Hollander (chapter 6) and others argue that the sequence is not important nor necessary for diffusion to result.

The Yukl and Nemeroff (chapter 10), Luthans (chapter 11), and Sims (chapter 12) all highlight the Questionnaire/Observation crosscurrent. The Yukl and Nemeroff work is an excellent example of the effort required to develop and test a questionnaire to measure leadership behavior. This is followed by Luthans's argument for more emphasis on observing the behaviors of leaders and subordinates with the conclusion that observing is necessary now if advancements in our understanding of leadership are to be made. Sims follows with the more moderate view that both questionnaires and observation are needed and both can contribute to our understanding of leadership. This perhaps represents the appropriate resolution of the Questionnaire/Observation crosscurrent but as the introductory comments for part 4 indicate we all have our beliefs about appropriate research methods and while we may, to be polite, say that both methods are appropriate we tend to be deeply committed to our own preferred method, and resolution of this crosscurrent will be difficult.

The Model/Empirical crosscurrent is perhaps the most subtle of the three crosscurrents that surface about the issue of research methods. Perhaps it does not totally fit under the heading of how to study leadership since in theory research is the act of theory testing. However, the issue is one of integrating the division of labor that seems to occur between those who attempt to build theoretical models and those who attempt to test hypotheses that grow out of these models. Perhaps Dubin's (1978) distinction between descriptive research (doing research to build a theory) and hypothesis testing (using research to test a theory) is the more appropriate division. What emerges in this volume is the fact that the field is populated with researchers who have a preference for hypothesis testing. (We also lamented the lack of theoretical work in the 1977 volume.)

The model presented by Schriesheim, Mowday and Stogdill in chapter 7 and the critique of this model by Child and Hosking (chapter 9) brings to light many of the problems of model building in a world of hypothesis testers.

We are less optimistic about resolving the crosscurrents that relate to the question of how leadership should be studied. However, we feel that these polarities must be integrated to allow for continued advancement of the field. Perhaps the best we can offer now is the suggestion that researchers read or reread Marvin Dunnette's 1965 address to the American Psychological Association convention "Fads, Fashions, and Folderol in Psychology" (see Dubin, 1978).

In his address Dunnette suggests in a humorous yet insightful way the games researchers play that limit the advancement of their field rather than advance it. For example, under the title of "The Pets We Keep" he suggests we can become committed to one great theory or one specific method and our major effort becomes one of distorting research problems to fit our favorite theory or method. Dunnette suggested that in 1965 our method pets were "factor analysis, complex analysis of variance designs, the concept of statistical significance, and multiple regression analysis" (p. 269). Another game in Dunnette's list is the "Names We Love." This is the game of coining new words and labels to fit old concepts. (Is Quality of Work Life really job enrichment?) Dunnette concludes his list of games with some remedies that are as relevant today as they were in 1965. They range from giving up constraining commitments to theories and methods to pressing for new values and less pretense in academic environments.

We have suggested that the current state of the leadership field is in a period similar to what Levinson, in his theory of adult development, calls a transitional stage. A transitional stage is a time for reevaluation of the past structure building period and a time for integrating polarities important for the next structure building period. We have identified several polarities or crosscurrents that emerge from the chapters in this volume. We are somewhat optimistic that these crosscurrents can be resolved (we are more optimistic about some, less optimistic about others) in the next few years, and in the final chapter we point to some work currently under way that may help to accomplish a workable integration of crosscurrents such as these.

Before closing this introduction a further word is in order concerning the organization of the book. The previous discussion has emphasized the crosscurrents that appear relevant to the field of leadership at the present time. Traces of the crosscurrents we have identified are found in chapters throughout this volume. In order to provide as much focus as possible, the book has been divided into parts. Parts 2, 3, and 4 have been set up to group together chapters which highlight crosscurrents under the major issues: what is the purpose, what should be studied, and how should it be studied.

As we have shown earlier, some chapters highlight only one crosscurrent while other chapters may stress two or more. For example, Sashkin and Garland, (chapter 5) concentrate on both the Action/Discovery crosscurrent, which focuses on the purpose of research question, and the Lab/Field crosscurrent, which focuses on the how should it be studied question. This chapter could be placed in part 2, the purpose of research, or it could be placed in part 4, how should it be studied. Because Sashkin and Garland stress the linking of research and application, we chose to include their chapter in part 2.

Several other chapters presented us with similar choices. Given the breadth of issues raised in the chapters in this volume we tried to group the chapters into the part that best represented the authors' major focus. We believe that part 2 focuses primarily on the Action/Discovery and Practitioner/Researcher crosscurrents. Part 3 concentrates on what should be studied and part 4 on the how it should be studied question. Chapters in parts 3 and 4 highlight both of these questions and cover the Leader/Manager, Leader/Non-Leader, Leader/Group, Lab/Field, Questionnaire/Observation, and Model/Empirical crosscurrents.

This grouping, though imperfect, serves an important integrative purpose. In conjunction with the introduction to each part, it also helps to highlight the content of the various chapters while keeping with the crosscurrents theme.

Part 1

The Ralph M. Stogdill Distinguished Scholarship Award Presentation

Introduction

JAMES G. HUNT AND LARS L. LARSON

The chapter contained in this part is by Fred E. Fiedler and is entitled, "Organizational Determinants of Managerial Incompetence." Fiedler prepared the chapter in response to his receipt of the Stogdill Award and it reflects his latest thinking on leadership. In it Fiedler reports empirical data from a number of his studies suggesting that leader experience and intelligence have differential effects on unit performance depending upon the amount of interpersonal stress felt by the leader. The chapter is of interest for a number of reasons.

First, it uses no measure of either leadership style or behavior. Rather it uses traits (experience, intelligence) within a contingency framework (interpersonal stress). This is a sharp break with Fiedler's previous work which has almost invariably used the Least Preferred Co-worker (LPC) score—a leadership style measure. It suggests a metamorphosis of the trait approach which has received relatively little attention in the leadership literature since Stogdill's (1948) article virtually rang its death knell. As we show in our epilog, the trait approach is once more beginning to receive attention from other leadership researchers as well.

Second, this approach essentially takes a role perspective concerning leadership. That is, it treats leadership not simply in terms of an interpersonal influence measure on the part of the leader but rather as a part of the leader's total role as a manager. Thus, it looks at a subset of traits that influence a manager's role, given specified contingencies. In this, the thrust is consistent with the work of those who argue that a role emphasis is the appropriate one to take in the study of leadership (e.g., McCall & Lombardo, 1978a). Such an emphasis allows for a wider range of characteristics to be considered. A question may be raised, though, as to whether such a perspective really separates leadership from managerial behavior. As we shall see, this question permeates much of this book.

Third, if this emphasis becomes a major trend, it would appear to address the Practitioner/Academician crosscurrent. Leader characteristics such as these might well be easier to get a handle on and work with in real world organizations than such slippery things as perceptions of leader behavior and the like.

2

Organizational Determinants of Managerial Incompetence

FRED E. FIEDLER

As every student of industrial and organizational psychology knows, Stog-dill's (1948) review of the leadership trait literature showed a very low relationship between leader intelligence and leadership performance. Like-wise, there is no consistent relationship between leader experience and performance. The problem which these findings raise is as important as it is puzzling.

These results run exactly counter to the strongly held layman's belief that intelligent and experienced managers will perform better: Recruiters and organizations generally prefer intelligent and experienced managers to dull and inexperienced managers. And yet, the empirical research consistently shows median correlations between leadership performance and leader intelligence no higher than .20 to .30 (Ghiselli, 1966; Mann, 1959; Stogdill, 1948, 1974). This is most curious if we consider that the manager's job involves such activities as planning, evaluating, judging, coordinating, analyzing complex information, and making critical decisions (see Campbell, Dunnette, Lawler, & Weick, 1970, pp. 71–100). Many of these and similar functions are typically measured by intelligence tests (Butcher, 1968). It seems, therefore, highly unlikely that intelligence, which is basically the ability to solve problems, can be irrelevant to the effective management of organizations.

There is also no empirical evidence that leadership experience neces-sarily contributes to managerial performance. Such notable leaders as Joan of Arc, Alexander the Great, William Pitt, Charles Percy, and Robert Maynard Hutchins were highly effective, even though they were relatively young and inexperienced. And everyone knows of some managers who perform poorly despite their many years on the job. One review of 13 studies reported a median correlation between years of experience and task performance of $-.12$ (Fiedler, 1970), and the research discussed in this chapter provides further evidence that the relationship is low. Again, we must then wonder why previous encounters with management problems appear to be irrelevant or useless.

One possible answer is suggested by the many contingent relationships in the leadership literature. These lead us to expect that managers may well be able to use their intelligence and experience only under some conditions, while these abilities and knowledge may be unimportant or detrimental under others. In particular, our research suggests that the organization determines to a considerable extent whether an individual in a managerial position will appear stupid and incompetent, or brilliant and effective. The crucial variable, as we shall see, appears to be the stress in the interpersonal relationships between the leader and others and, most particularly, the stress with the leader's immediate superior.

Background

I became interested in this problem in 1959 when we conducted a laboratory experiment on group creativity (Fiedler, Meuwese, & Oonk, 1961). Four-man teams of college students were given the task of inventing fables from Thematic Apperception Test pictures. A version of the Miller Analogies Test measured intelligence, and the group's performance was evaluated by four independent judges who agreed quite highly in their ratings. We found that neither the leaders' nor the group members' intelligence scores correlated with group performance.

We subsequently analyzed data from studies of three other groups in which we had obtained leader intelligence scores. The criteria for each of these were as follows: a) for air force bomber crews, the circular bombing error scores, b) for tank crews, the "time in seconds to hit the target," and c) for army antiaircraft artillery crews, the "acquisition and lock-on of target" (Fiedler & Meuwese, 1963). Each of these team performance measures was an objective, "hard" criterion score.

Again, we found no correlation between leader intelligence and group performance. We did, however, consider the possibility that the leader's intelligence could have an impact on team performance only if the group members accepted and "listened" to the leader.

To test the above hypothesis, each set of groups was divided into those which sociometrically accepted their leaders' authority or showed evidence of cohesiveness, and those which did not. For those teams accepting them, leaders' intelligence and team performance correlated positively, that is, .26, .67, .57, and .54, for bomber, tank, and antiaircraft units, and the creativity groups, respectively. For the teams which did *not* accept their leaders, the correlations were $-.21$, $-.40$, $-.05$, and $.24$, respectively. As a group, the former correlations are significantly higher than are the latter.

Leaving aside the problems caused by small samples and different measures of leader acceptance, these findings posed a very important question. While it was easy enough to conclude that only the accepted leaders were able to utilize their intelligence, it was difficult to understand why three of the four correlations for the "nonaccepting" groups should have been in the *negative* direction. Barring a chance finding, this suggested two possibilities: One hypothesis was that the not-accepted leaders gave ideas a "kiss of death," and, since the brighter leaders were likely to make better proposals, they might have caused their groups to react by rejecting these better ideas. Another possibility was that the not-accepted leaders were made anxious and insecure because of their ambiguous status in the group, and their anxiety caused them to misuse their intellectual resources.

We tested these two alternative hypotheses in a laboratory experiment (Meuwese & Fiedler, 1967), in which three-man ROTC teams were required to work on two creative tasks. These were to write a new pay proposal for remunerating army and navy ROTC students, and to invent a fable to illustrate the need for a standing army in peacetime. The 54 teams were randomly assigned to three conditions so that 18 worked under low stress in which the procedure was made as relaxed as possible, and 18 under an internal stress condition which induced conflict between two army cadets and one navy ROTC cadet. The third set of 18 groups worked in an external stress condition in which three army cadets performed their tasks while a senior army officer, whom they did not know, rated their behavior and performance throughout the session. The groups' performance was evaluated by three independent judges.

A comparison of teams in which members sociometrically did accept and those which did not accept their leaders yielded no significant differences in correlations between leader intelligence and team performance. This suggested that the group's acceptance and presumed willingness to listen to the leader was not especially important in allowing the leader to use his intelligence. However, the mean correlation between leader intelligence and team performance was higher in the low stress condition than in the internal or external stress conditions, that is, $.41$, $.24$, $.13$, respectively. This suggested that the leader's anxiety might be the critical variable.

Since anxiety test scores had been obtained from all cadets two weeks before the groups were assembled, we divided the teams into six subgroups on the basis of the leaders' pretest anxiety scores. We then obtained correlations between intelligence and performance for each of the subgroups on the pay proposal and the fable task. These are shown on Figure 1. The

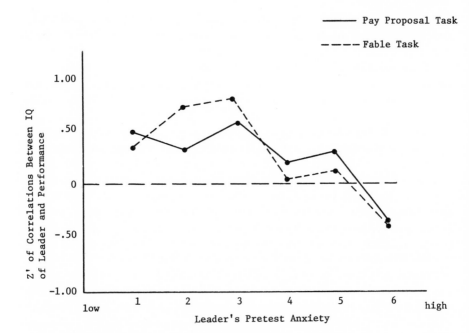

Fig. 1. Correlations between leader intelligence and group performance on the Pay Proposal and Fable tasks under leaders with different pretest anxiety

correlations between the coefficients and the preanxiety test scores were $-.77$ and $-.72$ (N's = 6, p = .10 for the pay proposal). Thus, the higher the leaders' anxiety scores, the lower were the correlations between leader intelligence and team performance. These findings suggested, then, that the leaders' anxiety interfered with the use of their intelligence and under high anxiety conditions caused a misuse of intelligence, while "acceptance" of the leader was of lesser importance. After letting this problem lie dormant for about 10 years, we began to worry about it once more. This led to a series of three studies, which are discussed here.

Infantry Squad Leaders

The first study in the series (Fiedler & Leister, 1977) dealt with 158 leaders of infantry squads. These eight to eleven-man teams constitute the army's basic fighting units. The leader of the typical squad is a staff sergeant (E-6) who supervises the men in the performance of their garrison duties and military combat training exercises. Most squad leaders are career soldiers who have been in the army from four to six years. They participated in a large longitudinal study (Bons & Fiedler, 1976) in which extensive questionnaire data were obtained from members of an entire infantry division.

The intelligence score of these men was based on the Army General Test (sample $\bar{X}=105$, SD $=14.56$), which is administered to all enlisted men at the time of their induction into service. The years in service served as the measure of their experience ($\bar{X}=5.6$, SD $=4.28$). The squad leader also made various ratings of subordinates, superiors, and their values and preferences. Relations with superiors were described by completing a ten-item semantic differential using such adjectives as pleasant-unpleasant, cooperative-uncooperative. The sum of these items was taken as an index of the squad leaders' relationship with the boss. One additional scale item ("stressful-nonstressful") measured the stressfulness of the relationship ("stress with boss"). Similar scores were obtained from leaders describing their relationships with subordinates and from subordinates describing their relationships with leaders (see Fiedler & Leister, 1977).

The performance of squad leaders was rated by two superiors, the platoon leader and the platoon sergeant, using an eight-item scale developed by Bons (1974). This asked the superior to indicate the degree to which the subordinate "is technically proficient," "performs well under pressure," "takes initiative to propose and carry out innovations relating to the job," etc. Inter-rater agreement as well as internal consistency of this scale were quite satisfactory (.65 and .92, respectively).

Intercorrelations among the relevant variables were low and accounted for less than 5 percent of the variance. In particular, the correlations between task performance and leader intelligence, leader experience, and stress with boss did not exceed .10, and in only one instance did the variable, stress with boss, correlate significantly with another main variable, namely, intelligence ($-.18$). The low magnitude of these correlations justified the use of stress with boss as a moderator.

The study was designed to test the hypothesis that certain variables in effect acted as a screen which prevented the leader's intelligence from affecting the way in which the job was to be accomplished. The sample of squad leaders was, therefore, divided as nearly as possible at the median of each of the screen variable scores, that is, above and below the median on leader experience, stress with boss, leader-boss relations, leader-group relations as perceived by the leader, and leader-group relations as perceived by the group. The leader's intelligence score was then correlated with performance for groups falling above and below the median of the screen variables.

The leader's stress with boss turned out to be the most important moderator, as was also borne out by additional analyses, and will be the primary concern in this chapter. For groups in which the leader reported low stress with boss, the correlation between leader intelligence and task performance was .40 (n = 72, p < .01), while the corresponding correlation for leaders reporting high stress with their boss was significantly lower (.07, N = 56). However, the average performance of these two subgroups was nearly identical (282 and 286, respectively).

That a stressful relationship with the boss should be extremely important to a leader is, in retrospect, not too surprising. The immediate superior is clearly one of the most important persons in one's working life. He or she not only assigns the task, but also assesses how well it has been performed. Without the superior's endorsement, promotion or transfer to a more desirable job is almost never possible, and a supervisor who is displeased or ill disposed toward a subordinate can make life unbearable. A stressful relationship with the immediate superior is, therefore, likely to be the cause for considerable anxiety.

To pursue this problem one step further, we analyzed the extreme groups, that is, leaders whose stress with boss score fell one or more standard deviations below or above the mean, and we considered the effect which stress with boss would have on the utilization of leader experience. The results of this analysis are shown in Table 1. As can be seen, the very low stress condition further increased the relationship between leader intelligence and performance. Interestingly enough, however, under very high stress with boss, the leader's experience also correlated significantly with performance. It appears, therefore, that the leader, who is rattled and disorganized by the stressful relationship with his boss may, in effect, fall back on previously learned behavior patterns. And while his ability to solve problems or to think creatively has been impaired, the highly stressed squad leader may compensate by using what he has learned in the past.

These findings raised several questions. First, how generalizable were these results, and were they specific to individuals who occupy leadership positions? Will they also apply to staff positions which do not require the supervision and direction of others? Second, will we find results of this nature at higher levels of the organization where leadership positions presumably make greater intellectual demands than are required of army squad leaders?

The Coast Guard Staff

A second study investigated how stress with the immediate superior affects the utilization of intelligence and experience by responsible staff

TABLE 1

Correlations between Leader Intelligence and Leader Experience
and Task Performance Ratings by Superiors

Leader's Stress with Superior	Leader Intelligence	Leader Experience	Performance Mean
Very Low[a]	.51**	.09	306
Very High[b]	−.01	.40*	308

[a]N = 28	*p < .05
[b]N = 27	**p < .01

personnel who provide ancillary and support functions for the line executive. We investigated a sample of 130 officers, petty officers, and civilian employees of a regional United States Coast Guard Headquarters (Potter & Fiedler, 1978). Subjects ranged from the chief of staff, chief marine engineer, chief of personnel, and so forth, who held the rank of captain, to petty officers who served as marine inspectors or assistants in staff sections.

Intelligence was measured by the Wonderlic Personnel Test (1977), a 50-item, 12-minute scale, which has been widely used in business and industry. Experience was measured by months in service. The performance rating was identical to that used in the squad leader study and was filled out by two or three of the staff officer's superiors. Subjects also described their job and the estimated percentage of time they devoted to each of 10 common task functions (routine administrative work, advising on policy matters, decision making, communicating with the public, etc.).

The stress-with-boss score was based mainly on items from the Leader Behavior Description Questionnaire—Form XII (Stogdill, 1963a). The staff member marked on a seven-point scale how much anxiety and tension he felt on the job as a result of the supervisor's behaving in a certain manner. These items (e.g., "He does not notify me of changes," "He does not give me enough authority to accomplish what is expected of me") yielded one major factor, which described a leader who placed the staff officer under considerable pressure to produce, while at the same time withholding needed guidance and support. The factor was, therefore, called "Double-Bind Stress" and constituted the stress-with-boss measure in this study. Intercorrelations among all relevant variables were low. The highest correlation, and the only one to reach statistical significance, was .18 (N=130) between experience and rated task performance.

The effect of stress with boss was first tested by correlating the staff officers' intelligence with their performance under conditions of high stress and under conditions of low stress with boss. These correlations were

TABLE 2

Correlations between Staff Member Intelligence and Experience with Task Performance under High and Low Double-Bind Stress

	Stress							
	High				Low			
	Intellectual Demands				Intellectual Demands			
	High	(N)	Low	(N)	High	(N)	Low	(N)
Intelligence								
Nature of Job:								
Decision Making	−.47*	(13)	−.14	(32)	.10	(19)	.24	(29)
Policy Advising	−.46**	(23)	.06	(22)	.27*	(29)	.07	(19)
Experience								
Nature of Job:								
Decision Making	.47*	(14)	.42***	(34)	.08	(21)	−.12	(33)
Policy Advising	.41**	(25)	.49**	(23)	.05	(34)	−.24	(20)

*p < .10
**p < .05
***p < .01

low, but in the expected direction (.16, N=60, and .27, N=48, p<.05). Of particular interest for purposes of this discussion is the question whether individuals whose jobs are intellectually demanding will be more strongly affected by stress with their superior than will those whose jobs are not highly intellectual in nature.

On the basis of the task descriptions, we therefore further divided the group into those who reported spending 10 percent or more of their time (roughly the median) on intellectually demanding tasks, that is, advising on policy matters and making policy decisions. Interestingly enough, these were uncorrelated task attributes, and there were very few individuals who were represented in more than one of these subgroups.

Table 2 presents the correlations between intelligence and performance and between experience and performance for staff members who a) perceived high or low double-bind stress, and b) performed tasks making high or low intellectual demands. Let us first consider the findings related to experience, which are indicated in the lower part of the table. These show (on the right side) that the staff officer's experience did not contribute materially to performance under conditions of low stress with boss. Under high stress with boss, however, experience, that is, time in service, correlated significantly with rated performance, thus supporting the findings of the squad leader study.

The pattern of correlations between intelligence and performance, indicated in the upper half of the table, presents a more complex picture. Here we find on the right side of the table that the intelligence of staff officers did not correlate significantly with performance when stress with boss was low, either in intellectually demanding or nondemanding jobs. Unexpected are the consistently high correlations in the *negative* direction when (a) stress with boss is high and (b) the task is intellectually demanding. These correlations suggest that high staff officer's intelligence was detrimental to good staff performance. It must, of course, be recognized that all individuals in staff positions are technically qualified and are likely to have the minimum intelligence and experience required for adequate performance. Our data show, however, that a higher level of intelligence was dysfunctional for intellectually demanding staff jobs, making the more intelligent individual look incompetent and the less intelligent appear bright. Our next study investigated whether this very unusual finding would be cross-validated in another sample of staff personnel, and whether line and staff management might use their intelligence and experience in a different manner under comparable conditions.

Battalion Line and Staff Officers

A study by Zais and Fiedler (1973) dealt with 44 line officers (i.e., company commanders) and 45 staff officers of nine army battalions. The typical army battalion consists of four to five companies, each commanded by a captain. The battalion commander is a lieutenant colonel who is assisted by his executive officer, a major, and a staff of four to seven officers who are in charge of personnel, intelligence, operations and training, supply, maintenance, and so forth.

In most organizations it is very difficult to compare line and staff executives. Self-selection as well as selection by superiors might favor individuals with certain abilities, interests, and background for a leadership rather than a staff position, or vice versa. In army battalions, however, every captain and senior first lieutenant is expected to serve in both positions at one time or another. The line and staff officers thus come from a common pool, as also shown by their nearly identical mean scores on intelligence, experience, stress with boss, and performance ratings.

The measures of intelligence, experience, and task performance were the same as those used in the Coast Guard study. The stress-with-boss

TABLE 3

The Effect of Stress with Boss on Correlations Between Intelligence, Experience, and
the Performance of Line Officers (Company Commanders) and
Staff Officers of Army Battalions

	Stress with Boss		
	High	Medium	Low
Line Officers Performance and:			
Intelligence	.01	.24	.56**
Experience	−.05	−.15	−.86***
N for IQ, Exper.	(13, 12)	(24, 24)	(7, 8)
Staff Officers Performance and:			
Intelligence	−.56*	−.30	.17
Experience	.42	.24	−.13
N for IQ, Exper.	(9, 9)	(27, 26)	(9, 9)

*p < .10
**p < .05
***p < .01

measure was a seven-point scale on which the individual indicated the level of stress in his relationship with the battalion commander. The scale points were from very high (7) to very low (1). A multiple regression analysis to predict the stress-with-boss score from various descriptions of the battalion commander's behavior indicated two main sources of variance: a) the pressure by the battalion commander for greater output and b) the unwillingness of the battalion commander to give the line or staff officer sufficient freedom to do his job. The stress-with-the-boss scale was thus conceptually similar, if not identical, to the double-bind stress measure in the Coast Guard study.

The data were analyzed by dividing the sample of 44 company commanders and of 45 staff officers into three subgroups on the basis of their stress-with-boss score, using 1 SD above and below the means as cutoffs. Correlations were then computed between intelligence and performance and between experience and performance for each of the subsamples. The results are shown on Table 3.

The correlations between intelligence and performance for line officers were quite similar to those obtained on squad leaders. In both cases, the positive correlations indicate that the leader was able to utilize this intelligence when the relationship was relatively free of stress but not when stress with the superior was high. The relationship between staff officer intelligence and performance also was similar to that previously reported for the Coast Guard staff officers, and especially for those with intellectually demanding tasks. Here, again, intelligence did not contribute under conditions of low stress with the superior, but, as in the Coast Guard study, intelligence was *negatively* correlated with performance when stress with the superior was high.

The correlation between experience and performance in the battalion staff officer sample was also similar to that of the Coast Guard study: Experience was utilized only when stress with the superior was high. Unlike the previous results, however, we found a strikingly high *negative* correlation of −.86 between company commander experience and performance under low stress conditions. Thus, having a stress-free relationship with his boss seemed to incapacitate or handicap the highly experienced company commander. One explanation for this curious finding might be that the command of a company continually presents new problems and calls for new solutions. The experienced officer, who perceives little or no pressure from his boss, may simply be content to plug in old remedies without too much concern for their appropriateness. This effect obviously requires further investigation to determine its generality.

Discussion

The principal finding of these studies is, clearly, that interpersonal stress, especially with the immediate superior, strongly affects the individual's ability to utilize his intellectual abilities and his knowledge. Creative thinking and problem solving require a relatively stress-free interpersonal environment. Experience, on the other hand, seems to be an important asset only when stress with the superior is high. This suggests that experience in managerial positions may serve mainly as a substitute for creative thinking when the ability to function intelligently is seriously curtailed by stress and the anxiety which this generates. Particularly anxiety arousing is the stress which places the individual in a double bind: Being pressed to do better while being prevented from exercising authority. Interestingly enough, stress derived from a difficult task does not seem to have this effect on intellectual performance.

The most intriguing question raised by the research concerns the negative correlations between intelligence and performance when stress with boss is high. It is easy enough to understand why there might be a zero correlation between intelligence and performance under these conditions, but a negative correlation implies that intelligence is actually detrimental to performance, that it hinders the individual from doing his job. This is particularly apparent in the case of staff officers.

We might speculate that the very intelligent individual needs to live up to his high expectations. Being blocked or frustrated by superiors, the unusually bright person might well look for the dramatic and original solutions which frequently do not work. He might also be more impatient with the highly detailed procedures and lock-step methods which the organization prescribes. In short-cutting these, he is more likely to get himself into difficulties than would the less intelligent person who plays the game "by the book." This would seem to be particularly important in staff positions which call for legwork and adherence to rules and regulations.

Most importantly, perhaps, the individual's usable or "operative" competence and know-how seem to a surprisingly large extent dependent on organizational factors over which he has only limited control. The operative problem solving ability and know-how, which are, after all, the main reasons for hiring an executive in the first place, are then not as much attributes of the person as they are effects of the organizational environment. How generalizable these findings might be to other organizations or, indeed, to the ability of children to perform in school, and to the creativity of graduate students and scientists, are questions which bear thinking about.

Part 2

The Purpose of Leadership Research

Introduction

JAMES G. HUNT AND LARS L. LARSON

The four chapters in this part focus on the Action/Discovery and the Practitioner/Researcher crosscurrents and highlight the "Purpose of Leadership Research" issue. Chapter 3, entitled, "Leadership Findings and Applications: The Viewpoints of Four from the Real World," consists of the invited contributions of four practitioners integrated within a framework provided by Elmer Burack. These practitioners: David Campbell, Center for Creative Leadership; Joseph Moses, A.T.&T.; Paul Patinka, Motorola; and Blanchard Smith, Kepner-Tregoe are all Ph.D.'s trained in the research methods of academicians and are currently actively involved in "real-world" settings.

Two major concerns implicit in the chapter are the identification of individuals with the potential to be effective managers and the training and development of individuals who are already managers for more effective management of organizations. It is important to note that the practitioners, with one exception, do not make any specific distinction between the terms management and leadership; the terms tend to be used interchangeably. Thus, they as did Fiedler, have taken what we earlier termed a role perspective concerning leadership. The one exception is Joseph Moses who emphasizes the small percentage of individuals in assessment centers who score high on the leadership dimension.

There are some obvious implications that come to mind as one reads this chapter. First, as far as these contributors are concerned, academicians do not seem to be focusing their research in areas that are of major concern to practitioners. Second, according to Moses, researchers should make a greater effort to distinguish between good leaders and average or poor leaders in the conduct of their studies.

Chapter 4, "How Normal Science Methodology Makes Leadership Research Less Additive and Less Applicable" by Chris Argyris adds to the concerns in chapter 3 by bringing out the Action/Discovery crosscurrent. Argyris is very concerned with helping leaders to "manage" their world in a better way. He suggests, as the title of the chapter implies, that current research methods do not lend themselves to such ends. The Argyris chapter and comments by Weick (see chapter 6) elicited a great deal of general audience discussion concerning several issues. While we have generally dealt with such concerns in our introductions to parts 2, 3, and 4, we felt that these, because of their greater complexity, could be more appropriately treated after the Argyris and Weick contributions. Thus their essence is summarized immediately after Weick's comments in chapter 6.

Marshall Sashkin and Howard Garland in chapter 5, "Laboratory and Field Research on Leadership: Integrating Divergent Streams," bring focus to both the Action/Discovery and Practitioner/Researcher crosscurrents. They identify several current trends in both laboratory and field investigations and suggest a paradigm that integrates the two methods of study and attempts to link research outcomes to the application and diffusion aspects that are too frequently ignored by the researcher. These latter linkages and feedback loops are an important part of their model and are frequently overlooked.

One issue that can be raised with the Sashkin-Garland model is the suggestion of a research sequence beginning with laboratory studies followed by field studies. It can be argued that this sequence is not helpful because there is a need to have a model of the real world before going to laboratory research. Field studies would help to identify the factors that are important in developing a model of the phenomena to be studied. Only after the model were made explicit could laboratory studies be used to refine and further develop understanding of the topic under study.

We have a concern that the underlying theme of the argument can turn into a lab *versus* field approach as opposed to a lab *and* field approach. The lab *and* field approach is prescribed by the model but the lab *versus* field approach appears to reflect current trends. We add our plea for more integrative approaches to leadership research.

A third issue of concern pertains to the nature of laboratory studies and the ability of the researchers to simulate "real world" conditions in the laboratory. This is, of course, a perennial issue and has been discussed many times (e.g., Fromkin & Streufert, 1976). Hollander in his commentary in chapter 6 has some interesting additional insights concerning this issue.

The chapters in this part reflect the crosscurrents that presently exist between research that is primarily concerned with discovery and research that is primarily concerned with application. The virtues of both positions are elaborated and one suggestion for bringing about integration of these crosscurrents is presented.

3

Leadership Findings and Applications: The Viewpoints of Four from the Real World— David Campbell, Joseph L. Moses, Paul J. Patinka, and Blanchard B. Smith

ELMER H. BURACK

This chapter has the purpose of identifying problems and potential in the application of leadership research and findings in various "real-world" settings. Encompassed within this focus is the broad question of problem areas encountered by organizations and their (potential) relationship to practitioner/academician interfaces. The illustration and crystallization of application and interface issues is provided by the four contributors through: a) descriptions of the organizational circumstances leading to the need or development of leadership models or approaches, b) classification of application approaches, c) bases for monitoring and evaluating program delivery, or d) assessments to determine the effectiveness of approaches taken plus unanswered questions, problems, and future directions.

It is important to note in passing that the nature of this chapter differs markedly from the usual presentations in the leadership symposia books. Most such presentations describe specific research projects, models and/or findings. However, organizational needs and real-world applications typically proceed along much more diffused lines. Approaches are judged on the basis of participant response and bottom line performance. Priorities are established by organizational circumstances. Thus, in this context "leadership" is often intertwined with various personnel processes and developmental activities—sometimes distant from academic research.

Contributors

It is also of importance to note that the contributors represent much more than "knowledgeable resource people." All are well known and recognized by colleagues for their expertise. David Campbell, Joseph Moses, Paul Patinka, and Blanchard Smith have all achieved distinction in applied areas of leadership, management development, or various areas contributing to organization effectiveness.

Moses' company, American Telephone & Telegraph, pioneered in developing systematic means for determining management potential, much of which has been encompassed by the Management Progress Study (Bray & Grant, 1966). Moses himself has published widely in this area. Motorola, too, has accomplished notable work in management development activities; Patinka has been deeply involved in developing systematic procedures for assessing individual potential along with approaches for developing this potential. Campbell's organization, the Center for Creative Leadership, has achieved distinction among leading practitioners in the United States for its comprehensive approach to individual development and leadership skills; Campbell has been importantly responsible for development in these areas. Some years ago the Kepner-Tregoe organization adopted the research and developmental approaches of Vroom and Yetton (1973) to what has now become a widely known program for developing managerial talent; Smith is directly and actively involved in this program and others focused on strengthening individual effectiveness.

Problems, Issues, Interfaces

The application of leadership research to real-world situations involves a transfer and diffusion process involving information and people. "Interfaces" are described as ports of entry or information transfer, plus transfer agents between academic and real-world organizations. However, it is not at all clear that the notion of "interfaces" is an apt one or whether in fact they even exist. This is an important issue addressed by several of the contributors.

Second, leadership research and modeling is often viewed in a rather pure light but knowledgeable practitioners and real-world needs often do not proceed along such clearly defined channels. For example, one consulting organization (BNA Communications) asks "What kind of a manager are you? What's your leadership style? How can you improve your managerial effectiveness?" In another organization, its well known president (personal communication), indicates that "the leadership model and approach taken by our consulting organization with clients is based upon a model developed by R. Tannenbaum and W. H. Schmidt. . . . a good manager develops the situation and people involved by choosing the appropriate leadership pattern. . . . we do not believe in one style of leadership being correct [for good managerial performance]."

In another organization, "leadership" is viewed in the context of diagnosing situations, increasing employee motivation, developing subordinates, and understanding the bases for organization effectiveness. Finally, with considerable candor, the president of still another organization (personal communication) indicates "I'm not clear on just how the leadership process corresponds to the management process, but I feel confident that there are some areas of overlaps." In short, the clarity of what constitutes "leadership" issues and need may differ widely between the academic and practitioner perspectives. Understanding this blurring of outlook or focus is central to the interpretation of "interface" problems and concerns.

Interfaces—Do They Exist?

"Past SIU symposia, whatever their academic and intellectual merits, have been so far removed from the pressure on the practitioner as to be useless to anyone running training programs or to anyone in leadership positions." (D. Campbell, oral comments, October 5, 1978.)

As we shall see, Campbell's expression of this point is echoed in various ways by the other contributors. Campbell has also noted that traditionally important institutions of leadership training—the military, chamber of commerce, and YMCA—have maintained active or growing programs in leadership with but only modest input from academics or professionals.

Managers versus Leaders: Are the Right People Being Studied?

As Patinka notes in his contribution, "managers are made by proclamation while leaders (and leadership) involve far more complex processes." Not only are leadership processes complex but some have expressed doubt as to whether the appropriate behaviors are even being observed for research purposes. Moses crystallizes the issues clearly based on his years of study and development of managers and the assessment of leadership skills: "In any given organizational setting, at any given level, no more than 25 percent of all incumbents possess significant leadership skills. . . . this is probably a conservative estimate based on data in a well managed organization which has given considerable attention to management selection." The notion of "significant" leadership skills is based on ratings of four or five on a five-point scale and assessments involving over 200,000 men and women. The focus of Moses' concerns is with *demonstrated leadership behavior*. Thus Moses' "Commandment" is logically deduced, namely that "thou shalt study leaders who are first *accurately* identified as leaders before attempting to build theories of leadership behavior."

Another key point made by Moses is that "leadership behavior is but one factor which contributes to successful managerial performance." Effective managers may compensate for weaknesses in one area with strengths in another. Thus, we are cautioned to avoid leaderless leadership studies *and* to recognize that the "work world" places a premium on successful managerial performance rather than solely leadership per se. Smith, too, echoes the latter point in referring to "managerial behaviors, and managerial leadership" patterned along the line of the situational variables and normative behaviors identified by Vroom and Yetton (1973). Patinka also calls attention to his company's interest in identifying the potential for successful managerial performance through the use of "biographical data." To the extent successful job performance is used as a central criterion for assessment or evaluation approaches, leadership becomes embedded in a far more complex process.

All of the contributions which follow frequently reflect the broader managerial rather than the narrower leadership perspective. Campbell's contribution is presented first, followed by those of Moses, Patinka, and Smith. Campbell's concern is to provide a short description of the CCL program. The other contributions take the form of short position papers, with varying amounts of editing for purposes of transition and uniformity.

Some Highlights of the CCL "Seven-Day Leadership Development Program"

DAVID CAMPBELL

The "seven-day leadership development program" at CCL reflects an attempt to operationalize the state of the art in contingency approaches with a strong theme of career development. Heavy emphasis is placed on expanding self-knowledge through assessment, exercises, didactic presentations, feedback, and future planning of individual careers. In the seven-day program, a large battery of tests is taken (involving personality, leadership style, etc.) prior to arrival at the site. Participants are processed in groups of 12 to 18 members. Briefly, the seven-day (on-site) program involves: 1) assessment center exercises, 2) inventory based on the Vroom-Yetton model, peer feedback, and decision making, 3) work with the Blake-Mouton and Fiedler models, lectures, and games, 4) discussion and skill building involving creativity, 5) giving *and* receiving feedback, openly and involving multi-media, 6) goal setting and individual career analysis, and 7) actualizing goal settings, small group discussions, and action plans. Subsequently, followup is undertaken as much as six months after conclusion of the sessions. The programs are less than 10 years old and were started by energetic lay people who saw important leadership voids.

For the most part "Division 14" types as well as leadership theorists and researchers have not been a part of these training efforts. Specific impacts of the training are difficult to assess. Participants have a feeling of euphoria and a sense of learning something practical. Past surveys indicate that former participants feel they are using the technique.

Lack of Application of Leadership Findings to Real World Problems

JOSEPH L. MOSES

Several years ago, John Campbell (1971) summarized the state of the art in management development. He noted that most of the literature reviewed for his *Annual Review* chapter on the topic was unimaginative, poorly written, and dull. In many respects, Campbell's comments appear as quite appropriate descriptions of the current state of affairs in the leadership domain as well. Without going into an elaboration of why much leadership research is leaderless, this presentation summarizes a number of observations which might make the efforts of future researchers more palatable for real-world practitioners and consumers of leadership knowledge.

Murphy's Laws and Peter's Principles are well known. Shortly, Moses' Commandment will be offered. However, before doing this, an observation is in order. This observation results from over ten years of real-world experience dealing with critical issues of staffing management jobs at different levels in one very well managed organization. It also results from work done in a variety of organizational settings in business, education, and government, both here and abroad. Finally, it results from frequent and continuous interaction with many colleagues struggling with similar staffing issues in their respective organizations. Over the years I have observed, measured, and trained hundreds of managers to assess leadership skills as part of assessment center programs designed to evaluate management potential. Managers in both research and applied settings, at levels of management ranging from entry into management to candidates for senior-level assignments have been assessed. Programs used to evaluate thousands of men and women have been designed, developed, and installed.

This experience has led to an observation which, if correct, has serious implications for future applications of leadership research. That observation is that *in any given organizational setting, at any given level, no more than 25 percent of all incumbents possess significant leadership skills.* The definition and measurement of "significant leadership skills" are obviously important, so let's digress for a moment and examine this issue.

As is well known, assessment centers have been widely used to help identify individuals with potential for further advancement. The technique has received considerable research attention and is well documented in the literature. For those interested in learning more about this topic, two books have recently appeared. The first, *Formative Years in Business*, was written by Bray, Campbell, and Grant (1974) and describes the seminal research of the Management Progress Study. The second book, edited by Moses and Byham (1977) is *Applying the Assessment Center Method* and describes how the technique is applied in different organizational settings and uses.

In an assessment center, leadership behavior is defined in terms of the extent to which an individual in face-to-face interaction can influence others to resolve effectively problems without arousing hostility. It is measured by direct observation of men and women as they participate in exercises designed to simulate the kinds of behaviors that represent performance in more complex and demanding situations. The exercises are carefully designed to reflect organizational demands as well as organizational complexity. A variety of techniques is used and which range from unstructured, highly competitive leaderless group exercises to highly structured, cooperative business games. The nature of the exercises used varies with the type of assessment program, its purpose, and application. The actual technique used is (or should be) based on a careful examination and analysis of behavior.

Assessment exercises designed to measure leadership are often tailor-made to reflect actual organizational needs. Often, the exercises enable direct observation over a period of several hours, and in some cases, several days. In addition to measuring leadership behavior a wide variety of interpersonal skills can be evaluated as well. These can include flexibility, persuasiveness, perception, and many others.

While the exercises and techniques designed to elicit leadership skills are an integral part of most assessment center programs, they are by no means sufficient. Actually, assessment requires a complex set of activities. As noted, a first step is a careful examination of behaviors which are related to successful job performance. These behaviors can be defined and described in terms of characteristics or dimensions of performance. Once these dimensions are designated, techniques are designed to elicit behaviors reflecting these characteristics. Measurement techniques are developed, an observational methodology is designed, and observers are carefully trained to record, report, and evaluate behavioral data.

Leadership behavior is one of many different aspects of management performance which can be measured in an assessment center. The measurement process, in a well designed assessment center, is quite complex. Numerous controls are developed and introduced to ensure the objectivity of the process and to reduce as many measurement errors as possible. Multiple techniques, evaluated by multiple observers, standardization of training, evaluation, and monitoring procedures are but a few of the many strategies used to make the data collection and interpretation as accurate as possible.

In many assessment centers, performance on a given dimension or characteristic is rated on a five-point scale ranging from one (low) to five (high). Considerable training is provided to each assessor to anchor these scales. Assessor training is often quite complex and uses live and videotaped examples of behavior, standardization procedures, and an assessment of assessor competency to measure and evaluate behavior.

The measurements used in assessment centers are quite complex. The measurement system is expensive, time consuming, often difficult to administer, but it also is quite accurate. The evaluation of abilities measured by assessment centers is probably the single most accurate predictor of subsequent success. This is an empirical statement, based on over 20 years of research concerning applications of this technique in over 100 published studies here and abroad.

Returning to the theme of the presentation, it was noted that less than 25 percent of all participants demonstrate significant leadership skills (defined as leadership ratings of four or five on our five-point scale). Over 200,000 men and women in both research and applied environments have been assessed in A.T.&T.; this result does not appear to reflect a sampling bias. Parenthetically, similar findings are reported by those in other organizations. In any event, this is probably a conservative estimate based on data in a well-managed organization which has given considerable attention to management selection.

The focus of these remarks has been on demonstrated leadership behaviors. The fact that only one quarter of incumbents at a given management level possess significant leadership skills may or may not be alarming based on one's viewpoint. As we all well know, leadership behavior is but one factor which contributes to successful managerial performance. It is possible for managers to be effective because they can compensate for weaknesses in one area with strengths in another.

However, this estimate of significant observed leadership behavior might be an extremely conservative one, since most organizations do not have a sophisticated selection process, or if they do, it has been recently installed and has not been used to select many of its incumbents. Instant validity for this observation can be obtained through naturalistic observation. Just examine any group (subordinates, peers, supervisors, political leaders, baseball managers) and apply the 25 percent rule. If a person is critically honest, that person may be quite surprised with the results.

The implications of this observation should be quite clear by now, and may explain why the title was chosen for this presentation. It leads to Moses' Commandment which is "Thou shalt incorporate individual difference measurement into your experimental design." Another way of stating this "commandment" is, "Thou shalt study leaders who are first *accurately identified* as leaders before attempting to build theories of leadership behavior."

Arguments have been made elsewhere (Bray & Moses, 1972) that much of our "research" is based on available (translate that to mean the easiest to obtain) measures. That is one reason why many criterion measures are poorly chosen, and why many validity studies are not impressive. It is beyond the scope of these remarks to elaborate on this point other than to note that there does not seem to have been a serious effort to obtain adequate samples of leaders in most of the research studies purporting to be evaluating leadership. Rather, one studies what is available. Sometimes these are college sophomores, sometimes these are managers—rarely however, are the subjects of intensive analysis evaluated to determine if they have the skills we are trying to study.

Current identification of leadership behavior, aside from assessment center evaluations, is weak. Self-report measures, biographical data, sentence completion blanks are apparently the best the field has to offer to date. These rely on inferred behavior. Somehow that is much less impressive than measures derived from observed behavior.

In closing, it is the hope here that we can do a better job of identification of leadership behavior as a basis for meaningful research. The techniques are there—they have been developed, refined, and installed. It is about time that they can be "discovered" and used in non-"real-world" environments.

One More Time: Are Leaders Born or Made?

PAUL J. PATINKA

Despite the early rejection of the trait approach, which if normal cycles are to be repeated should be "rediscovered" shortly, there does seem to exist the prevailing feeling that there is something in or about the leader that makes a difference.[1] The approach to the leadership issue based on this notion includes, in addition to management judgment, the assessment center approach, clinical assessment, and the biographical data approach. This presentation relates to a study of managerial leadership based upon biographical background.

As is the usual case with the biographical data approach, present management groups served as the basis for model development. This, of course, raises the question of whether the successful managers of today realistically can serve as an adequate model for successful managers in the future. The answer to this question can be approached in two ways. First, those managerial leaders who are successful today lived, worked, and developed through significant periods of changes which are probably similar in magnitude and type to the changes anticipated for the future. Is it not possible to assume, therefore, that other managers like them will be able to handle the changes and vagaries of the future much as their predecessors did in their time? Secondly, if present managers do not constitute the correct model, what is the correct model? In the absence of any reasonable way to answer this question, we can only assume that the successful patterns of the past are likely to be the successful patterns of the future.

Using present incumbent managers as the data base, the predictors, that is, questionnaires and tests, are related to the criteria, i.e., different levels of management success by an item analysis procedure which identifies items that differentiate between high and low success managers. The relationship between total scores to management success is then estab-

[1] The assistance of H. S. Peres in much of the developmental and statistical work is gratefully acknowledged.

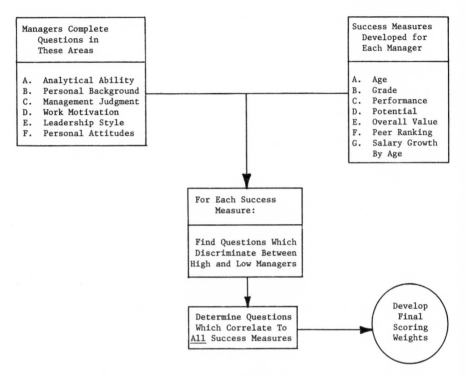

Fig. 2. Development of scoring keys for Motorola Personnel Inventory (MPI)

lished. Future administration assumes that individuals with patterns similar to those of successful managers have a higher probability of success and satisfaction in management in the given environment than those whose patterns are markedly different.

As shown in Figure 2 scoring keys were developed by relating the responses of the managers to a wide variety of questionnaire items after grouping those managers on the basis of a composite success index. With the sample size of several hundred managers represented here, a percent response difference of approximately 10 percent was considered statistically significant. Throughout the study, unit scoring weights were used. Figure 2 outlines the basic development scheme for the scoring weights.

The inventory referred to as the Motorola Personnel Inventory (MPI) was composed of the seven parts shown in Table 4.

In total, there were almost 3,500 possible individual responses. Of the many items and possible responses, only a few can be shown. For example, in the top portion of Table 5 are shown the results for a specific item from

TABLE 4
Motorola Personnel Inventory (MPI)

Composed of 7 Parts	Number of Responses/Questions[a]
1. Early Background	1003
2. Late Background	814
3. Organizational Problems	264
4. Work Values	568
5. Leadership Style	248
6. Personality Self-description	600
7. Concept Mastery Test	180

[a] These are responses for Parts 1–6; questions for Part 7.

the inventory section entitled "Early Background." The item reads, "During the years I was in high school, most of my spending money came from." Respondents were asked to choose from among the four alternatives shown in Table 5. The total group of managers was divided into thirds based on an overall composite evaluation referred to as the CPD success index. The results for the high third of the total group are shown in the column headed "High Success Percent Checking." The results for the low success group based on the composite index are shown in the column headed "Low Success Percent Checking." As can be seen, 12.1 percent of the high success group selected alternative A, while 7.8 percent of the low success group selected alternative A. Since the difference between the two is less than 10 percent, the future scoring weight for this item would be zero. On the other hand, 70.7 percent of the high success group selected alternative B, while 47.3 percent of the low scoring group selected B. Since the difference is greater than 10 percent in favor of the high success group, anyone selecting that alternative in the future receives a scoring weight of +1. Seventeen percent of the high success group selected alternative C while 34.2 percent of the low success group selected that alternative also. Since the pattern differentiates in the direction of the low success group, the future weight of that alternative is −1. In a similar way, all responses to the items were scored.

While it is impossible here to present any great number of items analyzed in this fashion, the lower part of Table 5 shows a few items from the "Later Background" of the inventory in contrast to the "Early Background" in the top part.

An attempt to describe the main theme running through this inventory in terms of the characteristics of the high performance, high potential manager would probably read as follows:

1. Background. The self-report of early background describes an en-

TABLE 5
Example Background Items from Motorola Personnel Inventory

Early Background			
	High Success Percent Checking	Low Success Percent Checking	Future Scoring Weight
During the years I was in high school, most of my spending money came from:			
A. Allowance from the family	12.1	7.8	0
B. My own earnings	70.7	47.3	+1
C. Partly allowance and partly earnings	17.0	34.2	−1
D. I did not have much spending money	0.0	10.5	−1
Later Background			
I have openly agreed with a subordinate who has: (mark all that apply)			
A. Broken a rule	29.2	10.5	+1
B. Gone beyond his authority	56.0	31.5	+1
C. Complained about an injustice done him	60.9	50.0	+1
D. Changed a method without consulting me	70.7	34.2	+1
E. I have never agreed in such situations	2.4	23.6	−1

riched childhood in terms of early achievement, recognition, decision making, diversified activity, and so forth, and this pattern continues into adult life.

2. Personal Characteristics. The most prevalent characteristics here are vigor, aggressiveness, self-confidence and resilience.

3. Motivation. The motivational pattern can best be characterized as task oriented, competitive, and seeking after utilization of skills, with minimal concern for job surrounds.

4. Management Judgment. Management judgment can be best described as incisive, motivative and characterized by long-range planning and the prediction of events as opposed to "far out" risk taking.

5. Leadership Style. The pattern here contains the apparent but not actual contradictory characteristics of firmness and flexibility with an underlying theme of strong goal orientation and the initiation of structure combined with a sensitivity to the nuances of interpersonal and individual differences.

6. Analytical Ability and Verbal Skills. In general, the group standing is above average compared to a normative group of college graduates.

When a multiple prediction equation was developed, it was found that the best single predictor of management performance and potential was Early Background followed closely by Later Background, for which it is an obvious antecedent. While it was not possible within a reasonable time frame to carry out any longitudinal studies, it was possible to correlate age with the various parts of the inventory as well as the composite success index. There is no significant correlation between age and any of these measured variables.

Obviously, an analysis of the type described above capitalizes on the positively correlated error variance. However, it should be pointed out that four separate samples were analyzed in the manner described and in each case, the results were remarkably similar to those discussed here. Furthermore, the scoring key for one group was applied to another of similar size and vice versa constituting, in effect, a double cross-validation. In both of these cases, the prediction equations held up very well.

Clearly, research of this type is more heuristic than definitive. Early indications are, however, that leaders, if not born, seem to be made early in their lives by their experiences up to and including high school. While a clear answer to the question is yet to be determined, indications are that there exist basic characteristics in people which can readily develop into necessary leadership qualities under the proper conditions. If these basic ingredients are not present, training for leadership might well be misplaced.

While many of the practical applications of the above findings are still in the experimental or hypothetical stage, the following figures illustrate possible uses that might be made of such data. Figure 3 shows a simplified version of how the independent measure of potential, the MPI, can be related to management judgment which must be accepted and recognized as an input to the decision making process. Clearly, where there is confirmation, that is, in the high-high quadrant and low-low quadrant, the actions are relatively straightforward. Where disconfirmation exists, that is, in the high-low quadrant or the low-high quadrant, neither input should be accepted. Additional on-the-job testing should be used to resolve the discrepancies. In a similar figure (Figure 4) potential is compared to performance and in this case, the actions become rather obvious. For example, for the high performer with high management potential, an individual career plan must be developed recommending promotion, rotation, educational programs, or specific assignments to further the continued growth of the individual. In the low-low quadrant where both performance and po-

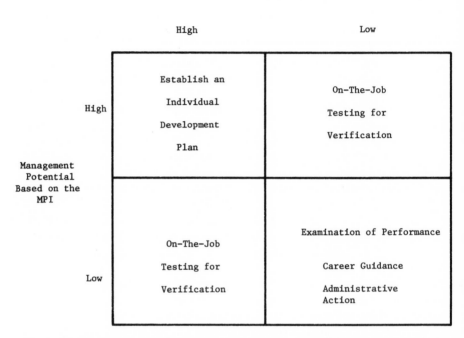

Fig. 3. Management potential (MPI)–management potential (management judgment) matrix

tential are low, administrative actions become necessary. The person with high performance and low management potential can be retained at the present level or by virtue of high performance considered for a development plan leading for advancement in a specialty. The second type of discrepancy is the low performer with high management potential, although such cases are probably rare. Such an identified person might require placement in a different type of work, special training to improve skills, or, most likely, an assignment to a different and perhaps stronger supervisor.

While it may remain with the academicians to resolve finally the issue of whether leaders are born or made, it is useful to know that certain background characteristics seem to be associated with leadership capability. This type of knowledge can aid significantly in career guidance, career planning, the design of developmental experiences, and the avoidance of mistakes costly to both the individuals and the organization.

Performance

	High	Low
High	Develop a Career Plan Promotion Rotation Education Program	Investigation of Causes Placement Training Change in Supervision
Low	Career Guidance Retain at Present Level Staff Specialist Development Plan	Administrative Action Placement Training Down Grade Termination

Management Potential

Fig. 4. Management potential-performance matrix

The TELOS Program and the Vroom-Yetton Model

BLANCHARD B. SMITH

The TELOS (a Greek term meaning goal directed or purposeful) program designed by the Kepner-Tregoe (K-T) organization is a two to two-and-one-half-day program based entirely on the Vroom-Yetton (V-Y) model of leadership choice. The program, ordinarily taught by organization employees trained by K-T, has the purposes of: 1) determining when and how to involve other people in resolving specific situations, 2) establishing differences between the managers' intuitive approaches and the V-Y model employing the latter's 30 standard case format, 3) assisting managers in formulating a personally effective leadership choice model and applying it to current job situations, and 4) working out individual developmental plans to build desired changes into the manager's work patterns. As with other situational approaches, no particular "best way" is prescribed; the program focuses on a limited facet of managerial behavior by presenting a cognitive, situational approach to managerial leadership.

Program Evaluation

In one form or another, there have been at least 40 evaluation studies of the program. Participant self-report items have followed the typical format of open-ended questions regarding plans or initial ideas for use of the approaches in the job; multiple choice questions have been used for specific topics and anticipated benefits. The evaluation framework will perhaps be clearer if three different evaluation phases are discussed.

Phase 1—The Start of Evaluation. Questionnaires of the type above were distributed during the latter moments of the course. They were distributed to 216 managers from 13 different organizations and took 15 minutes to complete. The results concerning anticipated benefits and comments on plans for using the TELOS ideas are given below.

Anticipated Benefits from TELOS Programs. (Each participant could report more than one benefit.)

72% said they found some specific things they would do differently.

67% reported the program should help them generally in their current job.

35% said the course should significantly increase their current job effectiveness.

51% reported that the course would help in their career development.

2% reported that the course was interesting, but no real value on the current job.

No one reported that the course was a waste of time.

3% did not answer this question.

Plans for Improvement. Eash participant was asked about a personal plan to use the learning from the course. (Each participant's response was coded to appear only once.)

1% reported they didn't intend to change.

5% said they weren't certain yet.

49% made a general statement about their plans.

19% reported they would use the model to plan specific job situations.

11% said they would be more participative.

6% said they would be less participative.

5% reported they would be more responsive to a specific situation variable.

4% said they would try a specific behavior (AI through GII) more frequently.

12% did not answer the question.

In reviewing participant responses, K-T program designers identified the strengths of the program as well as some areas requiring more data or information. Realistically, participant feedback is important—few programs survive in the face of (strongly) negative reactions and the likelihood of individual change being low. On the other hand, "positive" opinions "are comforting [yet] they fall short of addressing the question of behavior change," namely, "the comments are plans, what really happens?" "a certain euphoria exists during course attendance," and "social or political pressures exist to give positive evaluations without individual intent to change." These types of speculative questions or points regarding participant learnings and change led to a second phase of K-T analyses.

Phase 2—Training Effectiveness. As a part of his dissertation Robert Zimmer (1978) established a research design using test-retest procedures and control groups. Twenty sales managers from two American Consumer food sales companies were given TELOS training with a pretest of 30 cases to determine their approach to leadership choice. Six weeks later a different, but equivalent, set of 30 cases was given to test the effects of their TELOS training. Twenty untrained sales managers were given the same set of cases at the same times to control for any nontraining effect. Basic principles of experimental design and analysis were used to eliminate contaminating effects. The results are shown in Table 6. The trained group improved significantly on seven out of eight measures, demonstrating that, in fact, they had learned to use the TELOS model. The untrained group did not change at all, showing there were no nontraining effects. While the sample was small and limited, the results were evident. Three other less sophisticated studies reinforced these results; people could be trained to increase their correspondence to the Vroom-Yetton model on 30 standard cases.

Phase 3—On-the-Job Change. Follow-up questionnaires were used by some of the sponsoring organizations in conjunction with their company

TABLE 6
Average Scores—TELOS Sales Manager Evaluation

	Training Group (N = 20)		Control Group (N = 20)	
Measure	Pre	Post	Pre	Post
Average participation for all 30 cases	4.51	5.01*	4.10	4.38
Percentage of Guideline Violations				
Inadequate information	10	2*	14	14
Goal congruence	10	7	9	7
Unstructured situation	49	13*	44	42
Commitment	26	3*	24	26
Conflict	45	8*	52	51
Fairness	77	15*	90	75
Commitment priority	79	25	76	60

*$p < .05$

participants. One company's results are summarized in Table 7 based on six and twelve month responses with 100 participants (91 percent response).

Dilemmas in Evaluating Leadership Training

Most discussions of evaluation methodology center on technical difficulties. But, economic and sociological factors often shape evaluation efforts more than technological considerations. Evaluation costs money and time. The scientist's favorite alternative of control groups multiplies measurement costs while creating a guinea pig complex. The direct costs of such research are often exceeded by such costs as time away from job and impact on morale.

Many line managers are reluctant to incur those costs for the sake of research. We either must develop lower cost evaluation technologies or do a more convincing job of selling managers on the value of evaluation.

Self-interest complicates honest evaluation. If a manager is committed enough to initiate a leadership training program, powerful forces exist to confirm that judgment. The instructor and developer of the program want to prove positive results. This self-interest extends, of course, to the theoretician who initially provided the ideas for the program. A disciplined adherence to professional scientific inquiry is necessary to counteract these

TABLE 7
One Company's Follow-up Questionnaire Results

	Skills Needed by Managers			Effectiveness of TELOS in Teaching Skills		
1) Management Skills	Needed	Not Needed	No Response	Good	Fair	No Response
a. More effective leaderhsip techniques	89	2	9	56	42	2
b. Lead differently in different situations	88	1	11	78	20	2
c. Identify elements within a situation	85	3	10	58	38	4
d. Increase input from others to increase probability of success	84	2	14	71	29	0
e. Make decisions alone when information is adequate	84	6	10	70	28	2
f. Use participation as a development tool	90	1	9	58	39	3

2) Percentage recommending continuation of TELOS courses	95
3) Percentage indicating TELOS courses should be:	
Shortened to one day	19
Remain the same	69
Lengthened	13

influences. More pragmatically, outside researchers and duplication of studies are desirable.

The technological difficulties in evaluating any training effort are legion. Valid, reliable criteria for change, accurate measurement of change, and isolating those factors responsible for change have been extensively covered in literature (e.g., Campbell, Dunnette, Lawler, & Weick, 1970).

Some Key Issues

The program here as well as the other work in this chapter and elsewhere raise a number of significant issues ranging from basic research matters to practical application programs. Some of these are:

1. The multiple meanings of leadership. The global, nonoperational meaning of this term has been noted (J. P. Campbell, 1977). In fact, each leadership training program (and model) promotes its own definition. For example, the TELOS program presents a limited, relatively specific behavior in contrast to the broader Managerial Grid, Likert Systems or House path-goal approaches. Broad definitions complicate measurement.

2. Can leadership behavior be measured? The relatively specific TELOS with its situational base has some measurement advantages. Tests—such as used in Zimmer's research—can be designed to assess the use of the Vroom-Yetton model. Yet, even with this specific focus, several measurement difficulties exist: a) The Vroom-Yetton model provides a *process* for choosing behavior rather than prescribing one leadership behavior to follow. Therefore, an individual manager may mentally use the model to select leadership behavior; hence outside observers may only be able to guess how much of the manager's behavior, in fact, was conditioned by the TELOS program. While the use of TELOS jargon may be observed, some people contend that a language change is trivial. b) Managers report such observable changes as delegation or meeting frequency as a result of using the TELOS model. However, the direction of such change may vary between participants. One manager, prior to the TELOS program, may prefer to handle many situations alone; the observed behavior change for that person may include more involvement of others. A classmate of that manager—for reasons relevant to the Vroom-Yetton model—may react oppositely. Both learned to use the Vroom-Yetton model but behave in opposite ways. Therefore, any group statistic—or even individually oriented statistics that do not account for prior behavior—are spurious. This difficulty is not unique to the TELOS program but inherent in any contingency approach that does not prescribe one way to react to all situations.

3. Who reports the behavior change? The literature is full of shortcomings of self-reports (Sellitz, Jahoda, Deutsch, & Cook, 1965). And yet, other alternatives such as subordinate perceptions, or outsider observation have their own drawbacks (Stinson, 1977). Fortunately, the subjects of these studies are most often mature, responsible adults who are capable of making judgments about their intended or real behavior change. Nevertheless, the desire to please the researcher or respond to a socially acceptable answer must be guarded against in self-reports.

4. Contaminating the change by measurement. The act of measurement, unless done unobtrusively, may influence a person to change. The simple act of completing a questionnaire, in fact, brings to mind the training and may cause the participant to replan change. A subordinate rating of a leader has more influence due to increased supervisory motivation to change or altering subordinate expectations. If a desired change does occur, then the question becomes, "Was it the result of the training or the measurement methodology?" Interestingly enough, we are exploring subordinate rating of leaders as a tool for generating and maintaining behavior change and *not* because it is a more accurate measurement device.

5. *What is the value of that change?* The Western culture seems to prize leadership. But, putting an exact value on it has eluded most researchers. The operational fuzziness of leadership definitions, the fact that "leadership" is only one facet of a manager's job, and the lack of managerial performance criteria make most attempts at evaluation fall woefully short.

Questions to be Addressed
(By Elmer H. Burack)

It would be possible to develop readily a "cookbook" list of possible questions and issues emerging from those contributions on real-world applications of leadership results. This temptation aside, there are certain recurring themes which loom as major issues: 1) Significant problems are indicated at the "interface." Academic-practitioner interfaces appear vastly underdeveloped so that information transfer, working relationships, and follow-on work related to research and organizational need are clearly indicated. 2) Have really successful leaders or leadership situations been identified or are models and findings "diluted" with a host of other variables? If the latter, then how are they to be studied? 3) How are we to understand managerial performance vis-à-vis leadership performance and the notion of managerial adaptability to changing situations and compensating skills? 4) How are "real-world" programs to be evaluated which seek to develop leadership skills in particular or seek to achieve successful managerial performance generally? 5) Are "real" leaders evident at an early point in individual growth and development? Can leaders be developed, and how is change to be brought about if development is feasible?

Implications

More attention is indicated to identifying behaviors which can be accurately described as leadership activities. This matter is of major research significance and at the same time of substantial importance in the real world. Practitioners have a need for validated methodologies and instruments which can be used to deal with organizational matters. Yet at the same time, the requirement exists for establishing the conditions under which leadership behaviors and situations can be studied carefully and accurately and so that results (and instrumentation) can be transported to real world settings. What seems indicated here is the need for the academic to consider different research formats, perhaps along the lines of the assessment center described by Moses—and possibly in a *joint cooperative effort* with particular organizations. Evaluation of leadership applications as in managerial assessment and/or training indicate the need for multiple evaluation strategies. As Smith has suggested, multiple evaluation strategies are indicated with evaluation purpose and techniques aligned—but within the practical limitations of the setting—and the recognition of the trade-offs between economics, speed, and information needed.

4

How Normal Science Methodology Makes Leadership Research Less Additive and Less Applicable

CHRIS ARGYRIS

In the review literature such as the *Annual Reviews of Psychology* and Stogdill's (1974) review of leadership, there are three robust findings. First is that the number of publications (empirical and theoretical) is increasing significantly every year.[1] Second, the additivity of the research findings is minimal to put it minimally. Stogdill states, "The endless accumulation of empirical data has not produced an integrated understanding of leadership" (1974, p. 211). Third, the applicability to the central everyday problems of leadership is negligible. This berating of our research by ourselves has gone on for many years. Yet, as far as I can tell, it has had almost no effect upon the theories being produced nor upon the empirical research.

The explanation that is proposed here is that there is little influence because all of us have been educated to conduct research that follows the requirements of rigor and that these requirements will lead to research that lacks additivity and applicability.

Everyday Life and Scientific Activity: Similarities and Differences

Social scientists conducting research and human beings designing and implementing everyday actions assume that 1) life is ordered and causality exists, 2) public disconfirmability is a way of testing and learning, and 3) the more elegant (i.e., comprehensive and simple) a theory the better.

[1] I should like to express my appreciation for the thoughtful advice that I received from Clay Alderfer, Lee Bolman, and Richard Walton.

As Rychlak (1977) has shown, inquiry in science consists of 1) speculation (usually based upon theory), 2) testing of the plausibility of such speculation (usually in the form of "thought" experiments), 3) designing thereby an experiment which can show others the implication of the theory, and 4) carrying out the experiment. Recent research in human information processing (Blumenthal, 1977), social psychology (Weick, 1968), and theories of action (Argyris & Schön, 1974, 1978) suggest that human beings go through a similar sequence when they design their behavior and take action. Human beings have maps in their heads that help them to frame reality; they speculate about the validity of their maps; they design a course of action and take it with the view that their maps will not be disconfirmed. The operative metaphor therefore is that every person is a scientist, employing prediction and action to test his or her design.

There are two fundamental differences however between everyday life and research. The ultimate activity of life is to design and take action (action is behavior with meaning) while understanding (or explaining) and prediction are penultimate. The rankings are reversed in the practice of basic research. Understanding (explanation) and prediction are ultimate while taking action is low enough that it is relegated to applied research. Everyday action always occurs under on-line conditions such as inadequate time and information. Research is rarely conducted under on-line constraints. As Lewin pointed out years ago, he could easily have spent his life analyzing the moving pictures of the autocratic-democratic children's groups.

These differences are based upon some of the most fundamental features of everyday life and rigorous research. The sine qua non of rigor is precision. It is better to know something precisely and incompletely because with the advancement of knowledge more complete understanding will develop. Human beings, on the other hand, must always act under on-line conditions. They neither have the time nor the information to be precise. Their task is to be highly accurate with low precision. Moreover, since the information and time requirements needed to apply precise knowledge are greater than is usually available, the actor would have to be in control of the context in the same way as the researchers were of their research. Such control, as we shall see, would mean that the actor had a dominating authoritarian relationship with the others. Such a relationship, however, would influence the way the others would respond.

Human beings (and social systems) do not react benignly to the conditions created by rigorous research. This feature is more profound than the indeterminacy principle, which states that research methods can alter the data that can be obtained. Hence the electron microscope makes it impossible to assess the velocity and position of certain particles at the same time. The particle, however, is not motivated to create these problems. Human beings can be motivated consciously or unconsciously to distort data. Hence, some of the key requirements of rigorous research can trigger such motivations and do so in such ways that the subjects are unaware of their distortions.

The requirements to reduce the threats to validity may themselves be threats to validity. If true, it is an example of an inner contradiction, that is an activity that leads to effective and ineffective or desired and undesired consequences. In order to develop the argument, it is necessary to make explicit the view held about the nature of human beings and social systems.

A Theory of Action Perspective

The perspective underlying this chapter has been described elsewhere (Argyris, 1976, 1977; Argyris & Schön, 1974, 1978). Briefly, we differentiate between espoused theories and theories-in-use. The former are maps people have in their heads that refer to their beliefs, values, attitudes— that is, any meanings that they espouse about what informs their actions. The latter are the maps they use to design and implement their actions. The distinction between espoused theory and theory-in-use may be mis-interpreted, as was done by Chemers and Fiedler (1978), to be equivalent to the distinction between beliefs, attitudes, and values, on the one hand, and behavior, on the other. The difference between "do as I say" and "not as I do" is not news, as that age-old saying illustrates.

Our distinction is, we believe, more subtle. The theory-in-use is the map used to design behavior and not the behavior itself. For example, A may control B's behavior. Through education A learns of the negative consequences of this unilateral control and greatly reduces it. We have a change in behavior. But the values that A is "satisficing" could remain the same. For example, A may over or under control in order to win and not lose. If this were the case, the moment B made an error, A would return immediately to high control. Thus the theory-in-use never changed; only the behavior. This, by the way, is also our definition of a gimmick.

Model I is the label we have given to the theory-in-use found being used by most people. The *behavioral strategies* of Model I include advocating a position and simultaneously unilaterally controlling others and unilaterally protecting self and others from being vulnerable. All behavioral strategies are designed to "satisfice" four *governing variables* or values which are 1) to define in their own terms the purpose of the situation in which they find themselves, 2) to win and not lose, 3) to suppress their own and others' feelings, and 4) to emphasize rationality.

The governing variables and the behavioral strategies lead to behavioral worlds that are more defensive than unconflicted (low trust, low risk taking) where self-sealing processes occur that limit learning to single-loop. This, in turn, leads to ineffective problem-solving. Three criteria of effective problem solving are 1) to comprehend the variables relevant to the problem, 2) to solve the problem in such a way that it remains solved, and 3) to accomplish 1 and 2 without deteriorating the present level of problem-solving effectiveness.

It is useful to differentiate between single-loop and double-loop learning. Single-loop learning means the detection and correction of error that does not involve changing the underlying governing values or variables of our theory-in-use, or the governing values and policies of an organization's theory-in-use. Double-loop learning is detecting and correcting error which involves changing the underlying governing variables, policies, and assumptions (either of the individual or the organization).

The behavioral strategies of Model II (our candidate for double-loop learning) include combining advocacy with inquiry and minimizing unilateral attempts to protect self and others. The governing variables of Model II are valid information, free and informed choice, and internal commitment to the choice so that monitoring of its implementation occurs. The behavioral world now becomes significantly less defensive, statements become publicly disconfirmable, hence self-sealing processes are reduced, and finally double-loop learning is encouraged. To date, almost all people studied tend to be unaware of a discrepancy between their espoused theory and theory-in-use (again, many are aware of discrepancies between their espoused theory and their behavior).

There appear to be at least three reasons these empirical findings persist. First, Model I contains a proposition to the effect: If you experience people behaving incongruently with their espoused theory and they appear unaware of it, do not tell them because you run the risk of creating interpersonal difficulties and negative emotions (which would violate Model I governing variables). The second reason is that Model I theories-in-use contain rules that keep people blind to the discrepancy *and* unaware of the built-in blindness. In other words the blindness is not accidental; it is planned and systematic. The third reason of the unawareness is related to the nature of skillful behavior. Skillful behavior is that behavior that is performed effortlessly and with little conscious thought. Indeed, one can inhibit skill by requiring people to focus on their behavior explicitly (Reason, 1977). Skillful behavior is tacit (Polanyi, 1966). If skillful behavior is tacit, then the actors are not aware about what makes them skillful. Nor will they be aware of incremental units of error until the error becomes so large that they can no longer ignore it because it inhibits their effectiveness (Argyris & Schön, 1978).

To sum up: A basic characteristic of human beings in everyday life is that they tend to be unaware of the theory-in-use (not the espoused theory) they use for leadership; embedded in this theory-in-use are propositions to keep them unaware; the people around them are programmed not to inform them of the incongruities; the actors may be blissfully unaware or painfully aware of this fact, but, they are also programmed with the same theory-in-use, hence they cannot confront the lack of valid feedback; and finally if the behavior is skillful the program underlying it is tacit and not, therefore, consciously available to the actor.

People programmed with Model I will always create 0-I learning systems. These systems have several important features. 1) They make it highly likely that whenever the knowledge around any (human or technical) problem that is key in the organization is ambiguous, vague, and unclear, the result of problem-solving will be to make the knowledge even more ambiguous, vague, and unclear. We call this the primary inhibiting loop (Argyris & Schön, 1978). 2) They generate games at the individual, group intergroup, and organizational levels in order to protect the actors. They also generate camouflages to hide these games and camouflage to hide the camouflage. 3) Two results of these activities are double-binds for the individual and the organization. At the individual level, a loyal employee who might wish to surface the games could be ostracized. There is ample evidence of the danger of being a whistle blower. But, if they are loyal and do not surface the games, then they will feel that they are being disloyal.

The organization's double-bind is that activities that are created for survival will also produce deterioration. For example, people may distance themselves from threatening issues in order not to open up Pandora's box and blow the lid off the place. Since distancing means, in effect, no problem-solving on the causes of the problem, it assures that the causes of the problems will continue.

Certain Underlying Assumptions of Science May Limit Scientific Inquiry

The first inner contradiction to be explored is the following. The espoused theory of scientific research is that competent inquiry should not be limited. Yet, the assumption that research should focus on describing (understanding or explaining the world as it is) may lead to limits being placed upon inquiry.

If the task is to describe the universe, then the propositions will, not surprisingly, illuminate the universe as it exists. Such propositions would limit scientific inquiry to the status quo. But what is wrong with that if scientists are studying the universe as it exists? The problem is that the social universe is created by human beings; it is an artifact. Hence, there may be other universes that should be offered to human beings as options to explore. But to study such universes requires models that emancipate the researchers from inquiry primarily into the status quo. Such research would provide the "emancipatory function" that is needed in our world (Dachler & Willpert, 1978; Habermas, 1972; Normann, 1977; Rhenmann, 1973). Two examples. A contingency theory of leadership (or organizational effectiveness) may be valid in a Model I world but it will also lead to inhibiting individual and organizational double-loop learning (Argyris, 1972; Argyris & Schön, 1978). Dissonance and attribution theories may be valid in a Model I world but not in a Model II world (Argyris, 1969).

There is another way that rigorous research may unintendedly limit inquiry. If people programmed with Model I are unaware of double-loop issues, if the O-I learning systems in which they are embedded reinforce the unawareness, *and* if rigorous research methodology is (as we shall see below) also Model I, then how will the researchers ever discover what people are unaware of? If we do not discover these phenomena then we are not even fulfilling the presently accepted objective of describing the present nature of the universe.

For example, six presidents spent nearly 75 hours in learning about their leadership (using questionnaires, cases, tape recordings, and on-line observations). As a result they developed maps of their individual theories-in-use. Included in these theories-in-use were propositions about their relationships with their subordinates. Next, they were asked to design interventions (micro-experiment) to introduce Model II action in their back-home situations. The idea was for each one to strive to correct some aspect of his theory-in-use in order to be more effective. As a result of the exercise, they developed propositions that were contained in their theory-in-use (left-hand column below). As they began to design their interventions and to role-play them they began to unearth new data about their relationships with their subordinates which altered significantly some of the propositions of their theory-in-use. For example:

Before taking action	*While taking action*
I control high-risk decisions.	I control high-risk decisions, most of which are mine.
I withhold telling others how risky decisions may be.	I withhold telling others how risky decisions may be when I fear they may

	not consider them or become frightened by them.
I am not candid with my subordinates because I do not wish to hurt them.	I am not candid with my subordinates because I fear I cannot deal with their being or my being hurt.
I try to be non-directive to give people initiative.	I am non-directive because I do not trust answers given to direct questions.
I doubt if my subordinates would understand Model II.	I doubt if I understand Model II and could adequately defend it to my own inquiry.
I believe that subordinates have rights.	I strive to be considerate and hold in an authoritarian manner the prerogative to alter my considerate behavior.

Next, tape recordings of what actually happened were analyzed and we discovered even deeper issues about leadership effectiveness. For example, after the presidents' role-played but before they tried it out in their back-home setting, they had identified their fears of looking ineffective or weak in front of their vice-presidents. After they tried the new behavior in the back-home situation they realized that a deeper fear was the fear of fear.

It is important to note that this new learning occurred when people were exploring the use of a new theory-in-use (Model II). This exploration made their Model I skills inoperative. Having one's skills become inoperative leads people to see and experience meanings that they are unaware of because they are now placed in situations that are rare events (Model II). But, in order to design the seminars to move toward II, the researchers required models and research about the world as it might be (a normative position). Researchers would have to conduct what Warr (1977) calls "aided experiments" where the experimenters are themselves variables and where some of their models are normative.

Concepts Whose Meanings Are Rigorous and
Disconnected from Action Reality

Social scientists aspire to approximating truth. Truth, simply put, is publicly disconfirmable knowledge. In order to seek truth social scientists must always subject their knowledge to empirical test by others. The requirements imply that the research is repeatable by others. This, in turn, requires that 1) the concepts used are defined as unambiguously as possible, 2) the activities required to produce the results are explicit and reproducible, and 3) the results are precise (preferably quantitative) so that the criterion for disconfirmability is clear.

Let us focus on the first requirement of defining the concept as unambiguously as possible. Let us imagine the universe as containing a context of action. It is in this context that people design and take actions. This is the blooming buzzing confusion about which McCall (1978) and Lombardo (1978) write. We know that one of the most important features of the action context is that it is much more complicated than our information processing capacity can handle all at once. The universe upon which we attend must be broken down into more manageable units. We enact the environment in the sense that we assign it rules, norms, and other features to which we then attend (Weick, 1969b). Enacting an environment means including and excluding factors. Such choices are risky because they can be wrong. Hence the importance of disconfirmability.

Such choices also mean that concepts are abstractions. They are meanings, presumably selected from the action context, that are assumed to be useful for generalizing to many action contexts. Creating concepts therefore is creating knowledge that is distant from any given action context. The distant knowledge is necessary in order to comprehend and manage the action context. No human being and no scientist (acting as a scientist) can operate effectively without generating such distant knowledge. Again, human beings and scientists face similar problems. Human beings may use different rules to design their distant knowledge than do the scientists. I believe that the rules scientists use not only distance the concepts from the action context, they become disconnected from the action context.

For example, in the case of leadership research, one of the most frequent instruments used is the questionnaire. Much empirical and statistical effort goes into the designing and using of questionnaires. Consider the well-known research program known as the Ohio State Leadership Studies (Blum & Naylor, 1968, pp. 421–24; Fleishman, 1973a,b; Korman, 1966). In order to develop their leadership questionnaire, an original pool of 1,800 items was selected and studied empirically. Several factor analyses were made. The responses to the 150 items indicated two distinct groupings of supervisory behavior. They were labeled "Consideration" and "Initiation of Structure." This inventory, like any other similar instrument, tells the subjects where they "are" on these two dimensions. They could be high on one and low on the other, low on both, or high on both.

But what would happen if a supervisor, for example, wished to alter his behavior? Could he utilize the questionnaire to help him change? What is the relatively directly observable, action context information that he can obtain if he is to alter his behavior? For the supervisor to be told that he is high or low on "Consideration" and/or "Initiation of Structure" is to give him feedback that is not based on observable behavior. Even when the questionnaire is filled in by subordinates or others who have observed the supervisor as opposed to completion by the supervisor himself, it is made up of statements that are inferences from behavior. For example, the items with the highest loadings on "Consideration" are:

1. He expresses appreciation when one of us does a good job.
2. He is easy to understand.
3. He stresses the importance of high morale among those under him.
4. He makes those under him feel at ease when talking with him.
5. He is friendly and can be easily approached.

[Blum & Naylor, 1968, p. 422]

These items do not give cues regarding the actual behavior involved in "expresses appreciation," "is easy to understand," "makes those under him feel at ease." The variance of behavior that could be perceived to accomplish these may be very great. In one study, "Friendly and easily approachable foremen" (upon observation) turned out to be foremen "who left the men alone and rarely pressured them" (Argyris, 1960). In another study "friendly foremen" were those who took the initiative to discuss "difficult issues" with the men (Argyris, 1965). Lowin, Hrapchek, and Kavanagh (1969, pp. 246–47), in an attempt to prepare scripts related to "Consideration" and "Initiation of Structure" found it difficult to understand precisely the behavioral content of these categories, especially "Initiation of Structure." They wondered about the applicability of the concepts in the evaluation and education of supervisors.

There is another fundamental question. Distant knowledge that separates itself from the action context may also distance itself from issues of effectiveness; issues that are central for designing theories-in-use. In distancing themselves from the problem they do not ignore it, they simply make it implicit. The Dunnette-Campbell (1969) research implies that withdrawal and compromise is effective behavior for salesmen. Yet Blake and Mouton (1969) contend that the strategies for being a successful salesman (as identified by Dunnette and Campbell) may lead to long-run difficulties. For example, maintaining harmonious relations could be done at the expense of quality of the openness; being tactful and diplomatic could lead to a lowering of the salespeople's levels of aspiration.

Dunnette and Campbell could respond by noting that the assessment of effectiveness is an empirical matter. If compromise and withdrawal are ineffective strategies, research will tell us so and then the items can be altered. But, where is research conducted but in the "real world?" If the real world is Model I, then the test will always be limited to a Model I world. If the tests are limited in this way, then not only is the supervisor maintaining the status quo but the research is producing knowledge that maintains the societal status quo which feeds back to make the individual conclude that not changing may make good sense.

If the analysis above is valid, then we may hypothesize that citizens may hold the same doubts and concerns as we do. If so, then they may fill out our instruments with these attitudes. The responses people give in questionnaires and interviews are known to be influenced by the sense the questions make to them and by the degree to which they can profit from the results of the research. A question whose abstract definition appears to be distant from the subject's reality will tend to be seen, at best, as benign, and at worse, as annoying. Research results that are desirable for the subjects (e.g., learning about their leadership behavior) whose applicability gap appears to the subject to be too great to overcome, may also be annoying to the subject.

The subjects will seek to produce responses by using action context criteria and not distant context criteria. Hence a questionnaire or interview that appears to them to be disconnected from their action context may also induce a sense of bewilderment. But if they wish to cooperate, and since they probably hold Model I theories-in-use they may be predisposed to withhold their bewilderment. They may also be unaware of their confusion and hence not aware of the distortions. To the extent this is the case, their responses may be tinkering with the internal validity of the research.

But, if these distortions are not subject to further distortion, are we not describing valid behavior? The answer is yes, and that is the problem, for three reasons. First, we are describing behavior that is unrealizingly distorted and our generalization will be, as is the actor, blind to the distortion. Second, it is blind spots such as these that create many of the human communication problems that social scientists are trying to understand. It is one thing for subjects to be unaware of their distortion. It is quite another for scientific generalizations to contain the same ignorance.

Third, subjects who may wish to apply social science knowledge in order to become more effective or competent will not only tend to find it difficult to use the knowledge that is distant; they may find it dangerous because it is full of implicit distortions. At best, such knowledge may be used to maintain their status quo rather than change it.

The point is that basic research must be concerned with the production of distant knowledge but that knowledge should be directly connectable and usable in the action context. Such knowledge appears to have the features of being generalizable yet personal; known by many yet subjective; accurate yet ambiguous in meaning. These features can give us clues to the research that is needed in order to illuminate how human beings are managing their worlds by combining less precision with greater accuracy. One is reminded by Von Neumann's perceptive generalization that an important difference between the computer and the brain is that the latter can operate accurately with a sloppy calculus and under conditions of noise (Von Neumann, 1958). Where is rigorous science producing such a generalization?

Systematic Exclusion of Conditions Embedded in Many Generalizations

Conducting research is designing and implementing actions with intended consequences. This means that embedded in the conduct of research is a theory-in-use. Elsewhere, it has been argued that the theory-in-use of rigorous research is Model I (Argyris, 1968). For example, rigorous research occurs when (Edwards, 1954) the researcher unilaterally 1) controls the design and execution of actions, 2) defines the objectives, 3) controls the time perspective of the subjects, and 4) controls the experimental manipulations. Moreover, the technology recommended to minimize threats to internal and external validity (Cook & Campbell, 1976) also contains a Model I theory-in-use. These combined could lead to threats to internal and external validity; hence another inner contradiction.

But, the point to be emphasized in this section is that the theory-in-use is a necessary part of any generalization because it specifies the conditions under which it holds. Yet, the overwhelming amount of published research excludes this fact. For example, a proposition that such and such a reinforcement schedule can lead subordinates to react in such and such a way may well be valid, but it holds when the relationship between the superior and the subordinate is similar to the relationship between the experimenter and the subject.

The difficulty that arises when one tries to apply the knowledge is that the world created will be authoritarian and deceitful. For example, from the experimental research on persuasion and communication we learn to present one side of the argument when the audience is generally friendly or when your position is the only one that will be presented. If the audience is intelligent, present both sides; if not, present one side (Aronson, 1972; Zimbardo & Ebbesen, 1969).

If the strategies are to succeed, it is the leader who makes the diagnosis about "friendliness' or "intelligence" of the audience. Also, the diagnosis and the reason for the diagnosis will have to be covert. How do you tell the audience you are trying to assess them in order to decide what persuasion strategy to use? The use of the strategy will also have to be kept secret. How do you explain to an audience that you presented one side of the position because they were diagnosed as friendly and intelligent or dumb?

None of these issues was a problem to the experimenters because the theory-in-use of the experimental method is to legitimize the unilateral control and the deceit. Recently, questions have been raised about the ethics of this activity (Argyris, 1968; Kelman, 1969). The interesting thing to note is that the major solution to date has been to "debrief" the subjects after the experiment. Again, it is doubtful if debriefing is possible in the noncontrived world without washing out the results and creating new problems.

Jacobo Varela (1971) has utilized social science knowledge to produce remarkable results. One reason for his success is the rigor with which he has translated basic research into action. He translates rigorously the conditions created by the experimenter in the laboratory into the field. This means that he introduces the theory-in-use embedded in the experimental method which is Model I.

Two persuasion programs may illustrate the point (Zimbardo & Ebbesen, 1969). The first program was designed on the basis of experimental research on commitment. In the first step, the salesman skillfully piqued the storekeeper's interest and in the second step introduced him into the wholesale showroom. The showroom, unknown to the storekeeper, was an experimental laboratory where even facial expressions were systematically observed. The sales strategy was designed on the basis of what experimenters had done to subjects in order to produce commitment. For example, whenever the shopkeeper responded that he was favorably impressed, he was asked to give his opinion about that product. To commit him further, he was encouraged to elaborate the reasons why he liked the sample.

Moreover, uncut yard goods were sold by indirectly influencing the shopkeeper to compare the new designs with older ones. When the shopkeeper asked about the fabric, the salesman hesitated but eventually agreed to show him bolts of the fabric: "Once the retailer made this verbal commitment to see the material, and in addition put the salesperson through the work of presenting it, he had to justify his behavior. In such ways he very neatly *set himself up* for placing a big order" (Zimbardo & Ebbesen, 1969, p. 116). The sales results were excellent. The wholesalers then trained the retailers to adapt these techniques to use in persuading their customers, the unsuspecting housewives with irregularly shaped windows.

Some readers may believe that such a manipulation could not be repeated. After all, the retailers would now be less unsuspecting. Yet Varela was able to replicate his results through the design of a second-phase sales strategy which was even more manipulative and secret than the previous one. Varela, using reactance theory, educated salesmen to influence retailers to disagree with them. But in disagreeing with the salesmen's statements, the retailer was forcing himself to buy (p. 118).

Another difficulty is that the scientists remain blind to the requirements of their theory if it is to be used. Some of these requirements can be contradictory to the theory. For example, when Fiedler and his colleagues developed the handbook (Fiedler, Chemers, & Mahar, 1976) to apply their theory, they quite correctly focused first on diagnosing reality. Without this knowledge it would not be possible to tell which conditions existed (e.g., low task structure, high interpersonal tensions, etc.). They then admonish the user that diagnosis requires a high degree of trust and respect among subordinates and between the subordinates and the leaders. But trust and respect are associated with a high Least Preferred Co-worker (LPC) score for a leader. Hence to begin to use this contingency theory the user must begin with conditions that are not contingent *and* if they existed for certain conditions (high task structure and pressure) would be counterproductive (because a low LPC leader is most effective under these conditions).

There is also the problem of instrumentation for diagnosis. Fiedler utilizes questionnaires. Questionnaires, we have seen, create distance from the world of action. We may now add that questionnaires may also create distance between the leader and the subordinates. If there is trust and respect then why the mechanical instrumentation? If there is not trust and respect then by Fiedler's own advice, the diagnosis must be suspect.

To summarize: Rigorous research methodology contains a Model I theory-in-use. The theory-in-use is what creates the conditions under which the research results are produced. These conditions will always be Model I. The consequence, therefore, should be that whatever leadership behaviors are recommended, if one examines how they are implemented, the theory-in-use should be Model I. The result is a puzzle for the scientist. Leadership theories are overwhelmingly contingent in nature. If the present analysis is correct, the behavior may vary but the theory-in-use is the same.

Increasing Completeness Can Lead to Increasing Immobilization for Action

The research on information processing has made it clear that human beings can be immobilized by too much information as well as by the wrong information. Social science researchers may profit by reading the thoughtful literature by scholars in the field of information systems. These people are questioning whether the assumption of increasing rigor and knowledge is useful. They make explicit recommendations as to how to conduct research and design systems that are less rigorous and produce less information (Argyris, 1977).

The reason that these questions arise is not that these scholars aspire to being less rigorous. Indeed the quantification underlying many of the basic algorithms is several orders of magnitude above the quantification in leadership research. The reason is that, in addition to being rigorous, they have placed applicability high on their list of values. It is after many studies have shown clearly that the most rigorous models are not usable, that scholars have begun to redesign their views. They seek rigor that leads to applicable knowledge.

The reaction here to this problem is different. Instead of questioning our methodologies and our models, we question their results and continue to recommend the same methodologies and models. For example, at the end of his thoughtful and thorough review of the leadership research Stogdill (1974) makes recommendations for future research. In the section on leader-follower interactions Stogdill recommends the continued use of the conditional model (e.g., the type used by Fiedler). He then identifies 25 experimental and 6 criterion variables. If each of these variables is unitary in nature (an assumption which Stogdill explicitly doubts), then he states that at least 300 manipulations would be required to test the effects of the variation in each (p. 427). Stogdill continues by stating "the range of possible combinations of variables is very large indeed. It is not likely that any one researcher will be able to investigate the relationship between more than a few of the variables" (p. 427). In that one recommendation there is embedded enough work to keep many researchers busy throughout their lifetime to produce more handbooks where the future editors may be finding the same lack of additivity and applicability.

No one, to my knowledge, can store and retrieve the information in the handbooks, in an on-line manner. Moreover, even if they could, what would they do if they had to store similar amounts of information regarding other activities? Also, if it could be stored, how long would it take to diagnose the situation, scan one's brain, match a stored map with the present map of the situation, identify alternative actions, select one, and act? It is likely that the world would have passed by the leader while he was trying to cope with all these activities. This appears to be the reason that Chomsky is quoted as saying that if people were to follow rigorously the results of social science research, they would never get out of bed.

In a perceptive article on leadership, McCall calls for the reexamination of leadership research (1978). He makes a good case stating that the lack of additivity and usefulness of leadership research may be related to conceptual sterility and our asking the wrong questions. Then, when he presents his recommendations he appears to be remaining within the existing normal science research paradigm. McCall makes a plea for a further research in formalization, standards, selection, management movement, task interdependence, geographic dispersion, information and resource control, visibility, symbols, and job structure. He ends that paragraph by stating that, "these factors by no means exhaust either the range or depth or organizational influences on leadership processes" (p. 10). To this writer, this could be a plea for a new line of inquiry that will produce new findings embedded with the dysfunctionalities identified above.

In another perceptive article, Lombardo concludes, from a review of the literature, that 1) leadership is a complex set of behaviors, 2) the nature of managerial work is frenetic and capricious, 3) leadership involves making decisions with less-than-complete information, 4) the "situation" in which leaders work extends far beyond the work group to organizational and environmental demands, and 5) this "situation" is constantly changing (1978, p. 7).

I submit his conclusions are valid and that most leaders could tell us these findings without any research because they describe the action context that they experience every day. Finally, it is argued that if the above is true then it represents evidence (that will be continually reproducible) that the way we are going about studying leadership is a bit inefficient.

Lombardo would probably agree with these conclusions. He wants to study leaders as they "dash around" in the frenetic, capricious, changing world. I conducted such a study (Argyris, 1953) which I now see as flawed. Some of the factors that Lombardo proposes were observed, but the theories-in-use that the subordinates held were never mapped. Although I studied the pattern of relationships that they created, I never studied the learning system that they created. Lombardo identifies 12 leadership roles. He then wants to find out what leaders do to behave effectively in these roles. He hypothesizes that their cognitive/complexity features can make a difference. He also hypothesizes that their use of structures and power are also relevant, and hopes to learn about these relationships by placing leaders in simulated situations.

If I am not misunderstanding his strategy, he will simulate situations where leaders have to take on such roles as monitor, disseminate, take entrepreneurial action, shoot from the hip, persuade, etc. He will then observe their responses to see how cognitively complex they are, how they used structures and power. In order to produce generalizations, he will have to vary some conditions systematically. If so, then in order to be systematic he may be creating a world that is already significantly decomposed (less frenetic and capricious). Next, he will be faced with the problem of defining an effectiveness criterion. If he uses any perceptual measures, he will violate his own advice. If he uses some objective measure of an effective problem, he will have created an experimental problem that has the feature that most difficult leadership problems do not have—namely, an objective output measure.

None of this means that simulation should not be used; it means, I believe, that it should not be used as yet. The first step may be to take Lombardo's description of the frenetic changing world seriously, and observe leaders in their habitats to obtain the maps they hold, in order to create constancy among change. In the case of theory-of-action perspective, this would lead to mapping their theories-in-use. If the findings do not differ from the data collected to date, we would find that although there is wide variance in behavior there is little variance in theory-in-use. Also, we would find that there is little variance in the learning system in which leaders are embedded. Finally, we would find that the theories-in-use and the learning systems reinforce each other.

Conclusion

I began this chapter with the generalization that we are critical of the additivity and applicability of the research on leadership, yet not much seems to be done to correct the situation. An attempt was then made to show that the purposes of basic research and the purposes for everyday action on the part of human beings are consonant.

The difficulty arises in the rules for the conduct of rigorous research. By limiting research to describing the world as it is and by generating the present criteria to reduce threats to validity, a condition is created where 1) invalid generalizations may be produced whose invalidity is not ascertainable, 2) research methodology limits inquiry into the nature of the universe, 3) the concepts produced to understand the context of action can become disconnected from it, 4) there is systematic exclusion of the conditions embedded in many generalizations, and 5) there is an increasing probability of immobilizing actors by the knowledge that we produce.

These consequences are counter to the goals of science. As scientists we abhor generalizations whose invalidity is not ascertainable, rules that limit inquiry, and concepts that are disconnected from reality. Hence, the inner contradictions.

Every conclusion in this chapter can be shown to be applicable to sociologically psychologically oriented organizational theories, to political science decision theory and organizational theories, as well as to the behavioral theory of the firm. The research on leadership therefore is only an empirical example of a more comprehensive problem in social science (Argyris, 1978). The time has arrived, I believe, that the inner contradictions of rigorous research be taken more seriously.

5

Laboratory and Field Research on Leadership: Integrating Divergent Streams

MARSHALL SASHKIN AND HOWARD GARLAND

Prefatory remarks to a chapter are unusual.[1] The following are presented in response to an unexpected issue that arose in the review process, as we moved toward a final draft of this chapter. Some reviewers felt that our basic arguments had been made before by other authors. We were referred to these sources and found that this was not so, although our model is based upon a standard scientific research approach (e.g., Kaplan, 1964).

We would like to offer an observation on the above issue. Our primary arguments in this chapter are that: 1) everyone doing leadership research is at least vaguely familiar with the basic research model we present; 2) few, if any, scholars follow the model in their own research; and 3) a number of negative outcomes result from this, including a false conflict between laboratory and field methodologies which obscures the fact that the research model we espouse (Argyris, 1976, 1978) is not the basis for our behavior as leadership researchers. When these facts are stated openly, colleagues appear to go to considerable length to deny or obscure them.

We ask that before becoming wrapped up in the flaws of our model and our assessment of the literature, that the reader examine our basic premises with an open mind. Is there really nothing new in the following pages, or does one just want to ignore the issues that we raise in order to feel comfortable with a history of research in which these issues play little if any role?

---

[1] During the initial stages of the preparation of this chapter, Marshall Sashkin was Associate Professor of Management at Memphis State University.

Introduction

As students, most leadership scholars were thoroughly familiarized with the traditional scientific research model—observation is followed by theory, theory is followed by experiment, modified and refined, with a view toward pilot and eventual full-scale application of valid behavioral science knowledge. By any objective measure, the study of leadership has failed to produce generally accepted, practically useful, and widely applied scientific knowledge (Hunt & Larson, 1977). Thus, we are in the position of having a generally accepted paradigm, which does not seem to work. Why? We suggest two reasons.

First, the model has typically not been applied correctly. In particular, we see the field versus laboratory research "feud" as responsible for the lack of clear, valid scientific findings. In the behavioral sciences, laboratory and field research are both necessary and complementary. The specific details of the complementarity will be presented later in this report.

Second, we believe that any valid knowledge which is developed tends not to be applied, because universities do not train "linkers" (Havelock, 1968; Havelock, Guskin, Frohman, Havelock, Hill, & Huber, 1969), people who take scientific knowledge to users and help the latter put this knowledge into practice. Furthermore, we would argue that the reward system at academic institutions actually discourages systematic, large-scale application efforts; professors are promoted and tenured for researching or "knowing," not for applying or "doing."

In summary, the basic arguments of this chapter are: 1) Laboratory and field research approaches complement one another within the framework of the scientific paradigm outlined above. 2) Failure to train linking agents, coupled with an academic reward system which encourages "knowing," but discourages "doing," prevents any valid scientific knowledge we do have about leadership from being applied. In presenting these arguments we shall review field and lab research trends of the past decade, using some themes to illustrate our position and noting certain problems that might be dealt with through more careful application of the paradigm we have outlined.

We should explicitly note the determining value basis of our argument. J. P. Campbell (1977) observes that "while academic/researcher types can enjoy the luxury of being interested in leadership or repelled by it, as fashion dictates, real people must deal with it constantly" (p. 222). He goes on to say that "Discussion of the *purpose* for which leadership concepts and data are to be used is . . . notably absent" (p. 232). At another point in the same essay, Campbell argues "that judgments about the usefulness of a body of knowledge cannot be divorced from the purposes for which the knowledge is to be used" (p. 225).

We feel that Campbell has raised a crucial issue: why do we study leadership? Obviously there are many answers, and all depend to some extent on the individual researchers. In our case, we like to think that one reason we study leadership is that the knowledge gained can eventually be used to help organizations function more effectively and at the same time result in more "humane" organizations, i.e., organizations designed to meet the needs of their members to the greatest degree possible (e.g., Meltzer & Wickert, 1976). Thus, we believe in the importance of the ultimate practical utility of the research process. While the pragmatic can be overemphasized, as Argyris (1976) has noted, it is through the careful, conscious application of a research and diffusion process that makes use of the strengths of laboratory and field research, that we can try to insure that the results of a pragmatic value orientation are beneficial.

Complementarity

It is unfortunate that so many researchers, and not just in the field of leadership, see laboratory and field work as alternative options, or even worse, as exclusive of one another. Many writers have examined strengths and weaknesses of laboratory and field research methods (e.g., Festinger, 1971; Seashore, 1971; Weick, 1967). McGrath and Altman (1966) and more recently Evan (1971) have outlined models that incorporate similar sequences of laboratory and field research. In both cases some form of field observation precedes theory development which leads to laboratory experimentation and then to field validation. In neither case have attempts been made to interpret bodies of research within these models. Nor have serious efforts been made to use these models to guide the research process. It is clear that in the area of leadership, laboratory and field research have been two diverging streams, with the field by far the more heavily traveled, based on our literature search. Despite arguments in the preceding (Weick, 1965) and current (Fromkin & Streufert, 1976) decades for more laboratory research in organizational behavior, there is no evidence that an increasing number of leadership scholars have been more willing to enter the dark recesses of the behavioral laboratory. In a recent survey of the leadership literature (Hunt, Osborn, & Schriesheim, 1978) 81 percent of the studies cited were performed in the field.

Our position is that laboratory and field research are complementary, with the weaknesses of one being compensated for by the strengths of the

TABLE 8

Strengths and Weaknesses of Laboratory and Field Research Settings

Strength	Weakness
Laboratory	
True experiments are possible allowing for causal inference	Problems of external validity make it difficult to judge the practical significance of findings
Clarity of manipulation and precision of measurement are ideal for testing general theory	Weak manipulation of independent variables may lead to lack of effects
Relatively low cost permits creativity, "galumphing," testing hunches, etc.	Difficult to carry out research over extended time periods
Field	
External validity is less of a problem. The practical significance of results may be evident	Experimentation is very difficult, making causal inference a problem
Manipulations in field experiments have direct impact on the lives of participants	Manipulations tend to be less precise, creating difficulty of interpretation
Research over extended time periods is feasible	Relatively high cost discourages creativity, "galumphing," and basic research

other. Each of these research settings seems to be appropriate for gathering certain kinds of information, with the information gathered in one setting adding to, modifying, extending, and validating information gathered in the other. In Table 8 we present some of the more obvious strengths and weaknesses of laboratory and field research.

Perhaps the major strength of the laboratory setting is that it is well suited to experimental research (i.e., the manipulation of independent variables, control of other relevant variables, and measurement of dependent variables). Since experiments are the only safe method for drawing causal inferences, and since true field experimentation is quite difficult, not to mention costly, even when it is a possibility, the laboratory remains the most important setting for testing causal hypotheses.

A second strength of the laboratory setting is the ease with which it allows precision and clarity in the manipulation and measurement of variables. Related to this is the ability to control, in the laboratory, sources of variation that may be significantly related to the dependent variable of interest. Because the laboratory facilitates the refinement of experimentation to the point where researchers can specify exactly what variable(s) they have manipulated and measured, it is an ideal setting in which to test theory in its most general form.

Finally, the laboratory tends to be a much less costly setting for research than the field. The term costly is used here in both the economic and social sense. Real organizations cannot be damaged by the laboratory researcher, as they can be (and have been) by field researchers (Bennis, 1966). For this reason it is much easier to play or, as Weick (1977b) would say "galumph" in the laboratory. Basic research, creative research, playful research, galumphing, or whatever one cares to label it, is an important first step in the research process. It is a step ill-suited to field settings but well-suited to the laboratory.

Thus, we will make an assertion with which some, and perhaps many, will argue. We believe that the first step in testing theory about human behavior should almost always be taken in a laboratory setting. We have three qualifications. First, when "macro-level" variables are the concern (e.g., organization structure, technology, etc.) it may sometimes be more desirable to begin research in a field setting. Second, should a true experimental opportunity present itself in a field setting, the researcher should obviously not ignore this. Third, theory development may be assisted by field observation or, as Evan (1971) suggests, by obtaining case study or sample survey data prior to any experimental testing of hypotheses (see also McGrath & Altman, 1966).

Since a major thrust of the present argument centers on a particular stepwise knowledge development and diffusion process, we must caution the reader to avoid mistaking field observation for field experimentation. As noted earlier, the former is part of theory development, while the latter should generally follow laboratory experimentation (Lewin, 1948), although the laboratory work on which action-research is based may involve basic processes rather than specific applied issues (Frohman, Sashkin, & Kavanagh, 1976).

Despite the strengths of laboratory research which we have just reviewed, this method is not without a number of problems. One major weakness centers around the question of external validity (Campbell & Stanley, 1963). Basically, this question asks how much we can generalize the results of laboratory research to other settings, populations, and tasks? In this regard, we have the perennial charge of artificiality in laboratory research. Both Weick (1965) and Fromkin and Streufert (1976) have done excellent jobs in responding to this charge. We feel that in most cases, artificiality is an inappropriate and overused criticism. There is, however, one important problem with laboratory research in the area of leadership; how does one determine the practical significance of findings. It is possible that an effect observed to be significant in the laboratory would not hold up under conditions in which a large number of other variables were allowed to operate simultaneously. Also related to the question of external validity is the problem of getting subjects from a population of interest (e.g., practicing managers) into the laboratory.

Laboratory researchers have generally utilized those subjects who are most available, college sophomores. Although this may create a problem of generalization, it should be pointed out that college sophomores may be more heterogeneous with respect to characteristics associated with leadership than would be a group of managers chosen from within one company or industry, which is the kind of sample most often used in field studies of leadership. Considering that large numbers of college students, particularly those in business schools, will one day occupy managerial positions in a wide variety of organizations, there may be greater justification for generalizing from this population to "managers in general" than from a sample of managers studied within one "real" organization. This is not meant to argue away the potential problems of exclusive utilization of university students in laboratory research on leadership but, rather, to point out a relevant consideration which seems to have been ignored by many field and laboratory researchers.

A second problem for laboratory researchers is that the manipulation of independent variables in the laboratory may be too weak to produce an effect that might otherwise occur in a naturalistic setting. The problem of weakly manipulated variables has been greatly increased in recent years by the application of more and more rigorous standards for the treatment of human subjects in research.

Finally, it is very difficult to carry out laboratory research over an extended period of time. Most studies are severely time limited, and even a major laboratory simulation (e.g., Litwin & Stringer, 1968) is unlikely to last for more than a week or so.

Field research tends to be strong where laboratory research is weak. First, while problems of generalization are apparent in laboratory research, field settings allow one to do research in those situations and with those populations that are of immediate applied interest. In such cases there is neither a problem with external validity nor with assessing the strength and importance of effects. Field studies thus present good opportunities for determining the practical utility of effects. Such studies test the "washout" effect in the only way possible, an ongoing, complex situation (Weick, 1967). Second, although it is often difficult to manipulate independent variables in the field, these variables, once manipulated may have a strong impact on the participants under study. Generally, in true and quasi-experimental field studies manipulations, no matter how innocuous they seem, are of importance because they impact upon the everyday lives of participants. Finally, longitudinal research seems more feasible in the field than in the laboratory. In this regard, field experiments extending over a period of a year or more are not uncommon in the leadership literature (Hand & Slocum, 1972; Seashore & Bowers, 1970).

Just as we argued that the major strength of the laboratory setting was ease of experimentation, the major weakness of the field as a research setting is the difficulty posed by experimentation. Most organizations are quite reluctant to allow researchers the freedom needed to test causal hypotheses. (Interestingly, many of these same organizations are willing to pay consultants for the implementation of leadership training programs that have no scientific validity.) The vast majority of field research is, therefore, correlational, leaving the question of causality at best indeterminate and at worst erroneously asserted. Weick (1977) quotes DeNuoy (1966) as saying, "There are no independent variables in nature." Indeed, there are not. In the laboratory, researchers have begun to demonstrate that what had traditionally been thought to be causes by some researchers may be the results of what had been considered their effects (e.g., Farris & Lim, 1969; Lowin & Craig, 1968). One response to the problem of causal indeterminacy in field research has been the development and increasing use of sophisticated new analytic procedures (Blalock, 1964; Borgatta, 1969; Cappella, 1975). Such methods, however, are often applied inappropriately to data that do not, and cannot, fulfill the technical requirements for use of the methods.

Field studies are also weak with respect to precision and clarity of manipulations. In those few but very important field experiments that do exist (Coch & French, 1948) manipulations tend to be heavy-handed, so that while it may be possible to argue that the manipulation did have an effect, it is not possible to really determine what part of the manipulation was essential. Finally, the high cost of field research makes this setting less suitable for pilot testing, trying to verify hypotheses based upon hunch and insight, galumphing, and just playing around with ideas of one kind or another.

We have neither exhausted the problems with field or lab research nor defined all of the assets of each. We have tried to show that, in several important ways, laboratory and field research complement one another. This argument has been made by others (often implicitly), as we have noted. The models outlined by McGrath and Altman (1966) and by Evan (1971), in particular, are sound attempts to reconcile the issues we have detailed. We would argue that many of the current problems with leadership research can be usefully examined in terms of failure to follow some form of the basic model reviewed here. Using such a framework, we will review current prominent trends in leadership research.

First, we must add to our model a final phase—dissemination and utilization. We suggest that failure to seriously link research knowledge in the field of leadership to organizational applications, not on a single case basis but in terms of widespread practical day-to-day application, is yet another major cause of problems. Lack of application, as an expected, normal end-result of the research process, leaves the user out of that process. User-input is not, then, an input to theory development. An iterative cycle of research, based on user needs, is not then possible. We shall briefly describe the sort of diffusion and utilization phase that, we would argue, should be a part of an effective research process.

The Research, Diffusion, and Utilization Process

The research, knowledge diffusion, and utilization process may be characterized in terms of at least three phases. Although these phases are not "pure" and clearly separated from one another, we believe there is some evidence supporting this basic paradigm, as well as some degree of consensus among social scientists as to the desirability of using it (Havelock et al., 1969). An historical example may help in describing the complete model of the research, diffusion, and utilization process that is the basis for the present review.

Leader Emergence: An Example

Throughout the 1920s, 30s, and 40s one of the most important issues in leadership research was clearly that of leader emergence. The first research phase in our model, laboratory study, did not occur at this time, rather leader emergence was examined in field studies centered on the traits (psychological and physical) of leaders. The net result of these studies was the conclusion that a number of such traits are weakly associated with leader emergence, none to any practically meaningful degree (Stogdill, 1948).

Beginning in the late 1940s, Bales (1958) asked the same question in a series of seminal laboratory studies. He, too, found little evidence for the widespread existence of leadership traits. However, in devising a means for measuring leadership emergence, Bales invented what has come to be a tool in widespread industrial use for selection and promotion of managerial personnel, the leaderless group discussion technique (Bass, 1949). It was Bass who refined and extensively studied the technique in a long series of laboratory investigations (Bass, 1953; Bass & Coates, 1952). Bass used not only college students, but "real" managers in his studies. One of his most consistent findings was a significant relation between emergence as a leader in the leaderless group discussion and real-life leadership status (Bass, 1954). Thus, in the development of the "assessment center" (Bray & Grant, 1966), a technique for managerial selection and promotion, the leaderless group discussion was included as one of the "exercises" in which assessees participate. Assessment centers have since been shown to be reliable and valid devices for managerial selection and promotion (Huck, 1973; MacKinnon, 1975). The leaderless group discussion exercise is probably included in every assessment center now conducted.

We see in this example the three-phase research and diffusion process played out in full. The theoretical concern was leader emergence and phase one involved basic laboratory research, primarily by Bales and his associates. Some of this research was simply observational and exploratory, while in other research specific hypotheses were tested. Soon after the basic research began (1947–55) the second phase was initiated—refinement and research oriented field applications (Bass, 1953; Flanagan, 1961; Kiessling & Kalish, 1961). Finally, some time after this second phase had occurred came the third phase of widespread practical application (Bray & Grant, 1966). For this particular example, the process took about 20 years. Figure 5 illustrates the phases in this model.[2]

Although the model we propose is less sophisticated than some current models of research, development, and diffusion, our purpose is to demonstrate that: 1) laboratory research methods are most appropriate to phases in which field research methods are least appropriate, and vice versa, 2) problems of various sorts emerge when the model is not followed, either because one or another phase is omitted, or, more typically, when an inappropriate research method is the sole or primary approach to a particular phase.

Recent Research: An Interpretation of Trends

We will identify the predominant themes in recent lab and field research on leadership and analyze the development of these themes in terms of our simple-phase model. Our definitions of laboratory and field studies are basic: the former category includes all research done in vitro, in a controlled setting that has been created solely for the purpose of experimenting with or observing the dynamics of leadership behavior. Our field

---

[2] We do not suggest that this process was planned or intended, in this example, nor do we assert that the process is typically planned. However, it would seem that such planning would greatly facilitate the knowledge development and diffusion process.

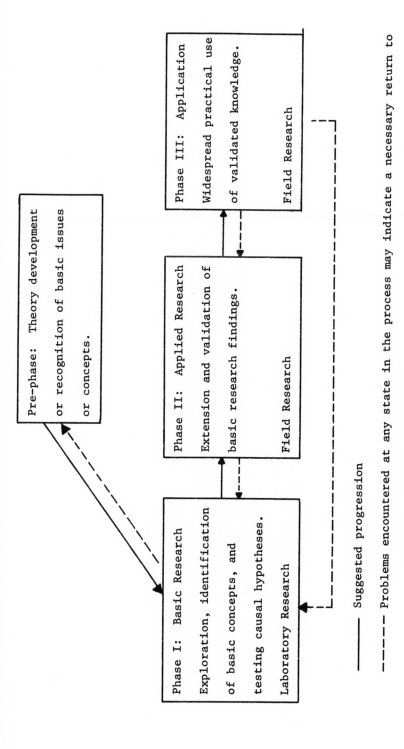

Pre-phase: Theory development or recognition of basic issues or concepts.

Phase I: Basic Research
Exploration, identification of basic concepts, and testing causal hypotheses.
Laboratory Research

Phase II: Applied Research
Extension and validation of basic research findings.
Field Research

Phase III: Application
Widespread practical use of validated knowledge.
Field Research

——— Suggested progression

‑ ‑ ‑ ‑ Problems encountered at any state in the process may indicate a necessary return to some earlier stage for further work.

Fig. 5. A model of the research and diffusion process

studies category includes all leadership research conducted in vivo, in real-life settings.

The primary selection criteria for this review were the authors' respective subjective perceptions. We each reviewed the leadership research literature of the past decade, one concentrating on field the other on lab research. Our aim was to perceive and extract the predominant themes, areas, or topics of study in the lab and in the field. Readers can accept or reject our judgments, but we are reasonably confident that we have caught —and interpreted—the flavor of the past ten years of leadership research.

Based on our earlier discussion, we were not surprised to find somewhat different trends in field as compared with laboratory research. What is somewhat unexpected, however, is the typical paucity of linkages between field and lab research. That is, the model we are using here is at least in part well known to researchers. In fact, an objection by some anonymous reviewers of this chapter to the presentation of our model was that nothing was new, since everyone knows and uses it. Thus, we expected to observe considerable use of the model. In fact, we found practically no such use. The few instances where we did find a fit with this model seemed to occur more through fortuitous circumstance than through planned research strategy. Since our aim was to identify, in each method area, the primary trends of the past ten years or so we did not attempt a comprehensive literature review. Rather, we show how studies in each of several primary theme areas result in a fit—or lack of fit—with the phase model we have described.

Field Research Trends

In our judgment, three themes stand out in field research of the past ten years or so, but in sheer number of studies (Hunt, Osborn, & Schriesheim, 1978), one theme is clearly dominant: the study of leader behavior as it relates to (and by implication, affects) subordinate performance and satisfaction, especially in terms of variables that moderate these relationships. In the vast majority of these studies,[3] leader behavior means the Ohio State Consideration and Initiating Structure scores, obtained via subordinate report on some version of the Leader Behavior Description Questionnaire (LBDQ). A second and more limited trend centers on trait measures of leadership, particularly using Fiedler's (1967) contingency theory. One new trait area has been opened recently by House (1977), the study of charisma. The third theme concerns a particular theory, the "vertical dyad"

[3] This judgment is based on our review of the literature; some supportive documentation can be seen in the recent literature review by Hunt, Osborn, & Schriesheim (1978).

theory of leadership recently put forth by Graen and his colleagues (e.g., Graen, Dansereau, Minami, & Cashman, 1973).

Leader Behavior and Subordinate Satisfaction and Performance

The history of research on leader behavior and subordinate satisfaction and performance is an interesting example of how the research and diffusion process can go wrong when the model we have described is not followed. The vast majority of field research studies on leader behavior have used the Ohio State dimensions, Consideration (C) and Initiation of Structure (IS) developed in field studies of the 1950s (Fleishman, 1953; Stogdill & Coons, 1957). These dimensions are, for all practical purposes, identical to the two behavior dimensions (i.e., "task" and "socio-emotional") identified earlier by Bales (1950) in laboratory studies.[4] C and IS behaviors are, of course, measured from subordinate reports rather than direct observation.

So far, so good; the Ohio State researchers clearly confirmed the predominance, in field settings, of the two basic leader behavior categories (or dimensions) first identified by Bales in the lab. However, the testing/extension phase from the mid-1950s to the early 1960s was disappointing. No clear relations were found between leader behavior (C/IS) and subordinate attitudes or performance. The relations obtained were either indirect (e.g., Fleishman & Harris, 1962, found a somewhat complex pattern of relations between C/IS and grievance rates, turnover, and absenteeism) or qualified and conditional (e.g., Kerr, 1973, found C related to satisfaction for employees moderate on "willingness to leave" but not when willingness to leave was very high or low), although there are weak general trends (Korman, 1966, found IS tends to be negatively related to a variety of criteria, including satisfaction and performance, while C tends to be positively related).

In attempting to explain these findings, Kerr and Schriesheim (1974) suggested that situational factors may *moderate* the relationship between C/IS and criterion variables. In fact, much of the field research literature from the mid-1960s to date can be characterized as a mad search for such moderator variables which regulate, condition, or attenuate the leader behavior (C/IS)—subordinate attitude/performance relationship. Unfortunately, no general moderators have been found.

---

[4] Some researchers would certainly argue that the various measures of these similar concepts show significant differences. We disagree, viewing such a position as equivalent to the situation of the entymologists arguing over the significance of differences among species of gnats based on eyelash length.

Despite the failure to find either direct or moderated effects of C and IS, two applied diffusion outcomes have taken place. One diffusion outcome has been the assertion that high levels of leader behavior on both dimensions (C and IS) lead to high subordinate satisfaction and performance (Blake & Mouton, 1964, 1978), despite extensive evidence that this is not the case (Larson, Hunt, & Osborn, 1976; Nystrom, 1978). The assertion has been developed into a well-known and widely used management training device, called the Managerial Grid.[5] This outcome should not be viewed in overly negative terms. Beer and Kleisath (1967), for example, found that Grid training for all supervisory and managerial personnel in a large plant improved managerial communication and problem solving by giving these people a shared language and knowledge base relevant to managerial problems and issues. Thus trainees did gain in understanding of leadership behaviors and, in particular, of their own behaviors. Finally, with Grid as with any training approach one should neither neglect nor downgrade the so-called Hawthorne Effect or, more generally, the placebo effect of telling trainees that they *will* become better leaders and getting them to believe it (see Shepard, 1975).

The second diffusion outcome occurred over the same time span but is only now becoming very popular (among managers; most academic researchers remain unaware of this second approach). This is the "life cycle" theory of leadership, developed by Hersey and Blanchard (1969, 1977) and now called "situational leadership theory." It is a direct outgrowth of the moderator search referred to above. Hersey and Blanchard (1969, 1977) assert that the developmental phase or maturity level of a group or individual moderates the appropriate combination of C and IS behavior levels. This assertion is based on their own logical arguments and has received no empirical or experimental test, in field or lab settings. Obviously, the need here is for experimental research in laboratory situations, a step in the basic research paradigm skipped by Hersey and Blanchard. We do not suggest that the effects of their approach are necessarily negative. Researchers do tend to agree that aspects of the situation are important for leader behavior. By training leaders to attend to certain situational variables, "situational leadership theory" may actually contribute to the trainee's improved control—management—of the situation. Whether this is so is, of course, pure speculation in the absence of any empirical evidence.

We suggest that one reason this research area—the study of the effects of leader behavior on subordinate attitudes and performance—has been

---

[5] Managerial Grid is the registered trademark of Scientific Methods, Inc., an Austin, Texas-based management training and consulting firm headed by Robert Blake and Jane Mouton.

fairly unproductive is its almost exclusive focus on field investigations (and applications). J. P. Campbell (1977) and Argyris (this volume) suggest that C and IS are constructs too far removed from specific leader behavior. If this is so, we suggest that the search for more concrete leader behaviors would best begin in, or return to, the laboratory. A reasonable place to start might, for example, be the 12 categories in Bales's (1950) Interaction Process Analysis framework, or the 10 factors in addition to C and IS measured by the LBDQ (Stogdill, 1963a). In any case, the failure of C and IS (or the various conceptually identical leader behavior categories) to be associated with subordinate behavior or attitudes in fairly consistent and *pragmatically useful* ways should lead us back to the laboratory, rather than to a widely divergent multiplicity of efforts to make sense of the current results through additional field studies and attempted applications.

We assume, of course, that the researchers' interests are on human behavior as a central aspect of leadership rather than as a peripheral factor. In the latter case, for example in examining technology or organizational structure as the primary causes of subordinate performance (and, perhaps, of leader behavior as well) one might do as Perrow (1970) and conclude that technology is the determining variable, to be studied in the field, while leadership is irrelevant.

The leadership researcher should return to the laboratory for further examination of task and relationship behaviors and their effects for reasons which to us seem obvious. That is, field studies are inconclusive and confusing; greater conceptual clarity is needed and can only be attached through true experimental designs, in laboratory settings. This is directly inferrable from the basic scientific research paradigm we detailed earlier. Despite this, field researchers look for salvation in increasingly complex and sophisticated research methodology (much of which we judge to be inappropriately applied) and in the mad search for moderators.

Despite this gloomy assessment, we note the recent development and testing of two theoretical frameworks concerned with the effects of leader behavior on subordinate performance. These are: 1) House's (1971) path-goal theory,[6] and 2) reinforcement theory or, as it is commonly called, "behavior modification" (Scott, 1977; Sims, 1977). The behaviorist approach is founded in many years of lab research (Skinner, 1953, 1976). Expectancy theory, too has a long lab research background (Lawler, 1973). Hunt and Larson (1977) have observed that these two frameworks may be

---

[6] This approach is, in essence, nearly identical to the various "expectancy theory" models, of which perhaps the best known is that refined by Campbell, Dunnette, Lawler, and Weick (1970) from Vroom's (1960) original theory.

considered alternative forms of the same basic approach, that is, application of the law of effect (Thorndike, 1913) to behavior in organizations. This argument is presented in detail in Mawhinney and Ford (1977).

Both of these approaches fall in the category of leader behavior as it affects subordinate behavior and attitudes. They are concerned with specification of desired subordinate performance behavior, and leader behaviors that involve, first the definition of reward "contingencies" for desired subordinate behavior (e.g., if production exceeds X amount a pay bonus will be awarded) and, second, the delivery of rewards when subordinate behavior is as desired (e.g., actually giving the employee a bonus check when production level X is exceeded).[7] In addition, the path-goal and reinforcement approaches both meet with J. P. Campbell's (1977) suggested need for greater specification of behavior.

Although the path-goal approach predates reinforcement theory (as applied to leadership) by more than a decade (Georgopoulis, Mahoney, & Jones, 1957), only the latter has been subjected to applied field tests, in the sense of using the approach to determine leadership behaviors. Path-goal theory has been tested in real situations, with generally positive results (see House & Mitchell, 1974, for a summary of the results of these studies), but has not been applied in formal *experimental* field studies. In fact, House (personal communication) has commented to the effect that further laboratory experimentation is needed, since so much of the path-goal literature is based on field observation and cross-sectional correlational tests (which cannot determine causality). This judgment conforms to our own, based on the model presented earlier, although we would suggest that limited experimental field applications of path-goal theory are also justified.

While reinforcement theory has had more experimental field application than path-goal theory, these efforts have, in our view, been rather crude (see Luthans & Kreitner, 1975) and further applied tests should be far more sophisticated (Mawhinney, 1975).

Trait Theories

The rather dismal conclusions of Stogdill's (1948) classic survey of research on leadership traits seem to have killed off the trait approach to the study of leadership some thirty years ago. To be sure, an occasional trait-based study still appears (e.g., Palmer, 1974), usually with no significant findings. Two trait-based theories do exist, one as a theory in the process of development (House, 1977), the other in a far more advanced—and hotly

---

[7] This example is extremely oversimplified. For clear presentations of these approaches see House and Mitchell (1974), Scott (1977), and Sims (1977).

debated—state (Fiedler, 1967, 1971, 1972, 1973). We can say little regarding House's (1977) theory of charismatic leadership, since the propositions he has developed await empirical testing. Most could and, in our view, should be examined in lab studies, although this method presents some difficulties for testing some of the propositions.[8]

Fiedler's Contingency Model is placed in this category because it began (Fiedler, 1954) as an explicitly trait-based approach, and because the greatest proportion of research studies (including the earliest ones) have been field studies.[9] This approach has probably stirred more controversy in academic circles, among leadership researchers, than any other. Furthermore, anyone with more than a passing interest in leadership research is generally familiar with Fiedler's work. We shall not present the model in any detail here but we will give our summary evaluation. Even severe critics (Schriesheim & Kerr, 1977) agree that Fiedler's theory has been of benefit to the field of leadership research. We would go somewhat further and conclude, as does Peterson (1978), that, "Given the complexity of Fiedler's predictions, the amount of empirical support they have received is surprising."

Fiedler's theory presents an almost Sphinx-like puzzle. Most critics admit empirical results are consistently (if often weakly) supportive of the theory. Yet we do not know what the key predictor trait variable, the Least Preferred Co-worker (LPC) score, really measures (except in terms of Fiedler's assertions), nor do we really know why the theory works (except, again, for Fiedler's speculative rationale). We suggest that one reason these key issues remain unknown is the inability of field studies to shed light on them and the failure of Fiedler to become deeply involved with experimental lab studies. In this regard, one of the few studies that provides hints about the nature of the LPC measure is a laboratory study by Fishbein, Landy, and Hatch (1969) whose results suggest that LPC is an attitudinal measure having properties similar to those expected of an attitude. Researchers seem to react negatively when asked to accept colleagues' theories and interpretations as matters of faith. We are not surprised at the vehemence of some of Feidler's critics. And, we emphasize that Fiedler has contributed to these reactions through the field research strategy he chose to follow.

Most recently Fiedler and his colleagues (Fiedler, Chemers, & Mahar, 1976) have developed materials and training programs based on Fiedler's

---

[8] That is, some of House's propositions involve charismatic leader behavior that might be impossible to create in a laboratory setting.
[9] Note that we interpret LPC as a trait approach here, while Hunt and Larson provide a somewhat different perspective in their introduction to part 1.

Contingency Model. Schriesheim and Kerr (1977) have, figuratively, raised their arms in horror at this development. While we are skeptical that the positive outcomes Fiedler (Chemers & Fiedler, 1978) and his colleagues (Csoka & Bons, 1978) have reported for this training approach can be attributed primarily to the theory, we are neither horrified at his applications nor do we doubt the positive effects of these efforts. Rather, in a vein similar to our earlier speculation regarding Blake and Mouton's (1964, 1978) applications, we suggest that the positive outcomes Fiedler and others report may be due to the increased awareness of, appreciation for, and ability to affect various aspects of job situations (e.g., one's own power or power sharing, task structure, etc.). Unlike Schriesheim and Kerr (1977), we do not anticipate that leaders will purposely make situations worse, in order to fit them to their LPC styles. Control over the situation is, however, likely to be a very useful skill, regardless of LPC in particular or the Contingency Model in general. Finally, we suggest that Fiedler's theory would benefit from a renewed focus on laboratory investigations designed to explore the meaning of the LPC measure.

Vertical-Dyad Linkages

The vertical-dyad linkage (VDL) model of leadership has developed over the past five years through the work of Graen and his colleagues (Dansereau, Graen, & Haga, 1975; Graen & Cashman, 1975; Graen, Dansereau, Minami, & Cashman, 1973). The VDL approach takes the superior-subordinate dyad as the basic unit of analysis in the study of leader behavior. The primary notion is that leaders do (and should) tailor their behaviors to best fit specific subordinates. Thus, the nature of the relationships between the leader and each of several subordinates may vary widely. This would be desirable, since different subordinates have different tasks, needs, and so forth. Thus, effective leaders are seen as those who vary their behavior patterns, depending on the superior-subordinate dyad under examination.

Work on the VDL approach is exclusively field-based with no lab background. Thus, it is not surprising to us that while the VDL model provides a viable approach toward leadership as a dyadic process and has demonstrated enough validity to be taken seriously, it suffers from results that are consistently weak and seem to have little practical utility. For example, in one study (Graen et al., 1973), the authors noted that "the observed relationships were too weak to sense the functions of (i.e., be useful for purposes of) performance feedback for individual members" (p. 620). We suggest that the key behavioral concepts should have been better examined in early lab studies. That is, there seems little doubt that leaders do, to some degree, tailor their behaviors to suit individual subordinates. The key term is *to some degree*. For example, such a process might logically be much stronger in an individual task type of work structure than in a group task structure, or for uncertain tasks (for which superior-subordinate interaction would be useful). However, we must again observe that the effect is weak. The various studies done by Graen and his co-workers indicate consistent significant support for the basic theory but the support is too weak to consider any applications of the theory to real-life settings.

This judgment may be seen by some as giving premature closure to a research approach that has recently been viewed with some optimism. Rather than suggesting that the approach be dropped, we suggest that well-designed experimental laboratory studies might prove useful, for example, in clarifying the relative importance of dyadic versus group-level effects of leader behavior.

Laboratory Research Trends

As was true for field research, our examination of the literature resulted in our identification of three broad areas of work in the laboratory. In only one of these areas does current lab research relate much to field work. The discrepancy, as noted earlier, is not surprising. Our diffusion model suggests that there should be such a demarcation, with initial investigations and explorations based on theory being conducted in the lab, followed, when appropriate, by field studies. Thus, lab studies *should* represent the leading edge of leadership research. Unfortunately, this does not seem to be the case, not because some lab research is not creative but because little of it seems ever to receive extension and testing in the field.

The three themes we discovered are: 1) the study of what affects leader behavior, with leader behavior as the dependent variable, 2) research on the effect of leader behavior on subordinate attitudes and performance (the major overlap with field work), and 3) studies of leader emergence.[10]

Leader Behavior as a Dependent Variable

Laboratory researchers have examined a number of potential causes of leader behavior and this field is probably the most plowed in the area of

---

[10] Earlier we used this topic as a good illustration of our proposed step-wise diffusion process. Laboratory research on leader emergence has, however, continued in one form or another without pause since about 1945, as shown by the work of Stein, Hoffman, Cooley, and Pearse in chapter 8.

lab research on leadership. It is particularly interesting that until very recently field researchers have shown no particular interest in causes of leader behavior,[11] choosing to examine leader behavior as a predictor rather than criterion variable.

Perhaps the strongest results in the area of causes of leader behavior involve the effects of subordinate behavior on leader behavior. Bandura (1977) has, as a cornerstone of his social learning theory approach, the notion that behavior, stimulus situations, and organisms are all *reciprocally causal*, that is, the three elements affect one another. The behavior of leaders is part of the subordinates' stimulus situation (Maier, 1974); likewise, subordinate behaviors are part of the stimulus situation for leaders. The reciprocal effects that one would expect based on Bandura's (1977) theory have been convincingly demonstrated in a series of independent lab studies (Ashour & England, 1972; Farris & Lim, 1969; Herold, 1977; Lowin & Craig, 1968). While Bandura (1977) has proceeded to various applications, the leadership researchers working on this topic have not. One of the more obvious applications, for example, would be attempting to train leaders to 1) be aware of the effects of subordinates' actions on the leader's own behavior, while 2) avoiding negative cycles of behavior (e.g., undesired subordinate behavior → punishing leader behavior → more negative subordinate behavior → etc.). Although what little field research exists seems to confirm the reciprocal effects of superior and subordinate behavior (Greene, 1975), much more extensive testing and application in the field is necessary at this time.

A second factor affecting leader behavior is *task structure*. Hill and Hughes (1974) found that leaders engaged in more C and less IS behavior in structured as opposed to unstructured task situations. Such a result is quite reasonable; a highly structured task does not require more structuring. House (1971) suggests that it is by engaging in such unneeded and inappropriate IS behaviors that leaders *reduce* subordinate performance, and his point is echoed by Fiedler and Chemers (1974). The leader training program developed by Fiedler et al. (1976) may serve to reduce such inappropriate leader behavior by cueing leaders to attend to the task structure variable. Field testing of the effects of task structure is needed and could indicate the desirability of incorporating in leadership training programs specific training on the appropriate and inappropriate use of IS depending on task structure.

---

[11] Fiedler (1967) and his colleagues did, for a time, attempt to measure the effects of differing situations on leader behavior. Results were extremely mixed, and Fiedler now speculates on leader behavior (with some occasional lab evidence being used) while focusing his argument on subordinate performance as the (assumed) outcome of leader behavior.

Leader Behavior and Its Effects on Subordinate Behavior

Although most research on this topic has been done in the field, there has been a fair amount of lab research as well. One set of studies, noted earlier, has examined Fiedler's (1967) Contingency Theory, providing somewhat mixed results (Fiedler, 1971). At this point we reiterate our suggestion that the basic concepts in the theory require further lab exploration.

Another area of lab study has involved looking at the effects of *leader behavior and attributes on subordinate compliance* (doing what the leader wants), with such attributes as leader expertise and leader reward/punishment power receiving particular attention. The original source for these studies seems to be the theory of social power developed by French (1956) and operationalized, in principle, by French and Raven (1959). It has been suggested that the more sources of power a leader has, the greater the leader's influence over subordinate behavior. Lab studies have demonstrated that leader acceptance or referent power (French & Snyder, 1959), leader competency, or expert power (Hollander & Julian, 1970), and leader legitimacy (Hollander, 1964) all affect leader behavior in that leaders make more influence attempts when they feel accepted, competent, and legitimate. Some research results suggest that increased leader expertise produces greater subordinate compliance (Hollander & Julian, 1970) but this relationship has not been well replicated (Herold, 1977; Michener & Burt, 1975; Oldham, 1975; Price & Garland, 1978b). Much stronger is the effect of reward/punishment power. There is no doubt that such power strongly affects subordinate compliance with the leader's wishes, at least in the lab (Herold, 1977; Michener & Burt, 1975).

All of these findings become far more complex when recent field studies are examined. Typically, it is *not* found that reward/punishment power relates strongly to compliance or performance, while expert and referent power *are* found to be related to compliance and performance measures (Ivancevich, 1970; Ivancevich & Donnelly, 1970; Student, 1968). Further research, especially lab research, seems needed in this area. At the present time, we can observe that these results illustrate the importance of our second phase—field testing and extension—prior to any large-scale applications of research findings, since a direct application of early laboratory findings in this area may have been premature.

Leader Emergence

Laboratory experiments on leader emergence have produced some of the most consistent, compelling, and powerful results in the leadership literature. Many of these studies have adopted a strict situational approach to leader emergence. Leavitt (1951) found that mere position in a communication structure was sufficient for leader emergence. Howells and Becker (1962) found that the spatial arrangement of group members significantly influenced leader emergence. The results of these two studies have theoretical and practical significance; they tell us that one can ignore all individual differences and predict with better than chance accuracy who will emerge as leader from a knowledge of individuals' spatial or functional positions within a group. Practically, these findings suggest that already appointed or emergent leaders might solidify their positions by keeping close to either the physical or functional center of things in their organization. This is consistent with the argument developed by Salancik and Pfeffer (1977) concerning the functional basis of power in organizations.

The most established hypothesis in laboratory studies of leadership is, unquestionably, what we call the "babble hypothesis" (Bales, 1953). Simply stated, this hypothesis argues that relative rate of verbal participation is causally associated with leadership, all other things being equal. In addition to a volume of correlational evidence from laboratory studies, there have been several experimental studies which, taken together, offer extremely strong support for this hypothesis. Bavelas, Hastorf, Gross, and Kite (1965) mechanically reinforced and punished low and high participators respectively for verbal participation in a discussion group. Low participators were found to increase significantly their rate of verbal participation in response to reinforcement. Furthermore, leadership ratings of these low participators made by the other group members significantly increased with increased participation.

Similar results have been obtained in at least five other laboratory experiments which have utilized varying group tasks, verbal participation manipulations, and measures of leader emergence (Ginter & Lindskold, 1975; Jaffe & Lucas, 1969; Smith, 1972; Sorrentino & Boutillier, 1975; Stang, 1973). These later experiments establish a degree of external validity for the "babble hypothesis" seldom achieved for other hypotheses either in the laboratory or in the field.

Leader emergence is still a subject of serious study, as shown by the work of Stein, Hoffman, Cooley, and Pearse presented in chapter 8 and related work summarized in chapter 14. These attempt to identify the details of the "babble" emergence process. There has been some field research in this area in recent years (e.g., Berkowitz, 1956; Elkin, Halpern, & Cooper, 1962; Rychlak, 1963), but most studies that have been done tend to be unintegrated and typically attempt to find traits (dominance, etc.) associated with emergent leadership. Success seems generally low (as measured by the results of the studies just cited).

Oddly, there seems to have been little application of the above results to the area of leader training. The example we gave of our research and diffusion process involved leader emergence in the leaderless group discussion (Bass, 1954), but no other applications are evident despite the strength of these results. One might then ask why no field tests or applications have occurred. To respond to this question we return to our model of the research and diffusion process.

Linkages in the Research and Diffusion Process

Why have some applications been widespread—and clearly traceable in terms of our simple research and diffusion model—while applications that one might expect have just not materialized? Our argument here is that the difference between application/diffusion failures (really lack of attempts) and successes can be attributed to the presence or absence of a *linking agent* (Havelock, 1968; Havelock et al., 1969), an individual—like Bass—who spans the gap between research and practice or, more generally, between "science and life" (Maier, 1974).

A positive step toward the development of more linking agents would involve more intense socialization of graduate students into the "scientist-practitioner" role (R. Campbell, 1978). In psychology this model has lately received little support from those who see themselves as pure scientists and is attacked (though often indirectly and, perhaps, inadvertently) by those who consider themselves to be practitioners. The scientist-practitioner training model also does not seem to be widely recognized as important by organizational behaviorists (i.e., scholars in schools of business, management, and administration).

We do not propose to solve this problem here. It is complex and not amenable to easy answers.[12] Others (e.g., Havelock et al, 1969) have devoted careers to the study of the broader problem of knowledge diffusion and utilization. We do suggest that if our efforts toward understanding leadership are to have meaningful outcomes we must develop a corps of linking agents, comparable to engineers, who are well trained in both science and applications.

A first step is recognition of a research and diffusion process that links basic and applied research. The model we present here is simplistic, yet it can prove useful. We have shown how it can suggest research directions—back to the lab; go to the field; and so forth—as well as reducing, if not eliminating the traditional mutual ignorance of field and lab researchers.

[12] See, for example, Sashkin, Morris, and Horst (1973).

Perhaps the thoroughly dysfunctional animosity generated by pointless arguments of which approach is "better" can be eliminated, by recognizing that each is better for specific purposes at certain points in the research and diffusion process. Perhaps field and lab researchers will not only talk to one another more, but will actually sequence their research in collaborative endeavors.

A second and equally important step is the recognition of the linking function. We suggested that Bass served such a function with respect to the emergent leadership research. Some researchers place little validity on other earlier (Blake & Mouton, 1964) and contemporary (Hersey & Blanchard, 1977) linking applications. We suggest that the recognition and purposeful control of the linking function, through the appropriate training of scientist-practitioners, is one way to improve the quality of future knowledge applications.[13]

One current illustration of the use of the research and diffusion and of the linkage process we have presented comes to our attention. This is the work of Vroom and his colleagues (Jago & Vroom, 1975; Vroom & Jago, 1975; Vroom & Yetton, 1973). Vroom began with a theoretical model, developed and refined his concepts through laboratory studies, extended the results via field tests, and is now at or near the point of large-scale application. Not without critics (e.g., Argyris, 1976), Vroom and his colleagues have been among their own strongest critics (Jago, 1978; Vroom & Jago, 1976).

The leadership decision approach developed by Vroom and his colleagues is representative of a new type of "limited-domain" theory. It does not pretend to explain all of leadership but rather is focused on one important aspect of leadership, that is, the decision-making process. We see the work of Vroom and others as one of the most hopeful indications that scientific knowledge about leadership can be developed and applied to improve organizational life. We argue that one reason for this is the use of the research, diffusion, and linkage approach roughly described in this chapter.

Conclusion

We have reviewed major trends in laboratory and field research on leadership. Our intent was not a comprehensive review but an outline of the most significant or obvious trends as we saw them. We noted three

[13] Many university professors have asserted to us that one or another program produces committed scholar-practitioners. Such assertions do little to alter real conditions, which consist of a hearty total lack of true linkers in the field of leader research and application.

trends for each research method: leader behavior effects on subordinate behavior (field and lab), leader traits (field), vertical dyad linkage (field), leader behavior as a dependent variable (lab), and leader emergence (lab). We were able to make some fairly specific recommendations regarding each of these trends, based on a scientific research, development, and diffusion model.

First, we believe that path-goal and reinforcement theories should receive further field application efforts, in controlled situations, while the path-goal approach may also require further lab investigation in order to be able to design applications that have a strong chance of success.

Second, we suggest that the basic variables of Fiedler's Contingency Model should be subjected to new, detailed laboratory investigations. Concepts such as group atmosphere and leader power should be investigated further, while the key variable of LPC should be studied in relation to actual behavior in highly controlled experimental situations. Another trait theory of sorts, House's (1977) charismatic leadership theory, deserves further study, first on an observational basis and then, to the degree possible, in controlled experimental laboratory situations.

Third, we think that vertical dyad linkage theory deserves further investigation, in the laboratory, with particular attention to a variety of possible moderator variables (such as task and organization structure).

Fourth, recent laboratory research has shown that leader behavior is dependent on a variety of factors, such as subordinate behavior and task structure. It would seem appropriate now to begin some field investigations in order to better identify those factors which are of greatest support in determining leader behavior.

Fifth, we find that some variables (such as certain types of leader power) that were, on the basis of laboratory studies, thought to affect strongly subordinate behavior do not seem to operate similarly in field settings. New laboratory studies would seem justified in such cases. These studies could be designed to explore the specific inconsistencies that have been identified.

Finally, we suggest that specific, in-depth consideration be given to the application of the leader emergence phenomena that have been identified and detailed. Such strong results should have practically meaningful application potential.

In this chapter our primary aim has been the development of a frame of reference that we believe can improve our understanding of and control over the research and diffusion process. We hope that those who disagree with our observations and judgments of research areas will nonetheless take seriously the model we propose for examining leadership research and the use of such research results.

6

Commentary on the Purpose of Leadership Research

Comments on Chapter 4

Some Thoughts on Normal Science and Argyris's Model I and Model II

KARL E. WEICK

One way to describe the Argyris chapter is that it needs some knots tied in the fabric out of which it has been fashioned.[1] The imagery of knots tied in fabrics or in handkerchiefs is Gregory Bateson's. He observed that in his own work he was often tempted to treat concepts as more concrete and more causally active than in fact they were, especially when those concepts were labeled with short words, like ethos, culture, economic, emotional.

When he was faced with a vague concept and felt that the time was not ripe to bring that concept into strict expression, Bateson would adopt a loose expression to refer to the concept. He would talk, for example, of the stuff of culture or bits of culture, or the feel of culture. "These brief Anglo-Saxon terms have for me a definite feeling tone which reminds me all the time that the concepts behind them are vague and await analysis. It's a trick like tying a knot in a handkerchief—but has the advantage that it still permits me, if I may so express it, to go on using the handkerchief for other purposes. I can go on using the vague concept in the valuable process of loose thinking—still continually reminded that my thoughts are loose" (Bateson, 1972, p. 84).

To understand the Argyris chapter is to introduce phrases like "bits of espousal," "traces of theory," "fragments of loops," and "bounded authenticity." It is tempting when talking about Model I, double loops, and es-

[1] Preparation of these comments was supported in part by the National Science Foundation through grant BNS 75-09864.

poused theories to treat them as tangible and causative when in fact they are not.

Consider for example the notion of theories in use. Alfred Schutz (1964) made a similar distinction when he talked about recipes for interpretation and recipes for expression. Schutz argued that newcomers to a group often are able to interpret what is going on long before they can express themselves convincingly in the same medium that they initially interpret. If one asks an individual, for example, to simulate a suicide note, he discovers that people who are nonsuicidal find it very difficult to accomplish this. The problem is that they write sentences that are much to complicated for a person under stress to generate (Osgood & Walker, 1959). While people can interpret and explain suicide notes, they are not able to convince others that they are in fact suicidal because this is a different activity the rules of which cannot be articulated. It is the point about inarticulateness that leads me to question just what Argyris is getting access to when he thinks he is getting access to theories-in-use. Many people would argue that theories-in-use operate at preconscious levels and therefore are incapable of being articulated. Nisbett and Wilson (1977) have recently argued that people can "tell more than they know" and that in fact they are largely unaware of the processes which Argyris argues make up theories-in-use (see also Smith & Miller, 1978).

A further complication is the fact that structurally theories-in-use may lack negatives, lack tense, contain no linguistic moods such as indicative or subjunctive, and be metaphoric. In the absence of simple negatives, organisms often have to say the opposite of what they mean in order to get across the proposition that they mean the opposite of what they say. If that is the way communication works in the absence of negatives, greater authenticity or more valid information simply is irrelevant.

Theories-in-use seem to function most efficiently when conscious thought is not essential to execute action. The essential economy that is accomplished here is the fact that if action is habituated, then conscious channels are freed up to deal with unexpected events that occur. Notice that if someone is concerned with making people aware of theories of action and of making more problematic that which used to be habitual, then there is the strong possibility that adaptability is reduced because all channels set aside for current adaptation are used up accomplishing in an intentional fashion activities which had previously been habituated.

The points here are several. What Argyris takes to be theories-in-use may well be explanations generated under the press of questioning that have no particular advantage or greater validity than do any other explanations that are generated under situational pressure (Mills, 1940). This possibility arises from the inaccessible nature of much that he seems to be talking about, an inaccessibility documented by other investigators. Furthermore, theories-in-use may be composed in such a way that, when they are articulated, the articulation changes them. Whether for reasons of economy or for reasons of being preconscious or for reasons of expressive subtlety that are unique to a culture, theories-in-use are not evoked by reflection or by confrontation or by questioning of assumptions. What is evoked is simply a different set of explanations for the same phenomenon

Argyris's concerns about science raise some interesting points. What Argyris regards as inner contradictions within science I would phrase differently as simply the necessary trade-offs that occur when individual scientists find they cannot simultaneously produce explanations that are general, simple, and accurate. When a scientist satisfies any two of those criteria, he necessarily violates the third.

Argyris's concerns about additivity are well taken, although I think there is another way to view that issue. A common way to think about understanding in science is to represent science as a maze. In this representation there are many different paths that one can take, but there is the expectation that all the paths lead eventually to one goal or one understanding of one nature. These two themes of unlimited outer accessibility and delimited inner meaning lend themselves to the maze imagery. What is disturbing is the possibility that at the innermost chamber of the maze one might find nothing. As Holton has said, "from a suitable distance, we cannot soundly claim that the historic development of sciences prove nature to be understandable in a unique way, as distinct from documentable, manipulable, predictable within limits, or technically exploitable. What has happened is that the ground of the unknown has continually been shifted, the allegory has continually changed" (1965, p. xxiii).

If areas of ignorance remain constant in size and continually shift, then it seems clear that we will not find much additivity in our research. But that is not so much due to the fallibility of the procedures or the fact that they are self-fulfilling prophecies but rather it is a commentary on the nature of the activity in which we are engaged.

I am also interested in whether it is true that if rigorous research, particularly experimentation, can produce Model I understandings that are self-reinforcing, it is also true that the current rush toward ethnography, thick description, and grounded theory might induce a Model II orientation. If Argyris wants to say that precise science reinforces Model I, I would imagine that he might also feel that ethnographic precision fosters Model II.

As a final aside, I am not so sure that people are currently debating whether to do away with science or not (Gellner, 1975), which is one way to read the current debates, but rather that what they are doing is working toward a new understanding of science and what it can and cannot do. From this standpoint we may have to learn to discriminate good from bad poetry rather than good from bad research. If inquiry looks more like appreciation or enrichment or description then this does not mean that we forego criticism. It means instead that we simply use a different kind of criticism.

On a different point, double-loop learning seems to mean raising questions about one's assumptions and becoming more self-conscious about the way in which one construes situations. The issues of win/lose, unilateral control, and suppression of negative feelings become reexamined as ways to deal with the world. Argyris equates double-loop learning with Deutero learning, but I think he is worried about a relatively minor form of Deutero learning. The more basic learning issue in Deutero learning is how people carve up their flow of experience.

Deutero learning was discussed in 1972 by Gregory Bateson and many of the ideas in the present section stem from his comments. Bateson started with a standard psychological question, "Under what circumstances will a dog learn to salivate in response to a bell?" and suggested that this question might be rephrased, "How does the dog acquire a habit of punctuating the infinitely complex stream of events (including his own behavior) so that this stream appears to be made up of one type of short sequences rather than another?"

Bateson's answer to this question is that if the dog is exposed to a Pavlovian conditioning situation a sufficient number of times, he acquires the habit of looking for contexts and sequences of this kind. He acquires a habit of punctuating the stream of events in such a way that in all new circumstances a Pavlovian sequence seems to occur.

To see the importance of this conjecture, contrast a Pavlovian situation with one that is an instrumental reward situation. The standard Pavlovian situation is characterized by a rigid time sequence in which a conditional stimulus always precedes an unconditioned stimulus. This sequence of events is not altered by anything that the animal or human does. In the Pavlovian Case, if there is a stimulus and a certain lapse of time then there is reinforcement. In contrast, the instrumental reward sequence depends for its occurence upon the animal's behavior. The unconditioned stimulus in this context is usually vague and it is only when the animal performs some action that a reward occurs. In the case of instrumental reward, if there is a stimulus and a particular item of behavior then reinforcement occurs.

The dramatic transition that one can make from these humble beginnings to the persistence of any theory-in-use or espoused theory is the extrapolation that prolonged exposure to Pavlovian situations and punctuation of subsequent events into Pavlovian sequences should induce a sense of fatalism. A person who learns to punctuate the stream of behavior into a Pavlovian sequence "would see all events as preordained and he would see himself as fated only to search for omens, not able to influence the course of events—able, at most, from his reading of the omens, to put himself in the properly receptive state, e.g., by salivation, before the inevitable occurred" (Bateson, 1972, p. 173).

The fatalism associated with Deutero learning and Pavlovian situations contrasts sharply with the kind of Deutero learning produced by chronic exposure to instrumental learning situations. An organism with an instrumental punctuation of life will, in a new situation, "engage in trial and error behavior in order to make the situation provide a positive reinforcement. If he fails to get this reinforcement, his purpose in philosophy is not thereby negated. His trial and error behavior will simply continue" (pp. 300–301).

This means then that the crucial shift is not from Model I to Model II, not from single-loop to double-loop learning, but rather from double-loop learning that reinforces the impression of opportunity, choice, and self-determination. Pavlovian sequences and their corresponding sense of induced fatalism, are less likely to produce change, reflection, confrontation, and striving toward authenticity than are learning sequences that are punctuated in an instrumental manner. The trick is not to get people to change the content of their theories-in-use or to line up their espoused theories with their theories-in-use, rather, the crucial intervention seems to be changing the fundamental way in which they carve up their flow of experience.

Aside from subtleties implicit in double-loop learning, there are other subtleties in Argyris's analyses of contexts of action. Argyris repeatedly talks about the complicated context of action and about people's efforts to decompose this complicated information into more manageable units. What Argyris ignores in all this emphasis on simplification is the equally effective alternative of complicating the individual. If we increase the variety available in an individual then that individual is capable of registering and managing more of the variety that is present in the complicated environment. True enough, people can deal with complexity by trying to restrict it but they can also deal with it by complicating themselves. Complication however frequently comes about when people seek contradictions, hypocrisy, ambivalence, and disagreement. Contradictory beliefs serve to sense more of the variation in the environment and this improved sensing heightens the adequacy of the solution. The principle here is that adequacy of sensing is a function of the number, independence, and degree of external constraint present among a set of sensing elements (Weick, 1978). Sand is a more complicated medium to register wind currents than are rocks. Sand has more independent elements that are externally constrained and I am arguing that in the face of the complexities in an action context, complexities to which theories and actions supposedly are addressed, one means to manage those complexities is to complicate the actor. What I worry about is the possibility that many of the changes being advocated by Argyris turn the actor into an even more simplified organism that is even less sensitive to variations in the action context.

To see this point imagine a world in which it is the case that believing is seeing. In the beginning there are beliefs and people see those things in the world that they believe in. Individuals who possess a greater number of independent beliefs should notice more in the situation around them than would be true for those individuals who have a smaller number of internally constrained and non-independent beliefs. And the way that people pick up independence of beliefs is to have images that do not associate to one another, do not flow into one another, are not consistent with one another, actively contradict one another, are ambivalent. All of the things that make for good rationality and tight logic make for simplified sensing mechanisms.

I think Argyris simply does not give enough weight to the fact that variety can be managed by complicating the observer as well as by simplifying the environment. And if he entertained that possibility, certain recommendations for the well-being of actors would probably change.

The Argyris chapter raises several additional issues that are worth discussing but I will simply list some of them in the interest of brevity.

1. Why is it necessary to assert, as Argyris does, that people *design* actions? People typically act and reconstruct after the fact some acceptable account of why they did what they did. Intention is loosely coupled to action under many conditions and it is not clear why, in this one instance, Argyris out-rationalizes those rational theorists who make him cringe. If there is one theme in social psychology these days it is the secondary importance of thinking before we act (Langer, 1977; Thorngate, 1976).

2. Argyris repeatedly asserts that people in everyday life act under on-line conditions such as scarce attention and scarce time which is precisely the cornerstone of the several notions such as bounded rationality, organized anarchies, garbage-can models, and loose coupling to which Argyris objects. What is the objection?

3. It is not obvious how someone could persuade Argyris to rethink his enthusiasm for Model II. If data showed that withdrawal and detachment were effective coping strategies and that internal commitments and confrontation were not (Warwick, 1975, p. 31) Argyris would simply say that is

another instance of Model I science finding Model I thinking and behavior in everyday life. For the sake of completeness, we need to acknowledge that if the world *is* Model I as Argyris assumes, then it is quite appropriate for science to look at this world with tools that are appropriate to its presumed quality and to explain how a Model I world works.

Some of the results of this inquiry admittedly set Argyris's teeth on edge because of his view of a better life. Back in 1977 I argued that the presence of Model I in laboratory studies can be an asset rather than a liability for laboratory researchers who are hard-pressed to demonstrate generality for their findings.

> One of the ironies of laboratory experimentation is that presumed liabilities turn out to be conceptual assets for organizational researchers. To illustrate, research participants are apprehensive about being evaluated, but so are ambitious employees. Laboratory tasks require limited skills, ignoring the "rest" of what the person brings to the laboratory, but the same holds true with a division of labor and partial inclusion. Relationships between experimenter and respondent involve asymmetrical power, but the same holds true for superiors and subordinates. Participants seldom know why they are doing the things they do in laboratories but employees often operate under similar conditions of ignorance and faith. Participants in laboratory groups seldom know one another intimately, but the same is true in organizations where personal transfers are common, where temporary problem solving units are the rule, and where impression management is abundant. People participate in experiments for a variety of reasons, but the decision to participate in an organization is similarly over-determined. Finally, people are suspicious of what happens to them in laboratories but so are employees suspicious as they become altered to the reality of hidden agendas and internal politics. [Weick, 1977b, p. 124]

The point is that subversion can be treated as trouble or as a datum to be explained. If Model I is predominant then science that documents Model I and its inadequacies is normal science. To fault science for its shortage of utopias, its failure to implant Model II, its timid emancipation, its basic conservatism is to assess science in terms of an idiosyncratic job description.

4. Argyris faults much scientific knowledge because it is distant knowledge, distant in the sense that it cannot be directly connected with the action context. But can knowledge be any different when it is impossible for a strictly general concept to be either accurate or simple. And, since an

actor's understanding of action is 1) retrospective, 2) fragmentary, 3) reflexive, 4) difficult to articulate, knowledge that is close to action will be difficult to preserve and convey without destroying the very qualities that distinguish it from distant knowledge.

I have been trying recently to sort out in my own mind the issue of application and I feel the contributions in this volume have moved that thinking along. I do not think application invariably means organizational development or change. Application can mean freezing activities that have an ill-defined form, providing labels, putting events into causal circuits rather than causal arcs, providing inputs that shape a climate of discussion for issues by practitioners, engaging in good conversation, writing aphorisms, upending Occam's razor, documenting why phenomena are elusive, and providing new beliefs so that people see new things.

Application may well also turn out to be basically an exercise in taxonomy. One of the things we could do on the basis of our information is to begin talking about differences in situations that seem to be homogeneous and then talk about those differences that make a difference and those that do not. For example, there seem to be feedback loops. On closer examination those feedback loops can be categorized into deviation amplifying and deviation counteracting feedback loops. And that categorization makes a difference because if the feedback loops are deviation counteracting then the counsel to managers is keep your hands off of them. And since managers like to meddle that is particularly good advice because they can easily undo the control implicit in those loops.

I think issues of application also get complicated because people who are interested in Model II views of the world seem to rely on Model I procedures to persuade people of the value of Model II formulations. This has been particularly well documented in Lisl Klein's (1976) new book *A Social Scientist in Industry* where in chapters 8 and 9 she talks about the invasion of Esso U.K. by the Michigan researchers who imposed System 4 whether Esso needed it or not.

I think normal science by definition is time consuming and boring. And these days people seem to be growing less patient and their attention spans seem to be shortening with respect to the products of normal science. We need to work toward a new understanding of science if we want to improve leadership research. Argyris's diagnosis is that science is basically a self-contained world that discovers the Model I assumptions that it imposed in the first place. That is a perfect example of enactment (Weick, 1977a) which pleases me no end, but if people are always doomed to see themselves seeing, and if truth is always relative to some inquiring system, then I think it is going to be much harder to beat those fundamentals than Argyris does. Perhaps the best we can do right now is to try to counteract our natural tendency to overvalue that which we can count and to undervalue that which we cannot.

Argyris's Response to Weick and Discussion

Argyris stated that there were two assumptions embedded in Weick's statements that he would like to surface. The first one was that espoused theory data (reflections, introspection) are as valid for inquiring and testing aspects of theories-in-use as are relatively directly observable data. Argyris found this not to be true in his own work.

The second assumption was that statements about the potentiality of human beings for double-loop learning can be questioned on the basis of research that does not deal with actual attempts to help subjects double-loop learn. Weick cited Schutz, Nisbett and Wilson, and Smith and Miller as evidence that people may be incapable of articulating their theories-in-use. Argyris reported similar results in his experiments. *But,* he pointed out the similar results were limited to the first stages of learning. During the latter stages, as in the case of the presidents, they were able to articulate their theories-in-use and, under specified conditions, be more effective.

Argyris noted that Weick hypothesizes that adaptability could be reduced by conscious on-line attention to theories-in-use. Again Argyris reported the same findings during the early stages of his learning seminars. However, he found that adaptability and effectiveness were enhanced as learning progressed. Argyris makes the point that there is agreement between the normal science research that Weick cites and action-science when the normal science research is compared with the beginning diagnostic or descriptive phases of action-science. Argyris and his associates disagree significantly only when they examine the data collected after time periods that normal science empirical researchers rarely use and when the empirical work includes theories-in-use different from Model I; hence it requires subjects learn to perform double-loop learning.

General Discussion

The general discussion following the Argyris and Weick contributions focused on three separate issues. The first was concerned with the purpose of research, the second on contingency and non-contingency views of leadership and the third on Model I and Model II clarifications.

Purpose of Research. There was lively debate on the purpose of leadership research. One point of view suggested that we use as a starting point a four-step process of problem solving. The first stage is the identification of a problem, the second stage is the discovery or invention of a solution, the third stage is the production or application of the discovery, and the fourth stage is the evaluation of the production phase. Using this paradigm it was argued that the purpose of research should be production (application) and that too often the purpose of research in leadership is for invention or discovery with no concern for production. Those on the other side of the question argued that not all researchers are interested in application and that they should be free to pursue their own interests.

It was suggested that if a manager were provided with all the "discovery" studies that have been done, he would be unable to implement anything or to take any action. Therefore, we ought to simplify, not elaborate. This view can be contrasted with Weick's suggestion that instead of simplifying the person and situation it might be possible to complicate an individual to a point that matches the complexity of the environment in which the person operates.

Argyris suggested that the problem was not complexity or simplicity but manageability and he emphasized that his Model II attempts to find a new way of managing the world. A point was raised concerning the complexity of Model I and Model II suggesting that Model II, since it causes people to examine their assumptions, is more complex and is the same as complicating the individual. Argyris responded that Model I and Model II approaches were equally complicated but that while Model II might lead a person to see the world as more complex it in itself was not more complex than Model I.

It was then pointed out that a function of Model II is to have individuals confront their inconsistencies and the presence of inconsistencies leads individuals to perceive more features of the situation which results in a more differentiated (complex) situation. Argyris argued that this was the theory of normal science, that is, if we differentiate the world more we will understand it better. He suggested that this might be appropriate if we are only concerned with discovery, but if there is concern with application this increased differentiation leaves people helpless. He argued strongly that with this normal science approach applicability is not possible to achieve. He suggested that if one takes the position of leaving the applicability question to the applied researchers and is only concerned with discovery then "self-fulfilling prophecies and incestuous in-groups" are created.

Contingency and Non-Contingency Views. A suggestion was made that a contingency approach might be appropriate. For example, in a mechanistic organization operating in a non-turbulent environment a Model I approach might be appropriate. However, an organic organization in a turbulent environment might call for a Model II emphasis. Argyris questioned this contingency view and cited an example of a mechanistic company in a non-turbulent environment that because of its Model I approach is in a great deal of trouble today. He also suggested that even managers in organic organizations behave in a Model I manner. Argyris expressed concern with contingency approaches to leadership because they promote the status quo.

Contingency theory proponents argued that one can change one's immediate organizational environment to suit one's own needs but that the organization will be continually changing. Thus, the leader will be required constantly to make adjustments. In the contingency theory proponents view this was not a static model.

Argyris argued that the theory-in-use of organization members has not changed and therefore organizations do not really change. He suggested that researchers report change because they are working with espoused data, not theory-in-use data. For example, size of organization and changes in the structure of organizations appear to have an impact on leader behavior because researchers have related these changes to the espoused theory of organizational leaders. He suggested that if one reviews transcripts of conversations with leaders 20 years ago and infers their theory-in-use and does the same with managers of today there will not be any change in their theories-in-use.

Model I and Model II. The third area of discussion focused on questions of clarification concerning the assumptions of Model I and Model II. Argyris was asked how the changing of a person's theory-in-use affects production. He responded that improved performance was not the right criterion for his approach. He is concerned with a theory-in-use that helps people detect and correct error in an on-line manner. Argyris also pointed out that people can change their behavior without changing their theory-in-use. A change in behavior may be a first step in changing an individual's theory-in-use but it is also necessary to look at how the change in behavior relates to a person's theory-in-use. He suggested that there is espoused theory and there is behavior. "Do as I say and not as I do" is not the concept that the two models deal with. Argyris stated that "there is an espoused theory and there's behavior and there's a discrepancy . . . there's a theory in the person's head that designs his having a discrepancy and he is unaware of that theory."

A question concerning the articulation of an individual's theory-in-use was raised during the discussion. The question was: If a person's theory-in-use cannot be directly inferred from his behavior, how can it be determined if he has changed from Model I to Model II? For example, if, after training in Model II, an attempt is made to determine a change in that person's theory-in-use, one gets an espoused theory and is caught in a circle. In summary, the theory-in-use that is in an individual's head has to be inferred and the question is how do we know that that is the theory in that person's head? Argyris suggested that the only way this can be done is to train people in Model II and then do research which makes predictions about the behavior of these people "back home" following the training. He also emphasized that these prediction studies need to cover a long-range four to five year period.

Comments on Chapter 5

What We Study and Where We Study It: Leadership Research in the Laboratory and Field

EDWIN P. HOLLANDER

Years ago, George Homans (1961) made the point that we "must not confuse the particular sort of situation in which research is conveniently carried on with the subject of that research" (p. 8). If leadership is what we study, then where we study it may not be as crucial as is made to appear. In practice, the fundamental task in studying leadership is to look at leadership phenomena and to try to make sense out of what is observed. Although they are different in various ways, laboratory and field research both contribute to the study of leadership.

The basic point of the Sashkin-Garland chapter therefore seems eminently reasonable and valid. Laboratory and field research should be better integrated. However, I do not believe they are quite as divergent as has been made to appear. Let me merely note that methodologically there are techniques used in leadership research which transcend the setting. One of these is observation, another is ratings or nominations by peers, and a third is attitude scaling. Furthermore, experimentation may be conducted in the field as well as in the laboratory.

Essentially, the question at issue is one of external validity with respect to application. Field studies need not necessarily have any greater claim on such validity than laboratory experiments. For example, a study of decision-making among the top executives of a particular organization may be less generalizable or applicable than a laboratory experiment on variables affecting group decision-making. It may also be that laboratory experiments on equity, or fairness, as perceived as an attribute of leaders by followers, may be quite pertinent (see Hollander & Julian, 1970, pp. 44–50; 1978).

The model of the research and diffusion process presented by Sashkin and Garland is built around the need for linkage, the slogan for which is essentially "Be a linker." Although the model is presented as a description of a sequential process, it actually *prescribes* the process rather than describes it. In short, the model is normative, and the actuality may not match it. An instance is that laboratory experimentation does not necessarily precede field research. The sequence may be quite the reverse. Another consideration is the reality element which Karl Weick (1969a) notes; that is, as a "broker of ideas" the social psychologist requires sponsorship and social support if the linkage between knowledge and practice is to be made.

There is also the issue of intentionality regarding a research approach. In fact, the choice of field or lab research may be dictated by circumstances, rather than by personal predilections. If I may personalize for a moment, my own research on leadership began by necessity in the field when I was on active duty as a psychologist assigned to the Naval Air Training Command at Pensacola during the Korean War. I was interested in laboratory experimentation as a graduate student, but did none of it on leadership until *after* I had completed a fair amount of field research in the navy and then went to my first academic position. It never occurred to me that a prior step to fieldwork was to study the phenomenon of leadership in the laboratory, as the model suggests.

In that connection, I am reminded that the pioneering research on leadership by Lewin, Lippitt, and White (1939) is often cited as an instance of laboratory experimentation opening the way to field research. Actually, it was not a laboratory experiment but a field experiment. The boys' clubs were real enough, they met recurrently over a period of several weeks, and the situation was quite involving. The circumstances were quite different from those of a laboratory experiment. In addition, it is worth mentioning that the boys studied in this research were 10 and 11 years old, but that the research findings frequently have been generalized well beyond to adult groups. The reference in the chapter to the classic field experiment by Coch and French (1948), also raises questions of generalizability. Critics of that experiment, such as Gomberg (1965), have pointed out flaws which undermine its external validity quite severely. While it grew out of Lewin's seminal work, it may not be the best example of diffusion, even though the value it espouses may be commended.

Although I certainly concur with the authors' point about gaining knowledge about leadership so as to make organizations more "humane," I would go even further. In my view, the study of leadership is significant to the health and well-being of organizations and the people who populate them. Leadership is the most central process affecting these outcomes, as I have recently pointed out in a new book (Hollander, 1978a, especially ch. 6).

Let me turn now the strengths and weaknesses of laboratory and field research which are set out in Table 8. Many of these considerations have been dealt with elsewhere, and special attention has been given to laboratory experimentation as it applies to organizational processes by Fromkin and Streufert (1976) and Weick (1977b). I do not intend to cover that terrain, but instead to comment on just a few essential points. For instance, it is surprising that "weak manipulation of independent variables" is listed as a failing of laboratory research. It has been my impression that, if anything, there are strong and even unreal effects in the lab. One is reminded of Hovland's (1959) long-standing comparison of the differential effects of laboratory and survey studies in attitude change, with the laboratory showing the greater impact because of the greater vulnerability of subjects there. This fits the general observation about how the "demand characteristics" of experiments may tip the balance toward compliance by subjects (see, e.g., Rosenthal & Rosnow, 1969).

Perhaps a greater weakness of laboratory experiments is that the groups studied have no past or future, unless the latter is induced. In one experiment on this point (Lewis, Langan, & Hollander, 1972), a group discussion task centered around urban problems was used. Half the participants were told that they would have future interaction, that is, that the group would have an extended life. Cross-cutting this treatment, the attractiveness of the decisional alternatives in the problems was varied. Where the participants believed that there would be future interaction, and the alternatives were of relatively equal attractiveness, based on our pretests, we found the greatest conformity to the group's majority judgments. By contrast, the lack of any anticipation of future interaction, coupled with unequal attractiveness of the alternatives, gave the highest level of nonconformity by participants.

The significance of this finding rests primarily in what it reveals about the greater pressure which may exist to conform to majority judgments in persisting groups. There are easily understandable reasons why this may be so. A major one is that disagreement is more costly in continuing interaction, compared with the cost in short-term interaction. A person who takes a different stand may be obliged to defend it later, and that represents a cost.

This particular experiment also is illustrative of the utility of the laboratory in helping to *sharpen our understanding* of the relationship between variables. Let me add that I am not wedded to the laboratory experiment as the method of choice, but I certainly wish to use it when that end is attainable. In such a case, we did a more recent experiment (Hollander, Fallon, & Edwards, 1977) on the succession of elected and appointed leaders, which is a phenomenon deserving more study than it has received. The results have some interesting implications for additional investigations. For instance, it was found that successors were identifiable as having been influential in the early stages of the group's life. They did not emerge suddenly in the election condition, but clearly had built a following before reaching the leader "threshold."

In another laboratory experiment (Gleason, Seaman, & Hollander, 1978), it was possible to create groups of male students composed of one high, one low, and two who were medium on the Machiavellianism Scale. The hypothesis of immediate interest was that those high in Machiavellianism would be more likely to show ascendance in the low structure condition (Geis, 1968). We did not find that as a significant effect, but we did find that those who were medium on Machiavellianism were significantly preferred as leaders, as against those who were at the extremes. In general, this research followed the injunction to study the relationship of personality and situational factors which was urged in a critique of leadership research (Hollander & Julian, 1969), a decade ago.

There is another technique which transcends the particular situation, that is, the use of critical incidents. Developed by Flanagan (see 1954) to evaluate bomber pilots in World War II, the technique has been used successfully to describe the major variables distinguishing effective and ineffective flight crew commanders and managers, among others (Fivars, 1973). Recently, the technique has been used to get at those relational qualities of leadership which stand out in distinguishing good from bad leadership (see Hollander & Neider, 1978). While still in an exploratory phase, the primary finding of this work was that for good leadership, the characteristics noted for appointed and elected leaders where differentiated by characteristics of fairness and smoothness in interpersonal relations, seen as more critical lacks in appointed leaders than elected ones. Obviously, this bears further investigation, which is now being done. Perhaps most essential in my view is the need to pay more attention to the study of process and to the perceptions of context by the participants in leadership events, whether in the laboratory or the field.

Part 3

What Should Be Studied?

Introduction

JAMES G. HUNT AND LARS L. LARSON

This part and a portion of Dubin's overview in part 5 focus on the "what should be studied" issue. The Leader/Non-Leader and Leader/Group crosscurrents are highlighted in the three chapters contained here. In addition, other crosscurrents are touched upon where relevant and other important considerations are treated in some detail.

Chapter 7, entitled, "Crucial Dimensions of Leader-Group Interactions," brings together research in leadership and research in groups. It was begun by Chester Schriesheim and Ralph Stogdill. Following Stogdill's death, Richard Mowday joined with Schriesheim to continue work on the model. The model represents an early attempt to bring together these sometimes divergent streams of research.[1]

The Schriesheim, Mowday, and Stogdill model and the commentary by Child and Hosking allows us to raise at least two important issues about models in general. One centers upon the purpose of building models and the other on the criteria or standards to be used in evaluating models. Models may be developed for such purposes as guides in designing research, training people in the development of behavioral skills, and making prescriptions to leaders on improving the performance of work groups. It can be argued that very few models have been developed to the point where they can be used as a basis for training or for making prescriptions to leaders. Critics suggest that many researchers do not take seriously the question of how people are going to use their model. (The Action/Discovery crosscurrent.) A suggested solution to this Action/Discovery crosscur-

---

[1] Some readers may be interested in a practitioner-oriented contribution by Hunt and Osborn (1979, in press) which treats some of the same points as the Schriesheim, Mowday, and Stogdill model.

rent is that model developers should think about such uses from the beginning stages of model development.

The second issue centers on the effort needed to develop models. The one-shot model that is presented, criticized and then dropped without further developmental effort is all too prevalent in the field. To some extent these one-shot approaches serve the purpose of stimulating thought for future models and serve a useful research function. However, the fact remains that there is little evidence that work is being done on comprehensive models. What steps are necessary to develop models beyond the one-shot phase and how are these models to be judged?

The Child and Hosking comments in chapter 9 concern the appropriate criteria for judging models, particularly those in the early stages of development. It can be argued that the Schriesheim, Mowday, and Stogdill model is being held to a set of standards that are intended for more advanced approaches. However, we agree that all models ought to eventually meet the kinds of standards Child and Hosking use to critique the Schriesheim et al. model. We are concerned, though, about how one can develop a model and get input on initial stages of development that is necessary for a later version without being held to standards that could discourage researchers from obtaining important input in the early stages of such development.

In chapter 8, entitled, "Leadership Valence: Modeling and Measuring the Process of Emergent Leadership," Timothy Stein, Richard Hoffman, Stephen Cooley, and Richard Pearse present a model of emergent leadership and a method for identifying the stages of the emergence process. Their approach goes beyond the previous participation methods of identifying emergent leaders by taking into account the responses of group members to leadership acts. Their approach also appears to hold great potential in the study and development of group problem solving and decision making.

The difference between the Stein and associates approach and previous studies should be emphasized. Previous studies of emergent leadership indicate a correlation between high verbal participation and leadership ratings (what Sashkin and Garland earlier termed the "babble hypothesis"). The relationship between leadership and participation appears to be based upon the number of leadership acts a person performs. Thus, the difference between leaders and non-leaders is a function of participation. The Stein and associates approach scores both the leader and the response to that leader's behavior. These response points are counted in the same category as an initiation of a leadership act and can "add to" or "subtract from" a person's valence scores. For example, in the category of "proposing solutions" if a person proposes a solution to the problem and someone responds, "That's a poor idea," this counts as a negative valence score for the individual who proposed the solution. Scoring is not limited to initiation because responses to initiation are used as a correcting device by adding points if an individual's influence attempt is accepted and subtracting points if the influence attempt is rejected. Thus, a highly verbal individual whose ideas are rejected will have a low valence score.

The model also has the potential to aid groups in problem solving. It involves thresholds such that as valence points accumulate for a particular person or for a specific solution, the group begins to believe that everyone thinks that person is the emergent leader or that everyone thinks that the solution in question is the correct one. This threshold can be crossed early in a meeting or late in a meeting. Groups are usually unaware that they have reached agreement on a solution until long after the threshold is passed. This threshold concept, as it pertains to acceptance of problem solutions, may be of practical use. If, for instance, a way of keeping track of solution valence in an on-line manner were developed a group could be informed that it was approaching a solution threshold. The question could then be asked, "Is this the solution you want?"

Such a use could also be of benefit for consultants in the timing of interventions. Catching behavior before it passes a threshold where it is consolidated and becomes automatic is crucial if a consultant's intervention is to be effective. With further development the Stein and associates approach might be useful for guiding a consultant in the timing of such interventions. Robert Lord's comments in chapter 9 provide an excellent overview of the model of Stein and his colleagues and highlight areas that need refinement and further development.

The chapters in this part represent two models in different stages of development. The Schriesheim, Mowday, and Stogdill model is in an early stage and is attempting to integrate the literature that focuses on the leader with the literature that focuses on the group (the Leader/Group crosscurrent). The Stein and associates model, which appears to be in a more advanced state of development, also focuses on the interaction between leader and group but is more narrowly focused on the emergent aspects of leadership (the Leader/Non-leader crosscurrent).

In spite of the differences in the two models it is interesting to note that both emphasize the different stages of group development as a part of their thrust. It is also interesting to note that, in addition to the earlier mentioned treatment of models, both commentaries raise a question about the efficacy of proceeding to a model at all without first devoting more attention to measurement of the underlying constructs.

7

Crucial Dimensions of Leader-Group Interactions

CHESTER A. SCHRIESHEIM, RICHARD T. MOWDAY, AND
RALPH M. STOGDILL

As Steiner (1972) has noted, groups appear to have gone out of fashion.[1] Following the large number of studies carried out on various aspects of small groups in the 1940s, 1950s, and 1960s, researchers appear to have lost their interest in groups in favor of investigations undertaken at the individual level of analysis. Steiner (1972) attributed the diminished interest in small group research, in part, to the fact that empirical research proceeded at a far more rapid pace than the development of theories capable of integrating the findings. Although the status of theory in the area of small groups has not changed a great deal in the intervening years, it is possible to detect the first signs of a renewed interest in the study of groups in organizations. In fact, a major question arising from the most recent meeting of the Academy of Management was whatever happened to groups? Several individuals, most notably Hackman (1976) and Leavitt (1975), have been influential in highlighting the apparent inconsistency between the rather limited way in which we treat groups in our empirical research and the theoretical importance we ascribe to groups in understanding individual behavior and overall organizational functioning. There seems to be little doubt that groups represent an important facet of organizational life and therefore an important area for inquiry. Thus, the development of a more complete understanding of individual behavior

---

[1] Ralph M. Stogdill passed away shortly after conceptualizing some of the basic elements of this chapter. One cannot replace a man of Ralph's vast knowledge, expertise, and insight in the leadership and groups area. The authors have not attempted to do so. Instead, we hope that this chapter accomplishes in some degree the basic mission that Ralph envisioned: to be integrative and provocative, to generate and stimulate additional work in this area.

and organizational effectiveness is unlikely to occur unless groups are given a more prominent role in our empirical research and conceptual models.

The major premise of this chapter is that substantial progress in research on leadership and management can be facilitated by greater attention to the role of leadership in the context of small groups and a greater appreciation of the interdependencies which exist between leaders and members of groups. Leaders emerge from groups or are appointed and have an influential role in determining the goal-directed behavior of the group and in maintaining social relationships within the group. Leaders are also influenced by the group, and the specific behaviors in which a leader may engage are highly dependent upon the characteristics of the group and its members (Carter, Haythorn, Shriver, & Lanzetta, 1950).

In the sections which follow, the role of groups in current approaches to leadership is reviewed, along with the reasons why we believe that a greater consideration of groups will facilitate the study of leadership. The literature on leadership and several important aspects of small groups is then reviewed, along with some illustrative moderators which may affect relationships among these variables. From this review, a tentative model of relationships among leader and group variables is developed, primarily as a synthesis. Finally, possible boundary conditions and limitations of the relationships highlighted in this chapter are discussed.

Current Trends in Leadership Research

It was noted above that there has been a marked decline in recent years in the publication of studies dealing with small groups. This seems indicative of a trend on the part of researchers to neglect all aspects of groups except productivity. The increasing emphasis on the importance of individual differences has directed attention away from the group and toward dyadic interactions between the leader and individual followers. This is evident in several current theoretical approaches to leadership. For example, the recently developed leadership models of House (1971; House & Dessler, 1974; House & Mitchell, 1974), Graen and Dansereau (Dansereau, Graen, & Haga, 1975; Graen & Cashman, 1975; Graen, Dansereau, Haga, & Cashman, 1976; Haga, Graen, & Dansereau, 1974), and their associates focus on interactions between the leader and individual followers to the exclusion of considering interactions between the leader and the group.

We do not wish to suggest that nothing of value can be learned from studies of interactions in the leader-subordinate dyad. However, we believe there is also much to be learned from studies of interactions between the leader and the group (cf. Fiedler, 1967; Fiedler & Chemers, 1974). Several considerations suggest the need and importance of studying interactions between leaders and groups.

First, work groups with appointed leaders in formal organizations develop role structures and exhibit various properties such as cohesiveness and motivation (Hare, 1976; Stogdill, 1974). Bales (1958, 1970) has shown that it is possible to observe different dimensions of group behavior in experimental settings where group members are required to interact intensively. The observational task may be more difficult in work groups where members are stationed at spatially dispersed benches or machines. However, even with such spatial separation of members it is possible for them to evaluate the properties of their group and for trained observers readily to detect differences among groups (Zaleznik, Christensen & Roethlisberger, 1958). The important point is that groups exhibit different characteristics and these differences may have important implications for group member behavior. Early leadership studies found that the impact of leader-group interactions on individual subordinates was substantial (Stogdill, 1974), and the fact that researchers in recent years have chosen to ignore these variables does not negate their importance. In fact, since the reaction of individual subordinates to the leader may be different in a group setting than when working alone, even individual (dyadic) analyses of leadership may benefit from taking the effects of the group into account.

Second, although a leader may not react alike to all members of a group, equity considerations may prevent large discrepancies in interaction patterns, and leaders may not have the time, energy, or skill necessary to diagnose the individual needs of subordinates and behave differentially toward each.[2] Also, if the leader singles out one or more subordinates for special treatment this in itself may be a reaction to the group as a whole. Coupled with this is the fact that individual group members, even though treated differently by the leader, may respond to such behaviors in consistent ways due to prior interaction patterns which produce reinforced histories and styles of subordination (Cummings, 1975).

A third argument for refocusing on the analysis of leader-group interactions deals with technological considerations. For one, group analyses may be more appropriate where tasks are sequentially and reciprocally

---

[2] This position is supported by numerous analyses. For example, it was shown in the early Ohio State leadership studies that reasonable agreement exists in the way subordinates describe their supervisors' behavior (inter-rater correlations group around .6; Fleishman, 1957; Fleishman, Harris, & Burtt, 1955; Halpin, 1957a), and that "subordinates differ more in describing different leaders than in describing the same leader" (Halpin, 1957b, p. 66). Recent studies support both findings as well (e.g., Evans, 1972; Jago & Vroom, 1975; Schriesheim & Kissler, 1978).

interdependent (Thompson, 1967) and where unit performance is more highly dependent upon group interactions and outputs than upon the contribution of any particular group member (George, 1962; Jacobs, 1970; Steiner, 1972). Further, where tasks are highly interdependent, group performance may be more easily measured than individual performance, reducing some of the measurement problems typically attendant to leadership-performance studies in general. With respect to jobs which involve pooled interdependence, the effects of the group on individual levels of performance may still be substantial. Studies such as those conducted by Gross (1953), Zaleznik et al. (1958), and others (e.g., Hilgard, Sait, & Margaret, 1940; Homans, 1946; Roethlisberger & Dickinson, 1939; Whitehead, 1938; Wyatt, Frost, & Stock, 1934) clearly indicate that group norms are often a more potent influence on individual and group performance than are individual, managerial, or organizational factors. Leader reactions to the group may therefore have a stronger impact upon members than reactions to them as individuals.

A final consideration, practically speaking, is that supervisors are more likely to be evaluated based upon the performance of their group than upon the performance of any one individual. Thus, for the development of practical prescriptions for those actually engaged in the management of organizational performance, leader-group interaction analyses appear to be a fruitful avenue for investigation.

Dimensions of Leader-Group Interactions

Based upon an extensive review of the literature, Stogdill (1959, 1965, 1972) identified three primary outputs of organized groups—productivity, drive, and cohesiveness. These outputs are the result of internal group processes and they are important in understanding leader-group interactions. This section briefly introduces these variables. Two types of leader behaviors and stages in group development are also briefly discussed. In the next section, the literature relating these variables is reviewed.

Group Productivity

Stogdill (1972) defined group productivity in objective terms as the number of units produced by the group or the dollar value of the group's output. Where objective criteria for measuring group performance are unavailable, subjective ratings of the group's productivity are thought to be acceptable. More recently, Steiner (1972, 1974) has analyzed group performance in terms of the difference between the actual and potential accomplishment of the group. Group performance is defined as the difference between the potential accomplishments of the group (i.e., the number of units a group would have produced if each member had worked as hard as possible and the efforts of different members were perfectly coordinated) and the unrealized accomplishment of the group (i.e., the number of units the group failed to produce because not everyone was highly motivated or member efforts were imperfectly coordinated). Steiner's analysis highlights the process losses that can occur when people work in groups rather than individually. For example, Ingham, Levinger, Graves, and Peckham (1974) found that individuals do not work quite as hard when paired with one or two others as when they work individually. Process losses in group performance also result from the selection of inappropriate task performance strategies, lack of agreement within the group on the group's goal, and poor coordination among group members. It is apparent that the leader of the group can influence the extent of unrealized group accomplishment through such leadership activities as structuring the task, rewarding performance, and coordinating member efforts.

Group Drive

Group drive has been defined by Stogdill (1972, p. 27) as "the degree of group arousal, motivation, freedom, enthusiasm, or esprit" and "the intensity with which members invest expectation and energy on behalf of the group." A similar definition of group drive is provided by Steiner (1972, p. 131). He defined group motivation as "the willingness of members to contribute their resources to the collective effort." Although French (1944) recognized the importance of group drive in his early work, subsequent research has most often studied motivation at the individual rather than group level of analysis.

Perhaps the most extensive investigation of group drive and motivation has been conducted by Zander (1971) and his colleagues. He views group motivation in terms of the group's level of aspiration. The level of aspiration chosen by a group is determined by a multiplicative function of the strength of the individual group member's desire to achieve group success or avoid group failure, the perception of the probability of achieving group success, and desirability of the outcomes resulting from successful task accomplishment (Zander, 1968, 1971). A group's level of aspiration is also influenced by previous success or failure on the task (Zander & Medow, 1963), and pressures for high performance (Zander, Medow, & Dustin, 1964). In general, it is believed that, holding task difficulty and the incentive value of successful task accomplishment constant, group performance is positively related to group drive (Zander, 1971). However, the extent to which high levels of group drive result in high group performance has been found to depend upon the nature of the task. This will be discussed further in a later section.

Group Cohesiveness

Group cohesiveness has been the subject of a large number of research investigations (Hare, 1976; Shaw, 1976). Integrating the research findings on the antecedents and consequences of group cohesiveness has been made more difficult, however, by the number of different ways in which the term has been defined and operationalized. Shaw (1976) identified three ways in which group cohesiveness has been defined—member attraction to the group, the level of group morale, and the coordination of group member efforts. A number of investigators have viewed group cohesiveness in terms of interpersonal attractions among group members. In an extensive review of the literature, Lott and Lott (1965, p. 2) employed Lotts' (1961) definition of group cohesiveness as "that group property which is inferred from the number and strength of mutual positive attitudes among the members of a group." A somewhat broader definition was provided by Festinger (1950) in viewing group cohesiveness as the group property resulting from all the forces acting on members to remain in the group. Finally, Stogdill (1972, p. 27) suggests group cohesiveness might be defined as "the extent to which the members reinforce each other's expectations regarding the value of maintaining the identity of the group."

This brief review of definitions of group cohesiveness suggests that it is a multifaceted concept. Adopting Festinger's (1950) approach of viewing cohesiveness as the result of all forces acting on group members to remain in the group, it is apparent that a number of factors can influence group cohesiveness. These factors have been broadly classified by Cartwright (1968) as falling into one of four categories: incentive properties of the group (e.g., attractiveness of group members and goals), individual motive bases (e.g., needs for affiliation and security), expectancies concerning the outcomes resulting from group membership, and the availability and attractiveness of alternative group memberships.

Leader Behavior

It has been argued that leadership research can be advanced by investigating interactions between leaders and groups. For the purpose of this analysis, leader behavior will be broadly defined in terms of two familiar summary dimensions—instrumental and supportive leader behavior. Instrumental leader behaviors are directed toward task accomplishment, while supportive leader behaviors are directed toward group maintenance (Stogdill, 1974). Defining leader behavior in this fashion lacks a certain degree of precision since a number of less global behavioral subtypes can be distinguished within each summary dimension. However, viewing leader behavior in terms of these two summary dimensions facilitates understanding by making the task more manageable. At the same time, it does not limit the use of more specific (less global) aspects of leader behavior in future analyses. In addition, using these two dimensions allows the use of the extant body of literature on leader-group interactions since, with few exceptions, this research has employed only global measures of instrumental and supportive leader behavior (Stogdill, 1974). Use of these two summary dimensions is also consistent with early research on role differentiation in groups (e.g., Bales, 1950), in which it was found that both "procedural" and "socioemotional" functions are associated with the leadership role. Finally, these two summary dimensions of leader behavior closely correspond to what has been identified as the two fundamental functions of groups—goal achievement and group maintenance (Cartwright & Zander, 1968).

Group Development

Bales (1950), Bales and Strodtbeck (1951), and Borgatta and Bales (1953) have demonstrated that groups undergo different stages of development and these stages appear to be closely associated with the group properties and leadership functions discussed above. Reviews of the group development literature by Tuckman (1965) and Heinen and Jacobsen (1976) suggest that four developmental stages are common across groups: 1) the formative or forming stage, 2) the differentiation or storming stage, 3) the integration or norming stage, and 4) the task performance or performing stage.

In the first stage of group development, group members are concerned with discovering the bounds of acceptable behavior within the group and establishing expectations about relationships among members of the group. It is in this stage that the group task, boundaries of the group, anticipated outcomes of group membership, and contributions of different members begin to be defined. In the second stage, group structure begins to emerge through the process of role differentiation. This stage is often characterized by a high degree of tension, conflict, arousal, and emotionality as members resist the imposition of structure and task demands. The third stage begins a process that reverses that which occurred in the second stage. Group cohesiveness is developed as members come to accept the group structure and the establishment of group norms to regulate behavior. Group communication improves and task discussions are characterized by a more open exchange of opinions and alternative interpretations of task-relevant information. The final stage of group development continues the processes begun in the third stage directed toward the accomplishment of the group task. Tuckman (1965) suggested that members accept roles that enhance task activities and engage in constructive attempts to complete successfully the group task.

Stogdill (1972) observed that group cohesiveness, drive, and productivity were closely related with the developmental stages of groups. The third stage in which roles are accepted and communication improves reflects the development of group cohesiveness. The final stage in which task-related activities are undertaken closely corresponds to group productivity. Finally, Stogdill (1972) felt that the arousal and tension characteristic of the second stage most closely reflected group drive, but that group drive appears to be present in each stage. The specific tasks to which the group is motivated to perform, however, may differ across the stages. For example, in the second stage group drive is directed toward evolving a structure for the group and in the third stage group drive operates to develop greater cohesiveness. In the last stage, group drive is directed toward the successful completion of the group task. It is also apparent that the two summary dimensions of leader behavior may reflect different leadership functions as group development takes place. Supportive leader behaviors would most closely correspond to the group's need to develop cohesiveness in the third stage, and instrumental leader behavior would facilitate group task accomplishment in the final stage of development.

Leader-Group Interactions: A Brief Review of the Literature

Having introduced some important variables in the sections above, it is useful to review the literature on the relationships among these variables. In this section, the relationship of instrumental and supportive leader behaviors to group productivity, drive, and cohesiveness is considered. In addition, the literature relating group productivity, drive, cohesiveness, goal acceptance, and group member satisfaction is also briefly reviewed. For more extensive reviews of this literature, see Stogdill (1974, especially chapters 32–39) and Hare (1976, especially chapters 1–4, 6–7, 10–11, and 15).

Group Productivity

A search of over three thousand empirical studies has failed to un-cover any single type of leader behavior which is consistently related to group (or individual) productivity (Stogdill, 1974). These results suggest that the extent to which a particular leader behavior is related to group productivity is conditioned by a number of situational factors and thus the leader behavior-group productivity relationship may be indirect. The lit-erature which is summarized below suggests that two general patterns of leader behavior (instrumental and supportive) influence group drive and cohesiveness, which in turn may influence group productivity.

Group Drive and Cohesiveness

Early behavioral researchers found instrumental and supportive lead-er behavior to impact positively on both group drive and cohesiveness (e.g., Lewin, Lippitt, & White, 1939; Lippitt, 1940), and subsequent investiga-tions have confirmed these findings (e.g., Likert, 1961, 1967; White & Lip-pitt, 1960). For example, Greene and Schriesheim (1977) studied relation-ships among instrumental and supportive leader behaviors and group drive (and cohesiveness) using a longitudinal design and 123 work groups. Using cross-lagged correlational, cross-lagged path, and corrected dynamic correlational analyses, both types of leader behavior were found to be causally antecedent to drive. However, beyond this and a few other studies, there is little evidence concerning the relative impact of different leader behaviors on group drive, so that it is not clear whether instrumental or supportive leader behaviors have greater impact on drive (Stogdill, 1974). Theoretical arguments can be made for a stronger effect of supportive leader behavior on group drive (e.g., Likert, 1961, 1967), but little empiri-cal support exists for this assertion. Indirect evidence of the importance of instrumental leader behaviors for group drive has been reported by Zan-der (1971) in his work on group level of aspiration. A number of factors which can be influenced by the group leader (e.g., feedback on perfor-mance, centrality of member work role, reward practices) have been found to impact positively upon group desire to achieve success.

The literature with respect to group cohesiveness is more clear and abundant. Although some studies have found only supportive leader be-haviors to be positively related to group cohesiveness (e.g., Lewin et al., 1939; Likert, 1961, 1967; Mann & Baumgartel, 1952), others have found only instrumental leader behaviors to be positively related (e.g., Berkowitz, 1953; Burke, 1966; Katzell, Miller, Rotter, & Venet, 1970; Keeler & An-drews, 1963; Stogdill, 1965). Furthermore, some studies have found both instrumental and supportive leader behaviors to be positively related to group cohesiveness (e.g., Christner & Hemphill, 1955; Greene & Schriesheim, 1977; Hemphill, Seigel, & Westie, 1951; Trieb & Marion, 1969). Although there are theoretical reasons to suspect that instrumental leader behaviors should exert a greater effect on group cohesiveness than supportive leader behaviors (through stabilization of group role structure), the empirical evidence does not support this and, in fact, it suggests that both types of leader behavior are necessary to ensure group cohesiveness. The importance of both types of leader behavior is also evident when the antecedents of group cohesiveness are examined (Cartwright, 1968; Lott & Lott, 1965). Instrumental leader behaviors may influence the incentive properties of groups (e.g., group interdependence, goals, and activities), while supportive leader behaviors satisfy the needs of group members, increase the attractiveness of participation in the group, and the expectation of rewards resulting from group membership.

It is worthwhile at this point to note also that instrumental and supportive leader behaviors are clearly not the only factors to affect group cohesiveness and drive. Such factors in member compatibility, physical proximity, stress, and group size have all been shown, for example, to impact upon group cohesiveness (Cartwright, 1968; Hare, 1976; Lott & Lott 1965; Shaw, 1976; Thomas & Fink, 1963). In addition, group drive is likely to be affected by a number of additional factors such as the nature of the task, feedback on the performance of other groups, and external pressures to perform (Zander, 1971). Leader behavior therefore appears to be only one of several sources of influence on group cohesiveness and drive. In some situations, other factors may exert equal or greater effects on group cohesiveness and drive than leader behaviors.

Effects of Drive and Cohesiveness

We have identified three group characteristics and two leader behaviors that are dynamically interrelated; instrumental and supportive leader behaviors generate group drive and cohesiveness, and these in turn lead to group productivity. However, the picture we have painted is still not complete, even given the crudeness of our attempted brushstrokes. We have not yet considered the subtle interplay of drive and cohesiveness on productivity, nor have we considered the effects of drive and cohesiveness on member satisfaction, turnover, and absenteeism. All of these relationships are important in understanding leader-group interactions.

Effects on productivity. Researchers have long been interested in the relationship between group cohesiveness and productivity (e.g., Seashore, 1954), because if the two were positively related one could argue that the display of supportive behaviors, which tend to increase cohesiveness, should also increase group performance (cf. Likert, 1961, 1967). While a straightforward relationship would make research on leader-group inter- actions far easier, the existing evidence indicates that such an unconditional relationship does not hold.

Although some reviews (Hare, 1976; Shaw, 1976) suggest that cohe- siveness is positively related to group productivity, other reviews suggest that the relationship between group cohesiveness and productivity is un- clear and conflicting (Lott & Lott, 1965). Available evidence suggests that group cohesiveness primarily influences the variation of performance with- in the group rather than the level of group performance (Cartwright, 1968; Schachter, Ellertson, McBride, & Gregory, 1951). In other words, highly cohesive groups are effective in enforcing the performance norms adopted by the groups but whether or not they perform at a high or low level depends upon the particular performance goals which are adopted. The performance goals of a group may or may not be congruent with the standards of performance desired by the organization.

Zander (1977) suggests that the level of group motivation (drive) may have a greater impact on productivity than cohesion, and that: "Members of a group may have, or may develop, a motivation concerned with the achievement of their group as a unit [group drive]. . . . Persons within such a work group become more concerned about the quality of the group's performance than about the quality of their own personal performance and develop a desire for group success" (pp. 46–47).

Furthermore, a careful review of almost 100 studies (Stogdill, 1959, 1972) concluded that cohesiveness and productivity tend to be negatively related under low drive and routine operating conditions, while they are positively related under conditions of high drive. Drive can be invested in strengthening cohesiveness or in furthering productivity, but it is unlikely to be effectively expended on both (Stogdill, 1963b, 1972). For example, Fiedler (1954), Torrance (1955), and Schacter et al. (1961) found that more effective groups tend to be less congenial and cohesive (i.e., energy spent on the maintenance of intragroup relationships decreases that available for productive output). In addition, Fiedler and Meuwese (1963) reported four studies in which it was found that leader ability and group produc- tivity were positively related only for groups high in cohesiveness. This was interpreted as reflecting the fact that leaders of uncohesive groups are forced to exert influence primarily on group maintenance, while leaders of cohesive groups were free to concentrate their efforts on group task ac- complishment. Finally, Greene (1976) performed a longitudinal field inves- tigation of 54 recently formed groups. Using the same causal-correlational methods as Greene and Schriesheim (1977, discussed above), group drive was found to be causally antecedent to group productivity, and group cohesiveness was found to cause group productivity, but only in those groups exhibiting high drive.

Effects on satisfaction, absenteeism, and turnover. While group cohesiveness and drive were viewed as having their primary influence on group productivity, these variables may also influence other group outcomes such as member satisfaction with co-workers, absenteeims, and turnover. In addition, the level of performance achieved by the group may have an important influence on how group members evaluate the group and their willingness to remain a part of the group.

The literature on the effects of group drive on member co-worker satisfaction, absenteeism, and turnover is sparse, so that it is difficult to draw more than speculative conclusions about such relationships. It is possible, however, that group drive indirectly influences these variables through its impact on group productivity. Cartwright and Zander (1968) suggest that successful group task accomplishment results in experienced gratification, increased evaluation of the group and attraction to it, and higher aspirations for group performance in the future. Members of successful groups are more likely to experience satisfaction, form a favorable impression of themselves and other members of the group, and wish to continue to pursue the activity on which the group was successful (Zander, 1968).

Considerably more literature is available on the impact of group cohesiveness on satisfaction with co-workers, absenteeism, and turnover. Numerous investigators have noted that group cohesiveness is positively related to satisfaction with co-workers (e.g., Exline, 1957; Gross, 1954; Heinicke & Bales, 1953; Marquis, Guetzkow, & Heyns, 1951; Van Zelst, 1952). This relationship is not surprising since interpersonal attraction among group members is an important component of group cohesiveness (Cartwright, 1968; Lott & Lott, 1965; Shaw, 1976).

The empirical evidence with respect to the relationship between group cohesiveness and member turnover and absenteeism is also reasonably clear. As Cartwright (1968) has noted, "there is considerable evidence in support" of the proposition that "various indicators of group attractiveness [i.e., cohesiveness] correlate negatively with turnover" (p. 103). In fact, all of the major reviews during the past twenty years or so have concluded that work group cohesiveness or attractiveness, or satisfactory group interactions correlate negatively with member turnover and absenteeism (e.g., Cartwright, 1968; Lott & Lott, 1965; Porter & Steers, 1973; Steers & Rhodes, 1978). Thus, while the effects of group drive on member satisfaction with co-workers, turnover, and absenteeism are less clear and may be indirect, group cohesion appears to be positively correlated with co-worker satisfaction and negatively related to job withdrawal.

Moderator Relationships

Thus far, we have considered a set of sequential relationships in which leader behaviors influence group cohesiveness and drive, which in turn are viewed as influencing the level of group productivity. Contingency theorists, however, would suggest that these relationships are likely to be more complex than previously indicated. Characteristics of the situation, task, group, individual group members, and the leader may moderate the relationships discussed above. Unfortunately, we have only vague ideas at best regarding the nature and scope of these conditional relationships. The list of potential moderator variables that may be relevant is undoubtedly large and thus beyond the scope of this chapter to discuss in a comprehensive fashion. For illustrative purposes, however, several potential moderator variables are discussed below.

As previously suggested, the extent to which the group accepts the organization's goals will determine whether or not group drive and cohesiveness are positively related to group productivity. Highly motivated and cohesive groups can be expected to work toward the goals adopted by the group. Jacobs (1970, p. 315) has noted that "the group norm apparently is simply more potent than organizational and supervisory pressures" in influencing the exertion of energy by the group and the direction in which this energy is exerted. Greene's (1976) study (discussed briefly above) supports this conclusion as well. In his longitudinal investigation, group goal acceptance was found to be causally antecedent to group drive, cohesiveness, and productivity. Similarly, other research has shown that changes in group-accepted production norms can result in increased productivity (Bronzo, 1968; Coch & French, 1948; French, 1950; Jenkins, 1948; Kelly & Ware, 1947; Lawrence & Smith, 1955; Lewin, 1948; Maier & Hoffman, 1964; Trist & Murray, 1960), and that groups may be less productive if they have agreed upon a lower production norm (Cartwright & Robertson, 1961; Lott & Lott, 1965; C. E. Warwick, 1964). In addition, Lott and Lott (1965) note in their review that co-worker standards of performance exert a strong effect on group output, and Shaw (1976) indicates that group members set goals for the group and that these goals measurably influence behaviors within the group (also see Horwitz, 1954; Zander, 1968, 1971; Zander & Medow, 1963; Zander & Newcomb, 1967).

Unless the goal adopted by the group is congruent with the goals of the larger organization, however, the efforts of the group are unlikely to result in high productivity. Group goal acceptance may also play another role. To the extent that the group accepts the goals of the organization, the role of the leader may change somewhat. When groups are highly committed to achieving the goals of the organization, some types of instrumental leader behavior may become less salient. For example, there may be less of a need for the leader to structure tightly the work of the group. In this situation, the leader may be free to concentrate on supporting the group's efforts and removing obstacles that may stand in the way of group goal achievement (House & Dessler, 1974).

The role of technology and the task on the leadership role and group processes has received considerable attention. At a more macro level of analysis, Dubin (1965) has suggested that technology to a large extent determines the appropriate leadership style. In unit or small-batch production organization, productivity appears to be positively related to leader consideration and sensitivity to the different needs of subordinates. In continuous or mass production organizations, on the other hand, productivity has been positively related to leader structuring of the task (cf. Fleishman, Harris, & Burtt, 1955).

The nature of the group task may also influence the extent to which group motivation increases group productivity. Zander (1971) reported two unpublished studies in which it was found that high levels of group motivation resulted in high group productivity on simple tasks but not on complex tasks. On complex tasks, high levels of group arousal may result in less care being taken in performing the task and thus lower performance. In addition, the nature of the group task may also determine the extent to which group versus individual motivation is the major determinant of group performance. Steiner (1972) has distinguished between group tasks in which the primary determinant of group performance is either individual performance or the combined efforts of the group members. On conjunctive tasks (tasks which require each group member to perform successfully essentially the same function), group performance is determined by the least competent group member; on disjunctive tasks (tasks involving a correct choice among possible alternatives by at least one group member), group performance is determined by the most competent group member. Zander (1971) has suggested that on these types of tasks the motivation of a particular group member may be a more important determinant of group performance than the level of group motivation. Finally, Zander (1971) also indicates that the nature of the task can be important in determining the level of motivation exhibited by the group. Group motivation is likely to be highest on tasks where the output of the group is attributable to the efforts of the group as a whole rather than one or two individual members. Research supporting this conclusion has been reported by Zander (1971), Zander and Armstrong (1972), and Zander, Forward, and Albert (1969).

The review presented earlier on the stages of group development suggests that variables related to group development may also moderate some of these relationships. For example, group size affects group development. As such, it will probably moderate the relationships between leader behavior and group drive and cohesiveness. Research has shown that the development and stabilization of a group's role structure becomes increasingly difficult as the size of the group increases (e.g., Slater, 1958). In addition, instrumental and supportive leader behaviors may aid in the development and stabilization of a group's role structure (e.g., Heslin & Dunphy, 1964), and a stable group structure is necessary for the development of group drive and cohesiveness (e.g., Borgatta & Bales, 1953).

Similarly, since group development involves a progression through stages over time, recency of group formation may also be expected to moderate leader behavior–group drive and cohesiveness relationships. Newer groups have less stabilized role structures and, based upon the earlier discussion of group development, the stabilization of structure within the group appears to be a precondition for cohesiveness to develop (Heinen & Jacobsen, 1976; Sherwood & Walker, 1960; Tuckman, 1965).

During the early stages of group formation members may want and accept more direction and guidance (e.g., Bion, 1949). Leaders may therefore exert greater impact on stabilizing group role structures in recently formed groups and thus have a greater impact on group cohesiveness. Greene and Schriesheim's (1977) longitudinal study (discussed earlier) obtained strong support for these two moderators. Instrumental leader behavior had particularly strong effects on group drive and cohesiveness in large groups and in recently formed groups. Supportive leader behavior, on the other hand, exerted causal effects on group drive and cohesiveness in recently formed groups. Thus, variables related to group development (such as group size and recency of group formation) should moderate relationships between instrumental and supportive leader behaviors and group drive and cohesiveness.

Clearly, this discussion does not exhaust the moderator variables that may be relevant to leader-group interactions. The moderator variables briefly discussed above are illustrative of the numerous possibilities that may exist and the complexity of the relationships being considered.

An Integrative Model

The survey of the literature presented above was brief, but the relationships suggested by this review may still be difficult to envision. For this reason, the major relationships discussed above are presented in the form of a model, both verbally and diagrammatically (see Figure 6). It must be noted, however, that this model should be viewed principally as a summary device. Although plausible relationships are proposed among the model's major variables, it excludes many of the subtleties involved in these relationships (Some of which were discussed above), as well as a large number of other possible variables and relationships (more is said concerning this below).

As our brief review of the literature indicates, the following conclusions about leader-group interactions appear warranted. First, leader behavior influences group performance through its impact on group drive and cohesiveness. Second, both instrumental and supportive leader behaviors directly (and positively) affect group drive and cohesiveness, although the strength of these relationships may be moderated by variables affecting group development (such as group size or recency of group formation). Third, group drive and cohesiveness interact in influencing group productivity. Fourth, the relationship of group drive and cohesiveness to group productivity is likely to be moderated by the group goal and the nature of the group task. Fifth, group drive, cohesiveness, and productivity are positively associated with group member satisfaction with co-workers and negatively associated with member turnover and absenteeism. Sixth, additional factors influence both group drive and cohesiveness, including various group development variables. From these conclusions, the model shown in Figure 6 was developed.

As shown in Figure 6, the model indicates that group performance is more highly related to the group characteristics of drive and cohesiveness than to leader instrumental and supportive behaviors. Leader behavior is viewed as influencing group drive and cohesiveness, but its effects are moderated by group development variables. Group goal acceptance (i.e., congruence between the group's goals and the goals of the organization) and the nature of the task moderate the relationship between group drive and cohesiveness and group productivity. Further, group drive and cohesiveness interact in influencing productivity. Following Stogdill (1972, p. 39), group cohesiveness and productivity are "negatively related under conditions of low [group] drive and under routine operating conditions" and "positively related under conditions of high group drive." In addition, satisfaction with co-workers, absenteeism, and turnover are more highly

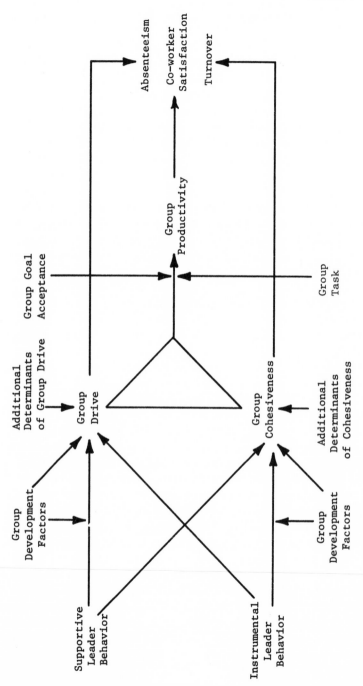

Fig. 6. Leader-group interactions model

influenced by group drive, cohesiveness, and productivity than by leader behaviors.

Boundary Conditions and Limitations

Boundary conditions. The relationships among leader behaviors and group characteristics summarized above are expected to hold only under certain conditions ("boundary conditions"). Although it is not possible to specify fully all of the boundary conditions associated with these relationships at this time (further research and systematization of the literature are necessary for this), several limiting factors seem obvious.

It should be clear that the relationships discussed above would be expected to hold only for clearly defined, task performing groups under the direct leadership of one individual, and not for loosely formed groups (i.e., groups in which the boundaries of membership are poorly defined) or groups that lack a clearly defined purpose. Also, the relationships deal only with task performing groups and not other types of groups such as informal social groups. Finally, as discussed in the section on moderator variables, the relationships dealing with group productivity are expected to hold only where performance is a function of interdependencies among group members (i.e., reciprocal and sequential interdependence; Thompson, 1967). Where productivity is determined by the performance of a single individual or where it is only the sum of individual performances, group drive and cohesiveness are likely to have less of an impact on group performance. This does not imply, however, that group cohesiveness and drive will not affect other importance dependent variables such as turnover and absenteeism.

As an illustration of the effects of a boundary condition, Schriesheim and Schriesheim (1978) studied relationships among group drive and cohesiveness, individual member motivation, and objective measures of group productivity, turnover, and absenteeism. Using a sample of 106 work groups employed as sewing machine operators (a highly independent task performance situation) and predicting the objective measures over a two-month interval, Schriesheim and Schriesheim found neither group drive nor cohesiveness to be significantly related to group output, while individual member motivation was significantly related. However, group cohesiveness and drive both obtained significant and substantial relationships with both turnover and absenteeism, as might be expected from the literature summarized earlier. Thus, a clear "boundary effect" was obtained with respect to performance. However, the effects of group drive and cohesiveness were still strong, but these effects were principally on job withdrawal behaviors.

Limitations. In presenting this model, an attempt has been made to portray the variables and their relationships in such a manner as to summarize accurately the literature and to provide a conceptual framework upon which to build for future research. We have not attempted to propose a theory of leadership, but have outlined what we feel are important variables and their likely interrelationships. Thus, while this model fulfills one requirement of theoretical soundness (inclusion of relevant variables and a reasonable specification of their interrelationships), it still must be considered only a framework for future exploration. This is because at least two requirements of theoretical adequacy have not been met: 1) The model does not contain a set of lawlike propositions which, taken together, fully and precisely specify all relationships among all variables. 2) The model does not provide for a strict procedure for determining whether a relationship is consistent or inconsistent with other relationships proposed by the model.

These deficiencies, while inherent in most current models, must be addressed in further development of this framework. Also, as noted earlier, future elaborations will need to specify further many additional variables and relationships as well. For example, we have not considered the dynamic nature of interactions between the leader and the group, and have not treated mutual and reciprocal causation of behavior. Since the available evidence indicates that reciprocal causation is likely under some conditions (e.g., Lowin & Craig, 1968; Lowin, Hrapchek, & Kavanagh, 1969; see Kerr & Schriesheim, 1974, for a review), it seems clear that this effect must be added to the model in the future.

Conclusion

Most research conducted during the past decade has been excessively narrow and limited. The relationships among leader behaviors and group and individual productivity and satisfaction have been extensively investigated, while group variables such as drive and cohesiveness have been largely ignored.

Perhaps this is because much of this research has been designed in terms of simplistic and incomplete theories of leadership, group dynamics, and employee satisfaction. This explains why much of the research which has been generated has produced negative results—leadership was hypothesized to affect variables to which it is not highly related. For example, why should leader behavior directly affect satisfaction with co-workers, pay, promotions, or the work being performed? There are no compelling reasons, yet most current leader behavior-subordinate satisfaction investigations routinely include these variables. On the other hand, little or no current leadership research is being conducted with group drive and cohesiveness, despite the fact that there are compelling reasons to believe that these are important variables which are caused by leader behavior and which, in turn, have strong effects on group and individual productivity and satisfaction.

Indeed, the medieval alchemists were determined in their efforts to transmute lead into gold, and we seem equally determined to compel direct relationships between leader behavior, group productivity, and certain types of follower satisfaction. In reality, the world of human nature may be structured in such a manner that no leadership behavior or characteristic is *directly* associated with individual or group member productivity. Although this may not be pleasant, it represents a distinct possibility which must be considered.

If the previous observations have any merit, we are confronted by a research problem of considerable magnitude and complexity. As noted throughout this chapter, there are numerous gaps in our knowledge of leader-group interactions and a whole host of possible variables and relationships needs to be investigated. Additionally, the existing research literature needs further systematization so that useful conclusions may be drawn about promising new independent, dependent, and moderator variables for future leader-group research. Thus, this chapter is really just a first step towards this end, and (to use an overused phrase), much more work is clearly needed.

In conclusion, research on leadership in small groups as well as on work groups in formal organizations should include measures of group drive and cohesiveness. Dependent measures should include satisfaction with co-workers, absenteeism, and turnover. Measures of group productivity should, of course, be included, as well as measures of instrumental and supportive leader behaviors. These variables should be included whether we are using contingency, path-goal, or any other type of design. Obviously, this chapter has not considered all the important issues in leadership research; as the title suggests, we have been concerned with crucial issues in leader-group interaction which affect whether or not our research will be optimally productive.

8

Leadership Valence: Modeling and Measuring the Process of Emergent Leadership

R. TIMOTHY STEIN, L. RICHARD HOFFMAN, STEPHEN J.
COOLEY, AND RICHARD W. PEARSE

Increased recognition has been given in the last twenty-five years to the fact that traditional bureaucratic methods of managing organizations are often inefficient and dysfunctional (Merton, 1957; March & Simon, 1958; Thompson, 1967). Rather than relying on adherence to strict departmental lines of authority or one-on-one relationships, the newer models of organization are designed to promote functional interdependencies by fostering links among people from different areas. Matrix organizations have been developed in which staff members have dual responsibilities, for example, the professional staff of hospitals, managers involved in several product lines (Davis & Lawrence, 1977). Task forces composed of people from several departments are brought together temporarily to solve a particular company problem. Temporary project work teams are often formed from a pool of people with relevant skills to perform needed work (e.g., mechanical and electrical engineers who jointly design equipment). These types of temporary structures coordinate the resources of the organization in a timely manner and avoid the barriers of bureaucratic lines of authority and divisional specialization.

One of the most significant dynamics of matrix organizations and temporary work groups is the issue of who wields influence in the group. Since many of the groups promoted by the newer organizational models are initially leaderless or lack the usual single authority structure, informal leaders are likely to emerge, or conflicts over leadership may ensue. An understanding of the leadership dynamics in such groups can provide a basis for diagnosing the sources of problems and for training in the skills of their effective self-management.

During the past 25 years substantial progress has been made in the understanding of how a group member emerges to a leadership position. In the mid-fifties and early sixties, Hollander (1958, 1961, 1964) developed his theory of idiosyncrasy credit and Stogdill (1959) and Bales (1953) published their reinforcement theories. During this same period, beginning with Carter and his associates (Carter, Haythorn, Shriver, & Lanzetta, 1950), many studies examined the behavioral differences between leaders and members. Unfortunately, the theoretical and experimental views of emergent leadership have never been sufficiently integrated. In this chapter we will develop a comprehensive model of how leadership emerges, describe a methodology for operationalizing it, and demonstrate its utility in accounting for a variety of phenomena by deriving a diverse set of testable hypotheses. The chapter will begin with reviews of the theories and the empirical research.

Literature Reviews

Reinforcement Theories

Reinforcement views have been developed by Bales (1953), Stogdill (1959), and Bormann (1969). In the Balesian (1953) view, the emergence process begins with a member making proactive statements which he feels contribute to the task at hand. The member will continue, expanding the scope of his comments by generalizing from the logical premises and emotional bases which underlay his original comments, provided that he is encouraged to do so or at least is not checked by negative comments. The group members generalize from these contributions and begin to expect further effective behavior. The expectations raise the status of the group member. At some point a generalization is made from the specific performance of the member to an ascribed position in the group. The member with the highest position is considered to be the leader.

Bales feels that two major types of roles (or positions) may emerge. The member who is perceived as having the best ideas and as doing the most to guide the discussion is the instrumental leader. The expressive, or socioemotional, leader reduces tension, reassures members, expresses solidarity, and is generally the best liked member.

Bormann (1969) adds two singular contributions to the reinforcement view. He provides a view of the overall process of emergence and describes the basis upon which members decide whose leadership behavior to rein-force. Emergence consists of three general phases: the elimination of those who are unsuitable, the selection of one of the potential leaders, and a probationary period during which the leader must continue to demon-strate his capabilities. Low participation, a lack of requisite skills, and taking a strong unequivocal stand are some of the screening factors. In the second phase, all but one of the remaining members are gradually eliminated. Factors leading to elimination at this level include: an inappropriate (auto-cratic or democratic) leadership style, sex (women are eliminated), irritat-ing personality characteristics, inflexibility, and an undue emphasis on either task or maintenance activities.

Stogdill (1959) places emphasis on two elements that receive only cur-sory treatment in the other views. First, he views the success or failure of the influence attempt to help the group attain its goals as the primary reinforcer. Second, both the initiator and the acceptors of the initiation are reinforced. The evolution of a leadership position is based on the initiation of actions which elicit acquiescence from other members. Thus, reinforce-ment develops mutually confirmed expectations of the roles of being a leader or being a follower in the ongoing group operations.

Idiosyncrasy Credit

The most prominent theory of emergent leadership is Hollander's (1958, 1961, 1964) idiosyncrasy credit theory. Hollander considers status to be the consequence of the positive regard, idiosyncrasy credit, in which a member is held by his peers. Initially, credits are based on the personal characteristics (e.g., social status) which shape first impressions. As time passes, credits are gained or lost depending upon conformity to group expectations and contributions to the task. Deviance and poor performance reduce the credit balance. As long as a positive balance is maintained, group membership is assured.

If a threshold of credits is reached, the member attains a differen-tiated role, that of group leader. The role is a set of special expectations toward that person. The leader continues to earn idiosyncrasy credits by conforming to the role expectations and to the general membership re-quirements. Hollander (1964) emphasizes three important aspects of the leadership role: providing structure and setting goals, maintaining a flexi-bility in handling new and different situations, and establishing proactive social relationships. Failure to meet these or other role expectations would result in the individual's loss of credits and possibly even the leadership role.

Behavioral Differences Between Leaders and Nonleaders

Simultaneous to the development of theoretical models of emergence, investigators have explored the behavioral differences between leaders and other members. In these studies, reviewed recently by Stein and Heller (1978) and Heller and Stein (1978), the group members' verbal interactions were categorized through content analysis according to the relevance of each statement to the ongoing group process (e.g., Bales's interaction categories; Bales, 1950). Emergent leaders and nonleaders were then compared on measures of each categorized type of behavior, or the measures were correlated with observer or peer leadership ratings.

The results clearly indicate that emergent leaders perform more task-related behaviors than nonleaders. Leaders were found to be significantly more active than nonleaders in 88 percent of the tests on problem identification, in 78 percent of the comparisons on proposing solutions to problems, in 70 percent of the tests on seeking information, opinion, or structure, in 63 percent of the comparisons on giving information or opinions, and in 55 percent of the comparisons of acts of initiating structure or procedures for group interaction or task accomplishment. The relationship of leadership status to the initiation of positive and negative interaction (group maintenance functions) was less consistent. Overall, leaders contributed significantly more positive initiations in only 25 percent of the comparisons and more negative initiations in 33 percent. Further analysis indicated that leaders and nonleaders did not differ in the *percentage* of their total behavior that was grouped within the tested categories. In short, in comparison to nonleaders, emergent leaders were generally more active, especially in defining the task and task-related problems, proposing solutions and procedures, and soliciting them from their peers.

While the above generalization is strongly supported by the data, the few divergent findings suggest that the relationship of the specific type of interaction to leadership status is at least partially situational. The following variables have been shown to affect the task-related behavior profiles of leaders: a) type of task (Carter et al., 1950; Hill & Hughes, 1974; Morris & Hackman, 1969), b) appointed or emergent leadership status (Carter et al., 1950), c) college and military groups (Allen & Ruhe, 1976), d) the authoritarianism of the leaders and followers (Haythorn, Couch, Haefner, Langham, & Carter, 1956a, b), e) popularity and the leaders' perceptions of their status (Borgatta & Bales, 1956).

This review of the various theoretical approaches to emergent leadership and of the empirical studies reveals a number of gaps in the theoretical frameworks and a need for associated methodological development. A direct measurement of idiosyncrasy credits ("the degree to which an individual may deviate from the common expectancies of the group," Hollander, 1958) is difficult. What is the person's credit balance at any point in the group's life? The reinforcement explanations have similar operational difficulties. The types of behaviors which, if reinforced, lead to leadership status and the types of responses that are reinforcing need to be specified.

Furthermore, the theories do not account for the frequently observed failure of a single leader to emerge (Fisek & Ofshe, 1970; Heinicke & Bales, 1953). Most theories point to the emergent leader's functional value to the group, yet the empirical evidence also suggests that leaders emerge at times merely because they are more powerful than the other members and personally dominate them. Carter (1954), for example, concluded that leadership was based on *both* task facilitation and personal prominence.

A comprehensive model is needed to account for the diverse phenomena of emergent leadership. Associated with that need is the need for a methodology which will permit making operational the central concepts and the testing of hypotheses derived from the model. In the remainder of the chapter we shall present such a model, a related methodology, and some testable hypotheses which illustrate their value.

A Valence Model of Emergent Leadership

The valence model of leadership emergence describes the process by which members of newly forming groups become differentiated until one becomes the leader.[1] We consider this process to be one facet of the developmental sequence by which a group establishes an interpersonal structure as the tool of task performance (Tuckman, 1965).

Tuckman's (1965) model posits four stages of task and interpersonal development, although Tuckman does not specify whether the four stages occur simultaneously at the two levels. At the interpersonal level, the members of the group first *orient* themselves to each other by testing their dependence on the group and observing each others' behaviors. In the second stage emotional *conflicts* arise, as the members resist each others' influence. These conflicts are resolved in the third stage when norms are

---

[1] The version of this model to be presented here will not deal with either the attachment or enactment of the formal leadership role. The conceptual and methodological issues of emergent leadership are sufficiently complex and problematic that we have limited our first efforts to them. However, extensions of the model are anticipated for future development (Hoffman, 1979, in press).

adopted which regulate the members' behaviors. The leader *emerges* during this stage, along with a norm of appropriate leader-member relations. Tuckman's fourth stage represents the functioning of a mature interpersonal structure which supports the group's task activity.

Although we shall adhere generally to the Tuckman developmental sequence, we prefer to view the development of an interpersonal structure as a problem for the group. We consider group development to be more like personality development than physical development, in that groups may fail to traverse critical points successfully (Erikson, 1968). Thus, many groups fail to reach maturity, especially with respect to the attainment of a mature interpersonal structure, and, even then, optimum task performance may not be achieved. With regard to the specific topic of this chapter, for example, many leaderless groups accomplish tasks, arrive at decisions, and so forth, without satisfactorily resolving the leadership conflicts which arise in the group.

The view that the establishment of such a structure is a "problem" for a new group allows us to apply to leadership emergence Hoffman's (1961) valence model of group problem solving and its extensions (Hoffman & Clark, 1979, in press; Hoffman, Friend, & Bond, 1979 in press; Hoffman & Maier, 1964, 1967) A brief description of Hoffman's model will enable the reader to understand better the use of his concepts in the leadership model.

The basic concept of the problem-solving model is the valence of a cognition. Valence is the force toward or against a particular cognition. Groups solve their problems by generating valence for a particular definition of a problem and, ultimately, for a particular solution to the problem. The generation of valence for both the definition of the problem and for the adopted solution, as measured from members' statements in the discussion, have both been shown to be implicit processes. By implicit, we mean the group may never explicitly state the definition of the problem or how much it favors a particular solution. Yet an implicit problem definition is used as a criterion for adopting a solution. The amount of valence generated by the group in discussion has been shown to predict accurately both the adopted decision and the members' satisfaction with it. For example, more than 90 percent of the groups in these studies adopted the solution with the highest valence and two-thirds of them adopted the first solution to accumulate 15 valence points, a value now considered to be the minimum needed for adoption. Members' satisfaction with the decision correlates positively with their individual valences for the adopted solution (Hoffman, Friend, & Bond, 1979, in press; Hoffman & Maier, 1964, 1967).

Furthermore, the group often does not define the problem before it begins to develop and evaluate solutions. The problem definition emerges, again implicitly, from the criteria used to evaluate the solutions suggested (Hoffman, Bond, & Falk, 1979, in press). As the valences for such criteria accumulate, the solutions proposed accumulate positive or negative valence according to how well they meet the most preferred (highest valent) criteria. It is important that the reader recognize that the process described neither fosters effective problem solving nor does it necessarily prevent it. If the problem is defined accurately and if the members are able to invent appropriate solutions to it, valence will accumulate for an effective solution. If not, the group will adopt a less effective one by the same process (Hoffman & O'Day, 1979, in press).

Emergent Leadership as a "Problem"

Applying this model to the process of leadership emergence, the group's problem is to determine the interpersonal structure necessary to accomplish the group's task. The solution to this problem involves the emergence of roles and the assignment of people to those roles. The above literature review suggests that leaders and members both perform task-facilitating functions, but that leaders perform them more often. Therefore, the group's problem in selecting a leader is twofold: What functions have to be performed by the group to accomplish the task? What member is best able or most desirous of performing those functions and of guiding and encouraging others to perform them? These two aspects of the group's leadership problem are related. The definition of the task-facilitating and controlling functions provides criteria for the selection of a member as leader. The leader is the person who is best able or most willing to perform those functions. The leadership valence model posits, then, that the group's activities will generate valence for a particular definition of the leadership role. That definition will provide criteria for the generation of valence for the concept of a particular member as the leader.

The processes of defining the leadership role and of identifying potential leaders occur simultaneously and implicitly as the group engages in its manifest task. Since the group almost never explicitly raises the need for leadership, the identification of necessary leadership functions occurs implicitly during the course of the interaction. The members' leadership qualifications are evaluated as they contribute to the discussion. However, just as groups often produce an incorrect solution to a problem, the members may also adopt a leader who is ineffective in facilitating the group's performance. They may misidentify the task requirements, misevaluate the leader's ability, or lack the ability or motivation themselves to resist the leader's attempts to control them.

The Orientation Stage. To further explain the simultaneous process of defining the leadership role and selecting a leader, we will delineate three phases of leadership emergence similar to Tuckman's (1965) stages of group development. In the beginning of a leaderless group whose members are homogeneous with respect to age, sex, and other status-related characteristics and are unacquainted with each other, all members have zero valence as leaders. Differences in status characteristics, if they are present, provide the basis for initial attributions of leadership potential (Berger, Cohen, & Zelditch, 1972). The higher status members may begin with some positive valence as leader and the lower status members begin with zero or even negative valence. This would be analogous to the pre-meeting valence for solutions brought into the group when the members have solved a problem individually beforehand (Hoffman & O'Day, 1979, in press).

During the orientation stage the members perform a variety of task-related functions—defining the task, suggesting solutions, recommending procedures to follow, guiding the discussion, and so forth. Through these acts, members announce their candidacies as leader. Because these behaviors indicate the willingness and ability of the speaker to help the group, they are presumed to add valence to the group's concept of that person as leader. In mixed-status groups people of higher status may feel it is their right or obligation to assume leadership and, therefore, to initiate activities which promote their leadership valence. Lower status members may wait for such initiatives and, by conforming to them, add additional valence to the higher status person.

These behaviors also begin to define the leadership role in that group. The group receives the implicit message that the function performed is necessary, in the speaker's view, to accomplishing the task. Through their responses to these attempts to influence, the members contribute valence to both the definition of the leadership role and to the person as leader. Agreement with or conformity to the suggestion adds positive valence both to the function and to the person. Disagreements with the suggestions or acts counter to them add negative valence to the function and to the person as leader. More complicated responses might add positive valence to the function and negative valence to the person as leader, or vice versa. Continued interactions of these types lead to further specification of the leadership functions, or, in Jackson's (1960) terms, to the crystallization of the leadership norm.

As the norm becomes crystallized, it also activates a more generalized concept of leadership consistent with the members' previous experiences with leaders in other groups. Although we assume that central to all leadership norms is the reciprocal dominance-submission relationship established between leaders and members, the generalized norm includes a variety of behaviors which express that relationship. These include not only behaviors which initiate activity or direction for the group or express the personal dominance of the leader, but also behaviors which are designed to enhance the personal rewards of the other members. The latter are likely to appear, however, only after one member's position as the emergent leader has been firmly established. As the established leader, he becomes the legitimate source of rewards and punishments from other members.

The Conflict Stage. If one member consistently and repeatedly initiates activity, guides the group, and controls others' behaviors, that member's valence will accumulate until it passes the candidacy threshold. Analogous to the adoption threshold found for solutions in problems-solving groups (Hoffman, Friend, & Bond, 1979, in press; Hoffman & Maier, 1964, 1967), the candidacy threshold is the amount of valence necessary for a member to be considered seriously for adoption as the group's leader. More than one member often exercises successful influence and gains sufficient valence to pass the candidacy threshold at about the same time as the first one, thus generating a leadership conflict. Sometimes this conflict becomes so intense that the group splinters into factions and ceases to exist, or at other times it precipitates a formal recognition of the need to elect a single person as the leader. Ordinarily, however, resolution of this conflict is achieved when one person accumulates sufficient valence to be adopted implicitly as the leader. An emergence threshold is defined as the amount of valence necessary to adopt a person as the implicit leader.

The Emergence Stage. The emergence stage begins after one member's leadership valence has passed the emergence threshold. At that point the group has implicitly adopted a leader who then continues to earn valence points and consolidates his position as leader. Such valence points would be similar to Hollander's idiosyncrasy credits and would be earned by continuing to exercise control over members' actions or by guiding the group to the accomplishment of its task. As the leader continues to accumulate valence, analogous to the affirmation of the group's decision in decision-making groups (Hoffman & Maier, 1964, 1967), we anticipate an enlargement of his repertoire of exhibited behaviors consistent with his concept of the generalized leadership norm. Even behavior deviant for a leader might be manifested, if the leader acquires enough valence to feel secure. In this way, the leadership valence model incorporates transitions from an essentially leaderless group to the implicit adoption of a formal leader who emerges from the ranks.

Patterns of Emergent Leadership

While these three stages of emergent leadership may be recognized, the ways in which leaders emerge may vary from group to group. Several possible patterns may be anticipated.

Pattern One. In some groups one member takes charge early by suggesting procedures or defining the problem or merely by controlling the discussion in such a way as to discourage others from participating. As he persists in such initiating and controlling behavior and as others in the group conform to the suggestions or yield to his control, his valence as leader increases rapidly past the candidacy threshold. If no other member also accumulates sufficient valence to pass that threshold within some reasonable period thereafter, the group will act as if the first person is the leader. The leader will initiate more acts consistent with the general leadership norm, since the members' previous compliance with his directions added valence to his self-concept as the leader. The members will conform to his new suggestions, since the valence of their concept of him as leader has been strengthened by his willingness to attempt to lead the group and the members' willingness to comply (Pepinsky, Hemphill, & Shevitz, 1958). Following his passing of the emergence threshold, the leader will not only act as leader consistent with the emerging norm, but will introduce new behaviors and even possibly engage in behavior deviant from other group norms (Hollander, 1964). The emergent leader essentially takes responsibility for the fate of the group, and the members surrender that responsibility as they are guided in performing the task.

This first pattern of leadership emergence is depicted in the graph of Figure 7. Person A is the emergent leader whose accumulation of valence has been described above. Person B initiates actions consistent with the general guidelines established by Person A, thus becoming his lieutenant. He operates as a proxy for the leader, especially in the emergence phase, to relieve the leader of the costs attached to exercising leadership. Person C is an average member who makes a few suggestions which are adopted by the group, but limits himself mostly to following the leader.

Person D accumulates negative valence for leadership early in the discussion. A person may accumulate negative valence as leader by engaging in deviant behavior, by making unacceptable suggestions or by verbally disqualifying himself by announcing incompetence for the task or an unwillingness to take responsibility for the group. The Conflict Stage is foreshortened in Pattern One, since only one member accumulates enough valence to pass the candidacy threshold. After possibly testing the erstwhile leader's competence or concern for the group, the leader will be en-

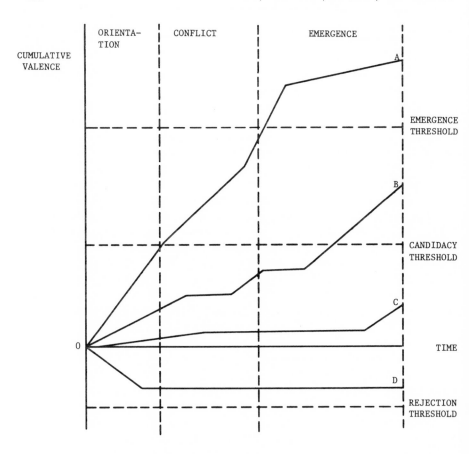

N.B.   The letters A,B,C,D stand for persons.

Fig. 7. Stages of leadership emergence: Pattern one

couraged to direct the group through requests for information or permission from the other members and by direct compliance with his requests until his valence surpasses the emergence threshold.

Pattern Two. If two or more members' leadership valences surpass the candidacy threshold and the differences in magnitude between them are small, leadership conflict ensues. Several possible outcomes may be anticipated. One of the two candidates may exert himself more or recruit followers or have a particularly attractive way of accomplishing the task, so he accumulates positive valence rapidly and surpasses the emergence threshold. Meanwhile the competitor's suggestions are ignored or mildly rejected

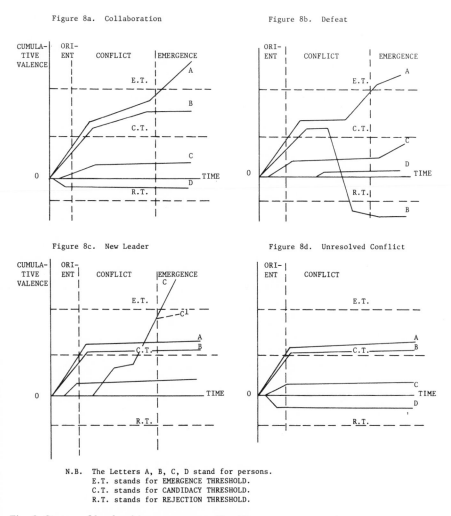

Figure 8a. Collaboration

Figure 8b. Defeat

Figure 8c. New Leader

Figure 8d. Unresolved Conflict

N.B. The Letters A, B, C, D stand for persons.
      E.T. stands for EMERGENCE THRESHOLD.
      C.T. stands for CANDIDACY THRESHOLD.
      R.T. stands for REJECTION THRESHOLD.

Fig. 8. Stages of leadership emergence: Conflict

so he fails to accumulate any more leadership valence. Figure 8 illustrates this pattern of conflict resolution graphically.

Figure 8 illustrates a somewhat longer conflict phase which is resolved by one competitor's accumulating negative valence as leader. That person's suggestions might be actively rejected, or the person might be attacked or withdraw in deference to the first person. As the rejected candidate's valence fails to accumulate or drops below the candidacy threshold, the remaining candidate can assume the leadership.

A third possible resolution to the conflict is the search for a third party acceptable to both candidates (Figure 8c). That person might make a new suggestion at some point in the fight which permits the group to turn to him as a means of resolving the dispute. By asserting control over the contenders and enhancing their contributions to the group's task, such a person accumulates sufficient valence to pass the emergence threshold.

Pattern Three. A third party may, however, merely provide a temporary respite from the conflict by mediating a particular dispute between the contenders. The contenders may prevent the third party from maintaining control long enough to acquire the valence needed to pass the emergence threshold (Person C^1 in Figure 8c).

In many cases the group fails to resolve the conflict even temporarily (Figure 8d). The result is either status inconsistency (Fisek & Ofshe, 1970; Heinicke & Bales, 1953) or the disintegration of the group into factions around the competing leaders. As noted earlier, in many groups some form of task accomplishment occurs even when groups fail to resolve their leadership conflicts. Some groups may disband, however, rather than yield to an unacceptable leader. The boundary conditions holding members into the group are too weak to sustain the leadership conflict.

Acceptance of the Leader

Although a leader of a group may emerge by one or the other of the processes just outlined, the members' acceptance of such a leader may vary considerably from person to person. We expect that a member's acceptance of the leader will be a function of that member's contribution to the leader's total valence.

The acceptance of the leader increases the willingness of the members to subordinate themselves to him, the resistance made to his being deposed in the face of group failure (Hamblin, 1958), and the scope of the power exercised by the leader. To the extent that one or more members resist the leader's influence attempts in particular areas, his legitimacy to engage in those activities as leader is questioned. He will receive negative valence points in response to such influence attempts, thus constricting his leadership efforts.

A Caution

Although the valence model of emergent leadership has used Tuckman's (1965) model of group development as its basic framework, this model differs from his in several important ways. Tuckman posits that the social structure forms to facilitate the problem-solving work of the group.

However, the present model is neither normative for, nor predictive of, the emergence of effective leaders by any external criterion, for example, the group's task effectiveness. Rather, the model is intended only to describe the process by which a group adopts (or fails to adopt) a single member as leader according to the members' own ratings. Although socioemotional issues may interfere with task accomplishment, their resolution may be achieved, in fact, at the expense of effective problem-solving. The member with creative ideas may be suppressed by the emerging leader in asserting his dominance over the group. The relationships between effective group problem-solving and the development and maintenance of social structures in problem-solving groups are part of a larger model presently being revised and developed (Hoffman, 1979, in press). The coding categories for leadership valence have been designed to be comparable with the effectiveness concerns of the larger model.

Testing the Model

Methodology

In this section the methodology currently being used to operationalize the leadership valence model will be described, hypotheses generated by this model will be outlined, and some preliminary descriptive data presented.

Valence Categories. The generalized leadership norm is assumed to be all behaviors exhibited by leaders in groups and accepted by the members. The specific norm will vary from group to group, depending on such situational factors as the task, the external status of the members, the place of the group in its environment, and so forth. The model's earlier assumption that crystallization of the specific norm results from interactions in the group implies that the group selects appropriate behaviors from a set defined by the general norm.

The set of behavior categories to represent the general norm was developed by organizing the behaviors identified with leaders in content-analytic and factor-analytic studies of leadership behavior (Carter, 1954; Stein & Heller, 1978). The scoring system consists of a list of behaviors grouped under five descriptive headings. The first two sets of categories— I. Identification and Solving of Task Problems, and II. Initiates, Directs, and Controls Group Procedure and Structure—are directly related to task leadership. Acts that relate to the task itself are scored separately from those related to the procedure or method to be used in accomplishing the task. The third set of behaviors—III. Direct Control over Others—includes acts of personal dominance, in which the member attempts to regulate the group's activities or to exercise control over other members. Positive socioemotional leadership behaviors are grouped under—IV. Support and Assistance. The member attempts to promote positive feelings among the members or encourage their efforts. The last set—V. Deviant Behaviors—identifies behaviors which are presumed to contribute negative valence to the member who initiates them, since they are likely to disrupt the group's task accomplishment or antagonize the other members.

Types of Acts. The behaviors are organized under three headings: initiations, positive responses, and negative responses. Both acts of initiation and responses to the initiations are scored in the leadership valence system. An *Initiation* is defined as any behavior on the part of a group member whose manifest or latent purpose is to facilitate accomplishment of the group's task or to control the activities of the members. Initiations are considered to be leadership attempts. The person performing the behavior receives one positive valence point for each attempt.

Certain initiations or leadership attempts call for responses from the other group members. A *Response* is defined as any reaction on the part of a noninitiating group member to an initiation or leadership attempt. Although the intensity of a response can range from extremely positive to extremely negative, at this point in the development of the valence method each positive response is scored as a single positive valence point. An act which fails to respond to an initiation and each negative response are scored as a single negative point. Because responses indicate agreement or disagreement with some initiation, the response valence points are assigned to the person who made the initiation. Responses which are also acts of initiation are also scored as initiations for the respondent. For example, Person A suggests that the members list possible solutions to a problem, and Person B responds by giving a solution. Person B's response is scored as a positive response for Person A in the category "proposes procedure." The response is also scored as an act of initiation for Person B in the category "proposes problems solution."

Acts of self-enhancement and self-devaluation—which flatter or denigrate the speaker respectively—are scored as positive or negative initiations. An act of submission to another, such as seeking permission, is scored as a negative response point for the person who is submitting and as a positive response point for the person being submitted to.

An example of the Scoring. Valence points will be assigned to the following fictitious interaction segment to illustrate the system.

PERSON A. I think Mr. Jones will make an excellent assistant director. (one point in the category of proposing a task problem solution) His resume indicates that he not only has the training, but he has the experience as well. (two points in the category of justification of task solutions)

PERSON B: I agree on Mr. Jones. (a positive response point for Person A in the category of proposing a task problem solution)

PERSON C: I don't agree. (negative response, proposing task solution, for Person A) Experience and training aren't the only considerations that we should take into account. (positive initiation point for Person B for evaluation of a task solution, and a negative point for Person A in the same category for the disagreement with his criteria) His record also indicates that he's single, and therefore probably unstable, and that he has a prison record, preferring to serve two years in jail rather than the military. (two initiation points in the evaluation of a solution criteria) I therefore feel we should consider someone else. (one initiation point in the proposing procedure category)

PERSON D: How about Mr. Lautenschlager? (positive reaction point for Person C in the proposing structure category, and an initiation point for Person D in the proposing task solutions category)

Ignoring the categories in which the valence tallies are placed, the total leadership valence scores are:

Person	Initiation Points	Response Points	Total
A	1, 1, 1	1, −1, −1	2
B			0
C	1, 1, 1, 1	1	5
D	1		1

The reader will note that only verbal statements are coded for leadership valence. Unverbalized indications of initiation or reaction, which might be seen in groups through direct observation or videotape—for example, head movements, facial expressions, gestures—have not been incorporated in the present system. Though research by Stein (1975) has shown that leadership status can be judged from visual information, the question of what specific nonverbal behaviors are indicative of such status has not been addressed in the literature. The authors are currently investigating the question in separate research. We believe that the paralinguistic cues and interaction provided by the audio recording will account for sufficient variance in the study of emerging leadership to permit us to test significant aspects of the leadership valence model. If this effort is successful, and when the relevant behaviors have been specified, we shall attempt to extend the methodology to include such unverbalized acts.

Experimental Groups. For our initial empirical tests of the model, we will

code the discussions of forty leaderless problem-solving groups of introductory psychology students. The groups were given a modification of the
Parasol Assembly Problem (Hoffman & Maier, 1964) and instructed to formulate a consensus solution. At the end of the 45-minute sessions, the
group members, two males and two females, were asked to respond to
questions pertaining to the members' leadership. Each group was tape-
recorded and transcripts were prepared to facilitate the valence scoring.

Hypotheses

The hypotheses listed below have been generated from the model.
They are designed to illustrate the utility of the leadership valence model
for integrating a variety of emergent leadership phenomena and for developing new principles. They also demonstrate the ability of the methodology to operationalize the concepts of the model and to measure aspects
of the process which were heretofore recorded in aggregate scores at best.

Hypothesis A: Post-meeting leadership ratings by group members will
be correlated positively with leadership valence points.

This hypothesis is, of course, fundamental to the model. Unless the
cumulative valence index predicts the group's choice of an emergent
leader, the model's value is dubious. Hypothesis A can be tested using multiple regression procedures. The leadership valence scores for each category will be entered as the independent variables. Peer ratings of leadership (for example, a rating of the extent to which each group member had
contributed to the group's leadership) will serve as dependent variables.
Since our literature review indicated that leaders were not differentiated
from nonleaders by socioemotional behavior, we expect that the socioemotional categories will not account for a significant amount of the leadership
rating variance. We also expect that the deviance categories will have
negative beta weights.

Hypothesis B: The valence scores, which include points for responses,
will yield a more accurate prediction of leadership status than will simple
measures of leadership attempts or of participation.

This hypothesis tests the model's proposition that the leader emerges
by engaging in *successful* leadership attempts, not just by continually attempting to control the group or engaging in unproductive conversation.
In this way the transactional aspects of the leader-member relationship are
measured by the valence index. To test Hypothesis B, a second set of multiple correlations can be calculated with the exclusion of the response points
from the categorical scores. The differences in the two sets of multiple
correlations can be tested for significance.

Hypothesis C: A rejection threshold can be identified such that those who fall below that leadership valence value will have a high probability of being eliminated by their peers as candidates for leadership.

Hypothesis D: A candidacy threshold can be determined such that those who have reached that valence level will have a high probability of being identified by their peers as candidates for the leadership position.

Hypothesis E: An emergence threshold can be determined such that a member whose leadership valence exceeds that value will have a high probability of being identified as the leader.

Hypotheses C, D, and E test the model's assumptions of the existence of three valence thresholds: rejection, candidacy, and emergence. If a member's leadership valence falls below the rejection threshold, that person's negative valence precludes his adoption as the leader. To be considered as a possible leader, a person's leadership valence must surpass the candidacy threshold. The emergent leader is adopted only from among such candidates when his leadership valence surpasses the emergence threshold. All emergent leaders will have accumulated more valence than the emergence threshold.

The principal difficulty with testing these three hypotheses is the identification of rejected, possible, and emergent leaders. Even where observers might identify an emergent leader, the lack of uniform acceptance in the group might not yield consensus about him. We intend to rely on the leadership ratings to identify the three types of members. Rejected members will be those who received the lowest peer leadership ratings. Candidates will have received high ratings (e.g., about five on a seven-point scale). Emergent leaders will be those who were rated highest by three-fourths of the group members.

Using these criteria, determinants of threshold values can be accomplished in several ways. Following Hoffman and Maier's (1964) method of determining the solution-adoption threshold, a cutoff point can be determined at which the probability is high, say .85, that only candidates will exceed that value. Similarly, the rejection threshold will be that point below which members have a high probability of being rejected. The emergence threshold can be calculated in similar fashion.

Hypothesis F: Little consensus about the leadership status of group members will be present in groups where more than one member has passed the candidacy threshold, but none has surpassed the emergence threshold.

This hypothesis tests the power of the model to predict with the same set of concepts not only successful leadership emergence, but also failures to achieve status consistency. Failure to resolve leadership conflict will produce disagreements in members' perceptions of who the group's leader is. To test Hypothesis F, Kendall coefficients of concordance can be used to measure consensus in the leadership rankings. The coefficients from groups in which a member has passed the emergence threshold can be compared to the values derived from groups with members who have only surpassed the candidacy threshold. The variance in the leadership ratings assigned the top members could also be used as a consensus measure.

These hypotheses are intended to be illustrative, not exhaustive. The model can also incorporate predictions about members with different initial statuses, the relation between participation and emergent leadership, and the nature of the leadership norm at different stages of the group discussion.

Preliminary Results

At the time this chapter was written, only a few transcripts of the problem-solving discussions had been prepared for coding. These were analyzed for total leadership valence, ignoring the separate categories, to determine, in a preliminary way, whether the principal hypotheses of the model had any merit, although we caution the reader that these are data from one coder only, whose reliability is as yet undetermined. Figure 9 presents plots for three groups of the leadership valences accumulated in successive 80-act segments by each of the four members. The graphs illustrate the utility of the method for describing the different processes by which leaders emerged in the three groups, as anticipated in Figures 7 and 8. Next to the total valence received by each member is that member's total leadership rating from his/her peers, in which they allocated 100 points among the four members.

It is readily apparent that the correlation between each member's leadership valence and his/her ratings are very high in all three groups. Furthermore, the results illustrate the usefulness of the valence concept in recognizing emergent leadership as a variable—as something often shared among members—rather than being an all-or-none phenomenon (Hoffman & Smith, 1960).

Even more interesting in terms of the utility of the model are the different patterns of leadership emergence exhibited in the three groups. In Group A the leader (Person 1) emerged early, having accumulated 60 points by the end of the second segment. His sudden increment in the next segment put him in clear control by the end of the third segment. It is possible that the flattening of this cumulative curve in the last segment identifies the Emergence phase, although that may represent only a termination phenomenon.

Group B shows a clear conflict pattern, somewhat like Figure 8a, in

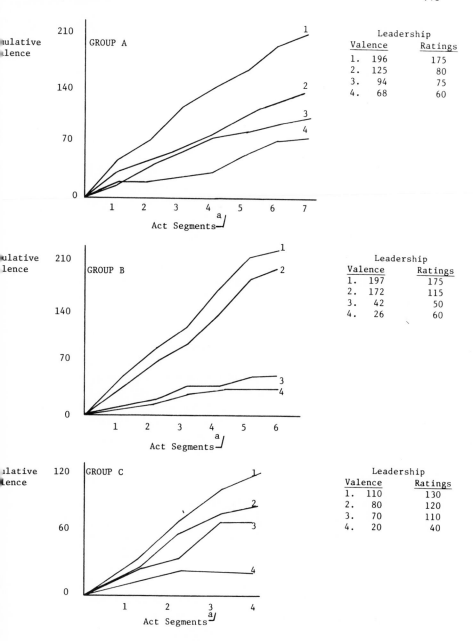

Fig. 9. Leadership valence patterns

which Persons 1 and 2 vied for leadership from the beginning of the meeting. Whatever the candidacy threshold may turn out to be, the valence curves for these two members clearly pass each potential value at about the same point in the group's discussion. The continued superiority of Person 1 and the failure of Person 2's curve to flatten—indicating no further accumulation of valence—suggest that Person 2 acted either as Person 1's lieutenant, or his competitor.

Group C also presents an interesting variation on the conflict pattern of Figure 8c. Persons 1 and 3 seem to have been in early conflict, but later Person 2 came into contention. This conflict established Person 1 as the leader, while Person 3 suffered a slight decrement in valence. This pattern suggests that Person 3 became Person 1's lieutenant in overcoming Person 2's influence, but did not supplant her as the leader.

The possibility of a candidacy threshold somewhere in the 40 to 60 range seems to hold for all three groups. In all three, the emergent leader was the first to accumulate more than 40 valence points. In the conflict groups (B and C) a second member also entered the candidacy range very shortly thereafter. Evidence for an emergence threshold is more tenuous and, since nobody accumulated negative valence, no rejection thresholds are apparent. An initial comparison suggests that total participation rates show less definitive relations to the ratings. The method also permits us to chart the emergence process and to determine the points at which members become differentiated. This measuring ability can identify correspondences between the emerging leadership process and the problem-solving process and, possibly, identify points of most effective intervention to facilitate effectiveness.

Conclusions

The leadership valence model presented here makes three major contributions: 1) It integrates a variety of phenomena which have been dealt with independently by different theories. 2) It generates new hypotheses, especially concerning stages in the process of emergent leadership. 3) It provides a methodology for operationalizing concepts and for testing hypotheses quantitatively. Moreover, our model and methodology differentiate among the members who are actively rejected as leaders, those who merely fail to accrue sufficient support to be considered, and those who compare actively with the emergent leader.

By identifying the development of a leadership structure as a "problem" for the group, the leadership valence model has capitalized on a model of the problem-solving process for tying the literature on emergent leadership into Tuckman's (1965) stages of group development. Similarly, in testing the model we were able to exploit the results of leadership behavior studies by creating categories of behavior which defined the generalized leadership norm. Initiations and reactions to those behaviors should provide a more valid measure of leadership valence than would total participation alone.

The method and the model provide a broad and integrated set of hypotheses and a way of testing them that no other model provides. The hypotheses listed in the previous section portray a variety of phenomena through a limited set of concepts which can be operationalized. Most of the hypotheses also illustrate aspects of the leadership emergence process which can be studied through this model and method, but not with traditional input-outcome designs. Furthermore, by recognizing which stage a group is in by this method, as shown in the preliminary results, we can design interventions and experiments to change the course of the group at appropriate times.

9

Commentary on What Should Be Studied

Comments on Chapter 7

Model Building and Contributions to Understanding

JOHN CHILD AND DIAN-MARIE HOSKING

The "tentative model" presented by Schriesheim, Mowday, and Stogdill represents the latest attempt to focus on leader-group interactions and their implications for certain aspects of organizational performance. In focusing on relationships between the leader and his group, Schriesheim et al. are following the perspective adopted by researchers such as W. C. Schutz (1958), Fiedler (1967) and O'Brien and Harary (1977). Perhaps the most similar previous work has been the system approach of Katzell, Miller, Rotter, and Venet (1970) who examined the relationship between various inputs (including leader behavior), group processes, and outcomes such as group problem-solving effectiveness and member satisfaction.

Our discussion of the Schriesheim et al. contribution centers on two related questions: How valid is their model, and to what degree does it advance our understanding of leadership processes and leadership effectiveness? We think it is particularly appropriate to pose these questions since the Schriesheim et al. chapter is not breaking entirely new ground. At the close of this commentary we also consider whether the best way of advancing our understanding of leader-group interactions is via model-building of the Schriesheim et al. kind.

The validity of Schriesheim et al.'s model and its contribution to understanding are discussed in terms of the following issues: 1) the nature of the literature from which the model is derived, 2) definition of key terms in the model, 3) the "type" of model being developed—for example, conceptual or operational, 4) the nature of the relationships postulated, 5) the sufficiency of the analysis, with respect to variables considered, and 6) the sufficiency of the analysis with respect to assumptions made about the contexts in which leader-group interactions occur.

The Nature of the Literature from Which the Model Is Derived

The literature from which Schriesheim et al. derive their postulates is extremely diverse. They state that they are prepared to sacrifice some precision in order to summarize the data; however, a good deal more than precision may have been lost. Take, for example, the concept of group cohesion—a variable which has been defined and measured in many different ways. The data from these measures do not necessarily correlate (Cartwright, 1968), and indeed, it is often unclear why they should. Such observations suggest, that if Schriesheim et al. had distinguished between the variety of conceptual and operational definitions they could have arrived at a different model (or models). One study which suggests how this might be the case was performed by Back (1951). Back varied the "base" of cohesiveness (interpersonal attraction, prestige of being a group member, and attraction to the task) and observed different patterns of group interaction to follow. These, in turn, might be expected to result in different outcomes (e.g., productivity).

The Definition of Key Terms

A second (and related) point is that, given Schriesheim et al. use terms which have been defined and measured in a variety of ways, it is often not clear what definitions they are using. A particularly serious deficiency concerns their failure to specify what they mean by the term "leader." In their second paragraph they comment that "leaders emerge from groups or are appointed." Elsewhere we get the impression that for "leader," read "supervisor." While we appreciate that a definition of this concept is problematic, *some* definition is required in order to assess the adequacy of the model.

Suppose, for example, that a person wishing to test the model defines the leader as the person with most influence over group activities. Such a "leader" might be the person appointed by management (e.g., the supervisor), or he/she might be an "informal" or "emergent" leader. One of Schriesheim et al.'s postulates is that leaders may behave in ways which cause low group drive and cohesion. These conditions are then hypothesized to lead to various outcomes such as high labor turnover. However, where emergent leaders are concerned, there is clearly another possibility not considered in the model—high levels of *leader turnover!*

The Type of Model Developed

Certain ambiguities exist which make it unclear whether the model is supposedly conceptual or operational. Schriesheim et al.'s use of the terms "supportive" and "instrumental" is particularly vague. These could be viewed as *concepts* for which it would be valid to substitute, for example, "relationships-oriented" and "task-oriented," or they could refer specifically to the dimensions *operationalized* in the Leader Behavior Description Questionnaire (LBDQ—Form XII) (Stogdill, 1963a). Support for the latter possibility is provided by the fact that Schriesheim et al. seem to regard the LBDQ as a valid means of testing their model. However, the discriminant and construct validity of these dimensions has been seriously questioned (see Schriesheim & Kerr, 1977). Consequently, use of LBDQ to test the model seems unwise.

This confusion between conceptual and operational levels, together with the absence of a clear definition of leadership, makes it difficult to discover what "type" of model is being proposed. Are the behaviors referred to those perceived by group members, by some independent observer(s), or by the leaders themselves? The question is important because different sources of description show little correspondence (see, for example, Ilgen and Fujii, 1976; Mitchell, 1970). This confusion causes further problems since: "If a theory is based on the subordinate perception of his/her leader's behavior, perceptual measures should be used. If the theory incorporates the totality of leader behavior, perceptual scales alone will not suffice" (Stinson, 1977, p. 115). In other words, we suggest that this lack of clarity makes it difficult to test the model. In addition, it makes it difficult to assess how well the model fits existing data: Different relationships might be expected between the variables depending on the source of description.

The Nature of Relationships Postulated

The fourth area of comment concerns Schriesheim et al.'s postulates—starting with hypothesized relationships between the inputs (leader behaviors) and the mediating, structural variables. It seems that "supportive" and "instrumental" behaviors are regarded as having *independent effects* on group drive and cohesion (but not for some unknown reason on group goal acceptance). However, previous research indicates that people's perceptions of, for instance, a leader's instrumental behavior are affected by the amount of support he shows and vice versa (Hosking, 1978; Lowin, Hrapchek, & Kavanagh, 1969). These findings seem to be reliable, and suggest that the model's postulates regarding relationships between leader behaviors, drive, and cohesion may need revising.

Schriesheim et al. conclude that both instrumental *and* supportive behaviors affect cohesion, although the literature they review is confused and does not justify this interpretation. It remains likely that, for example, only instrumental behaviors have any significant effect in certain circumstances, while in others, complex interactions occur between the two sets of behaviors. The link between leader behavior and group performance also requires comment. The way the leader behaves is depicted as a determinant of various group outcomes such as productivity and member satisfaction. These effects are conceptualized as indirect, being mediated by factors such as group drive and cohesion. However, the literature from which Schriesheim et al. derived their model does not provide a valid base for *causal* hypothesis since it is largely correlational. Furthermore, there are good reasons to suppose that the direction of causation is sometimes opposite to that postulated. For example, Schriesheim et al. view group productivity as *dependent* on levels of group drive and cohesion. The findings of researchers such as Sherif, Harvey, White, Hood, and Sherif (1961) and Fiedler (1967) show that productivity or task success also affect group variables. There is also evidence that differing levels of group performance influence the ways in which a leader behaves toward his work group (see, for example, Barrow, 1976). Schriesheim et al. acknowledge that other causal relationships are likely and should be included in the future, but one may ask why they were not incorporated at the model's inception? There is as much evidence on relationships between these variables as there is, for instance, on those between role differentiation and group cohesion. There seems no obvious reason why it should be ignored.

Schriesheim et al. argue that group drive and cohesion have an *interactive effect* on productivity. This effect is moderated by group goal acceptance and the type of task performed. Unfortunately, in the absence of a specification of task types, it is difficult to judge what would constitute disconfirmation of this part of the model. Schriesheim et al. hypothesize that group cohesion and productivity are negatively related when group drive is low and the "operating conditions" (task?) are "routine." Conversely, they postulate that high levels of group drive and cohesion promote productivity, but the necessary task conditions are not defined. Presumably, they are nonroutine. If so, the "groupthink" hypothesis presented by Irving Janis seems to contradict such a postulate. His analysis of policy-making groups with nonroutine tasks suggested that productivity (or more accurately, performance) is *impaired* in conditions of high drive and cohesion (Janis, 1972).

The Sufficiency of the Analysis with Respect to Variables Considered

In order to evaluate the model's validity, fairly extensive consideration of its sufficiency is required. Recall that the model is described as being concerned with "leader-group interactions." A reasonable response to this seems to be "where are they?" One "crucial dimension" seems missing—no attempt is made to consider the impact of the leader's behavior on what the group actually does: that is, *group behavior*. Perhaps, the model would be more "complete" if variables such as group drive and cohesiveness were viewed as conditions for a process category which is in turn linked to group productivity. Returning to "groupthink," Janis described the drive and cohesion of, for example, Kennedy's advisory group *and* the ways it behaved. He then linked these structural and process variables with group performance (and, incidentally, with leader behavior). The "groupthink" analysis also suggests that Schriesheim et al. fail to consider a sufficient range of leader behaviors. For example, Janis argued that Kennedy's behavior included encouraging uncritical acceptance of weak arguments, allowing certain representatives to dominate the discussion and failing to promote discussion of controversial views (Janis, 1972, pp. 43–44). A substantial literature exists demonstrating that these sorts of leader behaviors are influential in determining group performance on given kinds of tasks (see, for example, Hall & Watson, 1970; Maier & Sashkin, 1971). Consequently, these leader behaviors should be included in a model which purports to deal with leader-group interactions on a variety of task-types.

In arguing for renewed attention to leader-*group* interactions, Schriesheim et al. suggest that leaders probably behave in a relatively homogeneous manner toward the group, rather than "tailoring" their behavior to each group member. To support this view they quote correlations between subordinates' descriptions of their leaders' behavior, arguing that they show "reasonable agreement" (see their footnote 2). However, these correlations, which group around 0.6, account for little more than one-third of the variance in leader-behavior descriptions. One reason why this is the case might be that group members *perceive* the same behaviors in a variety of ways, depending on attributes which they (the subordinates) possess. Recent research has shown that this is indeed the case (Butterfield & Bartol, 1977; Hosking, 1978; and see the review by Schriesheim & Kerr, 1977).

Such findings suggest that the "types" of members a leader has in his group should also be included in a model of leader-group interactions.

There are other reasons why less than perfect agreement is found between subordinates' descriptions of their leaders' behavior. For example, the leader may actually vary his behavior in response to certain environmental cues (one of which might be the "type" of subordinate). Summary measures of perceived leader behaviors obscure such variations and neglect the importance of *timing*. While it is unclear how Schriesheim et al. conceptualize the role of leader behavior, they pay no attention to the possible importance of the leader doing the "right" things at *the "right" time*. Once again the work on small group decision-making provides some clues as to the possible significance of this variable. For example, Bales (1954) argued that more "successful" groups follow a certain pattern of discussion (assemble information → draw inferences → review proposals). The leader may influence that pattern by, for example, stating his views at the start of a meeting or withholding them till later (Janis, 1972). Leaders clearly do differ from each other in the way they pattern their behavior (see, for example, Sample & Wilson, 1965) and this may have a crucial effect on their group's performance.

The Sufficiency of the Analysis with Respect to Assumptions about the Situation

So far our comments have been confined to a discussion of individual, group, and task variables. However, as Melcher (1977) noted, organizational variables interact with leadership processes. Like most other leadership researchers, Schriesheim et al. largely abstract their model from contextual circumstances admitting that it is not likely "to hold under all circumstances." Unfortunately, contextual features such as management structure, socio-technical systems, and the nature of employment relationships cannot simply be dismissed by a disclaimer of general applicability. These aspects of context are always present in work organizations and they have a direct bearing both upon the conceptualization of variables incorporated in the model and upon the interrelationships between them. To ignore them is to imply that they are of no account.

Thus, there has been a marked trend toward multidimensional management structures, starting long ago with the line/staff distinction and culminating today with matrix organization. These structures not only generate multiple leadership positions; as "senders" for employee roles these leadership positions may also conflict. The single leader concept adopted by Schriesheim et al. is probably no longer the most common type in reality. Its utilization is therefore open to question.

Second, the abstraction from socio-technical systems also leaves out of account the question of how far the model applies in a situation of what Thompson (1967) would call "pooled interdependence," in which work-groups in any meaningful sense may not exist and where performance is purely individual. Schriesheim et al. recognize this particular problem. What they fail to consider are socio-technical situations in which the notion of an *appointed* leader has become redundant. This may be the case with the so-called "autonomous work group," the establishment of which is en-couraged by applying principles of Group Technology. Management re-lates to this kind of work group in terms that cannot readily be handled by the concept of leadership employed in their chapter. A classic case of work group "autonomy" arises with incentive payment systems which may lead to what is virtually a subcontracting relationship with management. Here again a very different concept of leadership is required.

Consideration of autonomous groups points to perhaps the most seri-ous blind spot in the Schriesheim et al. model. This is the total failure to recognize leader power and authority as problematic. Appreciation of the conflicts of interest and coercive elements embodied in employment rela-tionships (clearly analyzed in the literatures of labor relations and indus-trial sociology) suggests the power of the leader in the eyes of the group is a most significant variable. Nor have all leadership theorists ignored this issue. Leader position power has always been a major variable in Fiedler's analysis. Hollander's research (Hollander, 1960; Hollander & Julian, 1970) which draws upon exchange theory, points to another aspect of power relations: the leader's "legitimacy" in the eyes of group members. Here the possible interrelation of leader competence and degree of conformity to *group* goals is located in a recognition that group and managerial objec-tives may not be the same and that, within this area of tension, leaders are agents of groups as well as groups being agents of leaders. The present model only allows for the latter perspective, and offers no justification for so doing.

We suggest that its abstraction from contextual reality in this regard has direct implications for the validity of the model's conceptualization and portrayal of interrelationships. For example, the view of leader as agent of the group immediately suggests hypotheses of a kind that Schriesheim et al. do not consider at all, such as the following: High group drive and co-hesiveness support the maintenance of a single leader situation so long as the leader is successful in promoting group goals. If he is not successful, then high drive and cohesiveness will be conducive to the emergence of strong counter-leadership. This makes immediately intelligible the emergence and accretion of power to leaders selected by the group itself (e.g., union stewards) when appointed leaders fail to satisfy group objectives. As Hollander has argued, below a certain level of group success the leader simply ceases to be a leader. The doubtful validity in these respects of the Schriesheim et al. model appears to derive from a myopic focus upon a very narrow stream of previous research within the social sciences, and to be reinforced by the general managerial orientation of the chapter.

Our arguments so far may be summarized as follows: 1) Schriesheim, Mowday, and Stogdill treat a diverse literature as though it were homogeneous, 2) definitions of key terms are ambiguous, 3) confusion exists as to whether the model is articulated at the conceptual or operational level, 4) some of the postulated relationships seem questionable, as do the causal assumptions, 5) certain crucial variables are ignored which lessen the degree to which this is a model of leader-group interactions and cast doubt on the model's predictive power, and 6) there is too limited an appreciation of the assumptions made through ignoring the situation in which leader-group relations occur. The foregoing comments cast some doubt as to whether the Schriesheim et al. analysis represents a significant theoretical advance. Maybe one cannot hope for more from model-building which is so locked into existing conceptual and operational definitions within a relatively closed and narrowly bounded school of leadership research.

Model-building or . . . ?

A further question we posed was whether the best way of advancing our understanding of leader-group interactions is to engage in model-building. J. P. Campbell (1977, p. 23) suggested in the previous volume in this series that "the study of leadership has been hurt by over concentration on theory." One alternative to proposing new models, such as Schriesheim et al.'s (which is presumably intended as a step toward theory development), would be to devote more of our energies to grounding concepts and postulated relationships in empirical reality. It is therefore perhaps timely to return to direct observation, preferably of "natural" rather than *ad hoc* groups in order to ascertain through comparative studies: 1) the behavior actually pursued by actors who are assuming leadership roles, such as supervisors and informal group leaders, 2) the extent to which grouping characterizes the organization of employees, and 3) how leader behaviors tend to vary according to different group characteristics and other circumstances.

Much of science is based upon comparative observation. The additional dimension in the study of human beings concerns their ability to interpret and express the meaning of events including, of course, the meaning to be attached to the presence of an observer. This, however, presents an opportunity as well as a constraint—an opportunity to seek the interpretations which leaders and groups place upon the former's behavior in any given situation. Thus observation, accompanied by close verbal interaction with the people being studied, might well offer a particularly fruitful way out of the limitations which, it is generally agreed, are so evident in contemporary leadership research.

Even if it is felt worthwhile to engage in theory building before such studies are undertaken, there seems to be no reason why this should not take into account existing observational research into group behavior. Studies such as the research into work groups by Sayles (1958) and Roy (1952, 1953, 1954) in America, and by Lupton (1963) in Britain, and Crozier's (1964) research into the French postal service all offer useful indications about the relationship between leadership and group processes. We have a foundation of valuable observational research which should be used to direct future research and theory construction.

Comments on Chapter 8

Leadership Valence: A Transactional Measure of the Leadership Emergence Process?

ROBERT G. LORD

Recent thinking in the area of leadership emergence has emphasized the transaction between leaders and followers (Hollander, 1978; Hollander & Julian, 1969). Leadership has been conceptualized as a mutual influence process grounded in the shared perceptions of followers. However, our inability to measure adequately leadership transactions has hampered the empirical development of transactional models of leadership emergence. The measurement procedure developed in the Stein, Hoffman, Cooley, and Pearse chapter may help overcome this limitation since it focuses directly on the moment to moment interactions among leaders and followers. It permits precise recording of both an actor's behavior and other group members' reactions to it. Thus, this measurement technique appears to represent a significant methodological advancement in our ability to describe microscopically the processes associated with leadership emergence. Since their empirical results are preliminary, the findings of Stein et al. will not be discussed in much detail. Instead the focus will be on the theoretical perspective developed by Stein et al. and the utility of the methodology they employed.

Theoretical Basis

Translating Tuckman's (1965) developmental model into a valence model for emergent leadership presents serious problems that have not been adequately handled by the authors. First, the evidence for stage or phase related developmental models of group behavior is not compelling. The seminal study in this area (Bales & Strodtbeck, 1951) found only weak quantitative indications of distinct phases. Unlike Bales and Strodtbeck, Tuckman (1965) based his theory on qualitative rather than quantitative data which, for the most part, were from therapy groups. Thus, one should question the relevance of the data for the problem solving groups of Stein et al. Given this limited empirical basis, a descriptive approach rather than an a priori commitment to an orientation-conflict-emergence development sequence would have been preferable.

The problem with expecting such a developmental sequence, of course, is that it primes the researcher to interpret plausible evidence as support for a developmental model rather than to seek alternative explanations for findings. For example, relatively equal leadership valence and leadership ratings (chapter 8, Figure 9, Group B) may not reflect the existence of conflict as was suggested by Stein et al. Relatively equal leadership valence for two group members could reflect high task interest for these two individuals and co-operation (compliance) by other group members. Relatively equal leadership ratings may simply reflect a lack of behavioral differentiation between these two group members. Clearly, independent measures of perceived conflict and task interest would be needed to determine whether the pattern presented in Figure 9, Group B reflects conflict or equal task motivation.

A second problem with the model proposed by Stein et al. centers on the concept of leadership valence and its role in leadership emergence. Valence models of leadership (and decision making) imply that the development of valence preceeds and in part determines choice. It is equally plausible that leadership valence occurs after a leader emerges; valence may serve a dissonance reducing function or may reflect the cognitive component of the enacted organization suggested by Weick (1977a). Thus, valence may be a consequence rather than a determinant of leadership emergence. The implicit nature of the leadership emergence process noted by Stein et al. seems more consistent with this alternative interpretation of leadership valence.

Methodology

The definition of the construct of leadership valence is also problematic. Initially Stein et al. suggested that leadership valence was derived from group members' assessments of the leadership functions required by a task and the abilities of individuals to fulfill such functions. Thus, they implied a situation specific definition of valence. However, recent research suggests that leadership perceptions are based on more simplistic evaluations (Lord, 1977) since subjects rarely have the task experience to gauge the instrumental value of specific leadership functions. Moreover, in describing their operational procedure, Stein et al. seem to be measuring a different and more general conceptualization of leadership valence based on factor-analytic and content-analytic studies. Such valence is acquired by initiating normative leadership behavior by the reaction of others.

As operationalized by Stein et al., the *initiation* component of valence accrues from the production of behaviors corresponding to a "general leadership norm." This norm includes five classes of behavior—identifying and solving task problems, controlling group procedures and structures, controlling others, supporting others, and deviant behavior (which decreases valence)—derived from prior studies of leadership behavior. This norm seems to reflect a broadly accepted, culturally based definition of leadership similar to what others have labeled an implicit leadership theory (Calder, 1977; Rush, Thomas, & Lord, 1977). However, this component of valence would undoubtedly be highly correlated with the total amount of verbal behavior produced by an actor. Interestingly, quantity of verbal behavior is the most consistent predictor of leadership emergence yet uncovered. Thus, the crucial question in assessing the utility of this component of valence is whether it affords any incremental ability to predict leadership ratings over mere quantity of verbal behavior.

The *response* component of valence depends on the reaction of other group members to attempt leadership. If others comply with an initiator's requests, the initiator gains valence points; if others resist, valence points are lost. This aspect of valence measurement seems to be the major strength of the Stein et al. coding procedure, for it adds a component based on others' reactions to attempted leadership to the component associated with mere activity. Again, the most pressing empirical question seems to be whether this reactive component adds any unique ability to predict leadership ratings over the initiating component or over total verbal behavior. Unfortunately, Stein et al. have not yet empirically assessed this question, though they apparently will have the data to do so.

Conceptually, this latter component of valence, the portion based on others' reactions, seems to be quite close to what could be termed a behavioral measure of operating power or achieved influence. Thus, it could be easily integrated with existing conceptualizations of leadership as a social influence process (Hollander & Julian, 1969), social power (e.g., French & Raven, 1959), or operating power structures (Gray, Richardson, & Mayhew, 1968; Mayhew, Gray, & Richardson, 1969; Richardson, Dugan, Gray, & Mayhew, 1973).

The work of Gray and Mayhew is particularly interesting since they also have developed behavioral measures of achieved influence based on compliance to or rejections of attempted control. They use these measures to describe evolving control structures—a construct quite similar to emergent leadership. Moreover, they have developed a stimulus sampling model which does a very nice job of explaining emergent control structures as well as the development of behavioral differentiation in dyads (Gray & von Broembsen, 1974).

Two other methodological problems with the Stein et al. chapter should be mentioned. First, the primary dependent variable—leadership ratings—was obtained by having each group member allocate 100 leadership points among other group members. Thus, between-group differences in manifest leadership would not be reflected since each group's combined leadership score would be equal. Second, the constructs of candidacy and emergence thresholds were operationalized in a circular fashion. Presumably, group members "announce" candidacy or emerge as leaders by crossing these thresholds. Yet, operationally these thresholds seem to be identified by scanning graphs of leadership valence patterns to find the point at which eventual leaders were differentiated from other group members or potential rivals. Clearly, a more independent means of operationalizing both thresholds is needed.

In concluding, I would like to stress once again that the approach taken by Stein et al. represents a potentially important contribution to the leadership literature. The approach is new, so theoretical and methodological refinements will be needed; yet, by emphasizing and accurately measuring ongoing leadership processes numerous linkages with other important variables become possible. On the dependent variable side, future research should explore the relation of valence to different types of leadership ratings, to ratings of perceived influence or social power, and to causal ascriptions for task and interpersonal outcomes. On the independent variable side, future studies should assess the effects of group size, task experience, task commitment, and sexual composition on the differentiation across group members in leadership valence. In terms of the intervening process, the development of leadership valence, Stein et al. should partition leadership valence into two components: that associated with proactive behavior (initiation) on a leader's part, and that associated with reactive behavior (responses) by other group members. These two valence components may be related to different substantive variables, or they may exhibit differential relations to the same substantive variable. Such differences would be masked by a premature aggression of these two components of valence. Finally, since the measurement procedure developed by Stein et al. is new, descriptive studies exploring input-process-outcome relations among the variables noted above would be of great value to the leadership field. Moreover, such descriptive studies may lead directly to the type of integrative theories the authors have attempted to build. Prior commitment to a particular theoretical model, however, provides only an unnecessary perceptual constraint, since such models would be based on less precise and less comprehensive data than the Stein et al. measurement procedure seems capable of generating.

Part 4

How Should It Be Studied?

Introduction

STEVEN KERR, JAMES G. HUNT, AND LARS L. LARSON

The three chapters in this part address the Questionnaire/Observation crosscurrent and thus focus specifically on the way in which leadership is to be measured. Leadership research, like that in the social sciences in general has relied heavily upon information obtained via questionnaire. A number of particular failings of leadership questionnaires are discussed and addressed by Yukl and Nemeroff in chapter 10—"Identification and Measurement of Specific Categories of Leadership Behavior: A Progress Report." At least in theory, there is an important difference between the criticisms levied by Yukl and Nemeroff and that of Luthans in chapter 11 who argues: "The widely used . . . Ohio State, Fiedler, and Michigan questionnaires are not really measuring leadership behaviors. At best they are measuring the questionnaire respondent's behavior and perceptions/attitudes, not leadership behaviors: They require the respondent to reconstruct a leadership event within the predefined set of responses contained on the instrument."

That difference is that the shortcomings described by the former authors are potentially correctable, while Luthans's argument seems necessarily to be true of any questionnaire-based research technique. However, it is probably useful to look more closely at Luthans's argument, and to consider carefully what he proposes that we do instead. His suggestion is that we "observe leadership behavior *in situ*," that is, that we see how leaders actually behave in their natural habitat.

Therein, however, lies the rub. The fact is that inaccuracies in measurement may emanate from a wide variety of sources, and only a relative handful are caused by the use of questionnaires. For example, Yukl and Nemeroff refer to such measurement errors as leniency, central tendency, and halo. It is easy to show that the most commonly employed leadership questionnaires are plagued by these problems (cf. Schriesheim & Kerr, 1977). However, nowhere has it been shown that it is the use of these questionnaires that *causes* these problems to arise.

Certainly it is true that an inferior questionnaire may contribute heavily to measurement error. Furthermore, if we accept Luthans's argument, it is also true that even a superior questionnaire will not be trouble-free. The research literature concerning attributions and perception, however, gives rise to the inescapable conclusion that halo, leniency, and many of the other errors described are common to unstructured interviewing, eyewitness testimony, and other non-questionnaire-based methods of obtaining information. By what logic may we conclude, then, that Luthans's budding Leadership Behavior Observation System will be freer of these difficulties? The fact that "the few researchers in management that have attempted to use observational techniques have been quite pleased with the results"— noted in the chapter by Luthans—seems overly simplistic.

Therefore, the following points are worth keeping in mind in reading the chapters which follow: 1) The fact that psychometrically inadequate and atheoretical questionnaires have generated data of limited value does not prove that questionnaires are necessarily without utility. Yukl and Nemeroff's undertaking is impressive, and worthy of respect. 2) If efforts to develop superior questionnaires ultimately prove unsuccessful, or if it turns out that even superior questionnaires cannot increase the percentage of variance we can explain, then Luthans's caveats may prove prophetic, indeed. Unless and until this happens, Luthans offers a potentially exciting alternative—though not a substitute—and his effort should also be respected and encouraged. 3) Probably the most intelligent position to be taken, then, is to waffle just a bit and to adopt Sims's philosophy in chapter 12 ("Limitations and Extensions to Questionnaires in Leadership Research") that truth lies somewhere between the extremes. Sims points out that "questionnaires have often been used with virtually no consideration as to the theoretical relevance as to why certain variables should be salient in a particular organization situation." Again, however, this is no particular fault of questionnaire-based approaches to leadership. It would be equally silly, for example, to report observations without any conceptual or explanatory framework. What *all* these chapters are saying is that theory construction, development of adequate (questionnaire, observational, or other) measures, and programmatic research efforts are needed if *any* method is to succeed.

In this regard, Blau and Scott (1962) astutely observed long ago that we have only three ways of obtaining information about people: watching them; asking them questions; and examining their droppings. With so much yet to learn, and only three ways to find out what we need to know, it seems premature to discard anything until we know for certain that what remains will be adequate to the task.

In concluding the introduction to this part, two other points bear mention. First, (consistent with earlier concerns expressed in this volume) some would argue that even the above recommendations do not go far enough. They would admonish the researcher to be concerned with two further questions (Action/Discovery crosscurrent): "If I get the data, will they be helpful to those I want to educate and train?" "If I can describe reality, will it help me to manage reality?" Second, all of the chapters above appear to define the behaviors in question in relatively narrow and specific ways. Others, taking a role perspective of leadership while not quibbling with the ways of obtaining data, would probably argue that a wider range of behaviors ought to be obtained (Leader/Manager crosscurrent).

10

Identification and Measurement of Specific Categories of Leadership Behavior: A Progress Report

GARY A. YUKL AND WAYNE F. NEMEROFF

Hundreds of studies have been conducted on the relationship between leader behavior and leader effectiveness. Unfortunately, the results from this research have generally been weak and inconsistent. One reason for the slow progress of leadership research has been the lack of an accurate measure of specific leader behaviors. Most leader effectiveness studies have been correlational studies in which some measure of leader behavior is correlated with some effectiveness criterion. Without an accurate measure of relevant aspects of leader behavior, such research is unlikely to find meaningful results. Korman (1974, p. 194) has aptly summarized the importance of accurate measurement in leadership research: "The point is not that accurate measurement is nice. It is necessary, crucial, etc. Without it we have nothing." The present chapter describes the progress made so far in our program of research to develop a new and better measure of leadership behavior.

Perspective on Prior Typologies of Leadership Behavior

Over the years, many efforts have been made to identify and measure meaningful categories of leadership behavior. Unfortunately, each empirical study has found a somewhat different set of behavior categories. In past research, there has been little effort to determine if the results of one factor analysis could be replicated with different samples of respondents. Instead, researchers have typically done only one factor analytic study, after which they discarded many items not loading strongly on a few major factors and used only a much shorter questionnaire in any subsequent research. If another factor analysis was done at all, it was only done on the shortened questionnaire.

Another limitation of prior research on leader behavior categories is that it has not been guided by an adequate theory of leadership processes (Melcher, 1977). Without some theoretical guidance to help identify important aspects of leadership behavior, it is unlikely that many important behaviors will be well represented in the researcher's initial instrument. Most researchers simply collect a batch of old items from other questionnaires, write a few new ones, and then conduct a factor analysis on this mostly random collection of items to see what factors emerge. It is not surprising that meaningful factors are seldom found, or that the factors differ so much from study to study.

In questionnaire research on leadership, the most widely used behavior categories have been Consideration and Initiating Structure, which are measured by some version of the Ohio State leadership questionnaires (i.e., the LBDQ, the SBDQ, and the LBDQ-XII). (Hunt, Osborn & Schriesheim, 1978). Although the definition of Consideration varies somewhat from one version of the questionnaire to another, it has included items dealing with leader supportiveness, friendliness, consideration, communication, representation of subordinate interests, and praise for subordinate achievements. Initiating Structure has included items dealing with role clarification, establishing performance goals or standards, directing subordinates, production emphasis, planning, coordination, problem solving, and maintaining control. Several writers have pointed out that a few broad behavior categories such as Consideration and Initiating Structure fail to capture the wide variety of specific types of behavior exhibited by managers and administrators (Hammer & Dachler, 1975; McCall, 1977; Pondy, 1978; Schriesheim & Kerr, 1977; Yukl, 1971). The use of overly broad behavior categories masks the separate effects of specific components of the categories. In any given situation, some aspects of a broad category will be more relevant than other aspects of that category, and without measures of the specific components, it is very difficult to understand how the leader influences subordinate performance in that situation.

Of the currently available leadership questionnaires, the LBDQ-XII (Stogdill, Goode, & Day, 1962) measures the largest number of leader behavior categories. However, this questionnaire has several serious weaknesses. Psychometric deficiencies include a susceptibility to leniency and halo errors, unequal response intervals, and inadequate construct validity (Schriesheim & Kerr, 1977). Moreover, the LBDQ-XII fails to provide separate scales to measure some key aspects of leadership behavior, including coordination, planning, training, work facilitation, goal setting, decision participation, positive reinforcement, and role clarification. Finally, the LBDQ-XII includes some scales that measure traits and skills instead of leadership behavior (i.e., persuasiveness, predictive accuracy, and uncertainty tolerance). None of the earlier questionnaires satisfies the need for a set of scales that accurately measures a variety of specific and relevant aspects of leadership behavior. We initiated our research program to satisfy the need for a new and better leadership questionnaire.

Research Strategy

During the past two years we have followed a sequential research strategy similar to that used in the development of many psychological tests. Sets of items were written to measure several aspects of leadership behavior that appeared to be important and widely applicable to different kinds of leaders. Of course, we did not attempt to include every important kind of leadership behavior in the first version of the questionnaire, since to do so would have made the questionnaire much too lengthy and impractical. Instead, new categories have been added as existing ones are refined and shortened. In addition, we have tried to subdivide complex categories with two or more distinct components as the research progressed.

In the process of conducting our developmental research on leadership behavior, we have also tried to cope with several bothersome methodological issues. One issue was what format to use for the questionnaire items. The Ohio State leadership questionnaires use frequency adverbs as response choices for most items, the Michigan leadership scales in the Survey of Organizations (Taylor & Bowers, 1972) use magnitude choices, and other item formats besides these have also been used in leadership questionnaires. It was not evident at the beginning of the research program whether one format was superior to the others.

A second methodological issue was whether the respondent should be asked to describe how the leader behaves toward the respondent as an individual, or how the leader behaves in relation to all of his subordinates collectively. The possibility of differential treatment of subordinates is a reason for using the individual wording for items, since a researcher may be interested in how the leader varies his behavior from subordinate to subordinate. On the other hand, the collective wording lends itself better to behavior that involves more than a single subordinate (e.g., coordination, interaction facilitation, conflict management), and it is more suitable for inquiring about sensitive aspects of leadership behavior (e.g., discipline). A good case can be made for both kinds of wording, and it was not clear whether one or the other or a combination of both wordings should be used.

A third methodological issue was how to deal with response errors such as leniency, central tendency, and halo. These response errors have been a problem in prior research with leadership questionnaires (Schriesheim & Kerr, 1977). Another kind of response error occurs when an item is not relevant or the respondent doesn't know the answer but is still required to select one of the standard answers. Initially, it was not clear what approach would be best to minimize response errors.

In order to cope with these methodological issues, we included a variety of item formats and wordings in each version of the leadership questionnaire, and the results for the different approaches were compared. Other features of the questionnaire such as instructions and layout were also varied from one version to another in an attempt to obtain insights about the best way to handle the methodological issues. The process of testing and experimenting with different methods meant that we were intentionally increasing the ambiguity due to method variance and making it more difficult to find strong and consistent factors. Due both to method variations and content alterations, the questionnaire changed so much from study to study that it was not feasible to use a statistical procedure for testing factor equivalence across different samples.

Selection of Questionnaire Content

Three kinds of criteria were used in deciding what aspects of leadership behavior to include in the questionnaire. One major determinant of questionnaire content was the leader effectiveness model proposed by Yukl (1971) and subsequently revised and extended by him (Yukl, 1979). The model attempts to explain the influence of the leader on subordinate performance in terms of a set of intervening variables and a set of situational moderator variables. This model indicated the probable importance of several aspects of leadership behavior not represented by separate scales in most earlier questionnaires. these leadership behaviors include: 1) planning and organizing task roles to efficiently utilize personnel and equipment, 2) role clarification and goal setting to insure subordinates have accurate and unambiguous role perceptions, 3) training of subordinates to increase their task skills, 4) facilitation of subordinate effort by procurement of necessary resources and support services, 5) inviting subordinates to participate in decision making to increase decision quality and acceptance, 6) team building and conflict management to facilitate cooperation and teamwork, 7) a combination of goal setting, positive reinforcement (i.e., praise and incentives), and delegation of authority and responsibility to insure a high level of subordinate task motivation. The importance of the motivating, facilitating, and role clarifying behaviors is also indicated by other leadership theories (e.g., path-goal theory) and by some theories of work motivation (e.g., expectancy theory, goal theory, job enrichment theories).

A second basis for selecting behaviors to include in the questionnaire was a review of research on managerial effectiveness. The greatest importance was placed on research in which some aspect of managerial behavior was experimentally manipulated and found to be a potent determinant of subordinate performance. Since the Yukl model was itself influenced by this research, it is not surprising that many of the same behaviors ended up on the second list: 1) Goal setting has been found to increase subordinate performance in a large variety of organizations (see review by Latham & Yukl, 1975). 2) Positive reinforcement has increased performance in several organizations (see review by Hamner & Hamner, 1976). 3) Enriching subordinate jobs by giving subordinates more autonomy and responsibility has been found to increase motivation in some situations (Ford, 1960; Hackman, Oldham, Janson, & Purdy, 1975; Paul, Robertson, & Herzberg, 1969). 4) Training of subordinates has been found to increase skills and performance in many organizations.

We also examined the results of research on managerial effectiveness that used critical incidents methodology (see review by Yukl, 1979). The results from this research are very inconsistent, with many situation-specific behaviors among those found "critical." Nevertheless, some common categories of critical behaviors appear in a majority of the studies: 1) planning, coordinating, and organizing operations, 2) establishing and maintaining good relations with subordinates, 3) supervising subordinates (i.e., directing, instructing, monitoring performance), 4) establishing effective relations with superiors, peers, and outsiders, and 5) assuming responsibility for observing organizational policies, carrying out required duties, and making necessary decisions.

A third consideration in selecting aspects of leadership behavior to include in the questionnaire was our desire to maintain some continuity with the mainstream of previous research on leader behavior typologies. Even though the results from this research have not been very consistent, a few behavior categories appear with some regularity in the factor analytic studies, including considerate-supportive leadership, production emphasis, directive-structuring behavior, and behavior facilitating cooperation and teamwork. Sets of items on each of these behavior categories were included in the first version of our questionnaire. Most of the items were newly written, but some items from the Ohio State leadership questionnaires

(Fleishman, 1957; Halpin & Winer, 1957; Hemphill & Coons, 1957) and the Michigan leadership scales (Bowers & Seashore, 1966; Taylor, 1971; Taylor & Bowers, 1972) were included in order to facilitate verification of any correspondence between the factors we obtained and the factors found in the earlier research.

Factor Analysis Studies

Four separate studies with different samples were conducted to identify distinct, meaningful, and widely applicable categories of leadership behavior. The research methodology for each of these studies was a questionnaire survey with factor analysis of the item-response data.

First Heterogeneous Sample

The initial leader behavior questionnaire consisted of 70 items, with two different scale formats. The first format had frequency adverbs similar to those in the Ohio State University leadership questionnaires. The response choices were as follows: Never, Seldom, Sometimes, Usually, and Always. After referring to a study by Bass, Cascio, and O'Connor (1974), in which judges scaled frequency and magnitude terms, we selected frequency adverbs with scale values that were approximately equidistant and which had relatively small standard deviations for the judged values (see Table 9). Only the interval between scale values for Never and Seldom was substantially different in size. However, in a similar study Schriesheim and Schriesheim (1974) found that Seldom had a scale value nearly equidistant between the values for Sometimes and Never. No scale values were obtained for Usually in their study, but Sometimes was nearly equidistant between Never and Always. Thus, we were satisfied that the intervals were reasonably equivalent given the imperfect state of existing knowledge about scale values.

The second item format used magnitude descriptions similar to those in the University of Michigan ISR Survey of Organizations. Once again, the final choice of terminology was governed by reference to the Bass et al. (1974) findings. The response choices were as follows: Not at All, To a Limited Extent, To a Moderate Extent, To a Considerable Extent, and To a Very Great Extent. The scale values found by Bass et al. for comparable magnitude terms are shown in Table 9. The intervals were all of approximately equal size. Items with the magnitude format were placed in the latter part of the questionnaire following the frequency format items.

For each aspect of leader behavior covered in the questionnaire, nega-

TABLE 9

Scaled Values for Response Choices Similar to Those Used in the New Leadership Questionnaire

A. Frequency Adverbs			
Response Choice	Mean Value	Interval	SD
Always	58.0		3.5
Usually	39.2	18.8	3.1
Sometimes	19.4	19.8	2.9
Seldom	0.3	19.1	2.6
Never	0.0	0.3	1.4
B. Magnitude Terms			
A Great Amount	41.6		2.8
A Considerable Amount	31.4	10.2	2.9
A Moderate Amount	21.8	9.6	3.4
A Limited Amount	9.6	12.2	2.9
None	0.0	9.6	1.7

Note. Means and Standard Deviations of judged scale values are from Bass, Cascio, and O'Connor (1974).

tively worded items were written as well as positively-worded items. The effort to develop negative items was less successful for some behaviors than for others, and overall, the number of positive items was much greater than the number of negative items. Negative items usually had a frequency adverb format.

The questionnaire was administered to a sample of 203 night MBA undergraduate students who worked at regular jobs during the day. Their responses were factor analyzed with a principal components analysis using verimax rotation of components with eigenvalues larger than 1.0. Ten orthogonal factors accounted for 70 percent of the common variance, and nine of these factors appeared to represent meaningful categories of leadership behavior. The nine categories were labeled and defined as follows:

1. Consideration—the extent to which a leader is friendly, supportive, and considerate toward subordinates, looks out for their welfare, shows trust and appreciation, and is open and honest with them.

2. Direction—the extent to which a leader informs subordinates about their duties and job responsibilities, sets goals and establishes performance standards, and provides subordinates with necessary training and instruction.

3. Production Emphasis—the extent to which a leader emphasizes the importance of productivity and efficiency, encourages subordinates to attain a high level of performance, checks on their performance, and lets them know when it is not up to expectations.

4. Decision Participation—the extent to which a leader consults with subordinates and otherwise allows them to participate in making decisions, and the amount of influence over the leader's decisions that results from this participation.

5. Work Facilitation—the extent to which a leader obtains for subordinates any necessary supplies, materials, tools, equipment, support services, or other resources, and eliminates problems in the work environment and other obstacles that interfere with the work.

6. Autonomy-Delegation—the extent to which a leader delegates responsibility and authority to subordinates and allows them autonomy in determining how to do their work.

7. Conflict Management—the extent to which a leader helps subordinates settle conflicts and disagreements, restrains them from insulting or fighting with each other, and encourages them to resolve conflicts in a constructive manner.

8. Interaction Facilitation—the extent to which a leader emphasizes the importance of teamwork, and encourages subordinates to cooperate and be friendly with each other.

9. Positive Reinforcement—the extent to which a leader provides recognition to a subordinate, bases recommendations for pay increases and promotions on subordinate performance, and tries to provide additional rewards and benefits for effective performance.

Some representative examples of items for each factor can be found in Table 10. It is interesting to note that our Consideration factor in this first study was quite comparable to the Consideration factor found in the Ohio State studies, except for items on consultation, which loaded on Decision Participation in our study. Our Direction factor was somewhat comparable to the Initiating Structure factor found in the Ohio State studies. Although dominated by five role clarification items, other task-oriented behaviors also loaded on this factor, including two training items, a goal setting item, two coordination items, and a planning item.

The Interaction Facilitation Factor was only a weak secondary factor; the items loading on it all had higher loadings on Consideration. Positive Reinforcement was also a weak factor, with three items on providing recognition and rewarding superior performance by a subordinate. One praise item and two items on rewarding performance loaded on Consideration instead of on Positive Reinforcement.

TABLE 10
Some Representative Items with Factor Loadings in Four Samples

Scale and Item	Sample:	1	2	3	4
Consideration:					
1. Supervisor is friendly and easy to approach.		.80	.72	.71	.77
2. Supervisor is open and honest in dealing with subordinates.		.73	.68	.77	.57
Production Emphasis:					
1. Supervisor pushes for increased productivity.		.74	.56	.48	.70
2. Supervisor tries to keep subordinates working at their highest level of performance.		.63	.31	.76	.63
Decision Participation:					
1. Supervisor gets subordinate approval on important matters before going ahead.		.76	.65	.78	.55
2. Supervisor consults with subordinates before making major decisions.		.84	.60	.63	.72
Autonomy-Delegation:					
1. Supervisor allows me to determine what work procedures to use.		.56	.71	.59	.57
2. Supervisor permits me to use my own judgment in solving work problems.		.77	.65	.73	.73
Work Facilitation:					
1. Supervisor makes sure subordinates have the supplies necessary to do their work.		.77	.75	.61	.43
2. Supervisor tries to ensure that equipment is maintained in good condition.		.58	.66	.64	.45
Direction:					
1. Supervisor sets clear and specific performance goals for subordinates.		.55	.41	.55	.70
2. Supervisor provides subordinates with adequate training in how to do the work.		.63	.59	.54	.60
3. Supervisor lets subordinates know what is expected of them.		.71	.43	*	.51
Conflict Management:					
1. Supervisor tries to restrain subordinates from insulting or fighting with each other.		.71	.70	.43	.72
2. Supervisor tries to resolve conflicts and disagreements among subordinates.		.72	.80	.67	.65
Interaction Facilitation:					
1. Supervisor encourages subordinates to cooperate with each other.		.42	.66	.66	.81
2. Supervisor encourages subordinates to help each other in their work.		*	.69	.65	.31

TABLE 10—Continued

Scale and Item	Sample:	1	2	3	4
Planning-Coordination:					
1. Supervisor plans and schedules the work in advance.		NF	.80	.82	.63
2. Supervisor coordinates the work of subordinates.		NF	.53	*	.40
Positive Reinforcement:					
1. Supervisor provides praise for superior performance.		.49	NF	*	*
2. Supervisor tries to provide some kind of reward for superior performance by a subordinate.		.57	NF	NI	.55
Criticism-Discipline:					
1. Supervisor criticizes poor work by a subordinate.		NF	.72	NI	.38
2. Supervisor tries to discipline a subordinate with consistently poor performance.		NF	.60	NI	.79

Note. NF means no separate factor; NI means item not included; * means item loaded on another factor. More extensive information about factor loadings for each sample is available from the authors.

Second Heterogeneous Sample

The results from the first study were used to revise the questionnaire before administering it to another sample. In an attempt to sharpen the distinction among categories and improve their content validity, poor items were eliminated, weak items were rewritten, and new items were added. By eliminating poor items and some of the excess Consideration items, and by increasing the length of the questionnaire, we were able to add many items on aspects of leader behavior not represented adequately in the initial version, including planning, coordination, cooperation facilitation, communication, representation, controlling, and discipline.

Two new item formats were used in addition to the original ones. For items with the new formats, each respondent was asked to indicate how many times a specific behavior was observed during the prior year. The behaviors were more detailed for these "incident counting" items than for items with frequency adverbs or magnitude terms. The response choices for one new format were as follows: Never, Once or Twice, A Few Times, Several Times, and Many Times. The response choices for the other new format were the following: Never, Once, Twice, Three or Four Times, and Five or More Times. Another change in the questionnaire was the addition of a sixth response choice for all items, regardless of format. This option was Don't Know or Not Applicable.

The revised questionnaire was administered to a sample of 212 night students who were from the same two universities as before but had not been used in the first study. Their responses were factor analyzed using the same procedure. This time there were 16 orthogonal factors, and they explained 64 percent of the common variance. However, four of the factors were meaningless, with low factor loadings and only a few, dissimilar, defining items. Of the nine leader behavior categories identified in the first study, all but one (Positive Reinforcement) emerged as strong factors in the second study. Items on praise, recognition, and rewarding performance loaded on Consideration instead of forming a separate factor for Positive Reinforcement.

The addition of new items was apparently responsible for the emergence of a new factor for Criticism-Discipline. In the earlier version of the questionnaire, there was only one criticism item and one discipline item, and they both loaded on Production Emphasis. In this version there were five items, and they formed a separate factor. In the same manner, Planning-Coordination emerged as a factor apart from Direction. The beginning of a further differentiation of Direction was also evident. The Direction factor for this sample was dominated by four items on training, with only one item on role clarification and one on goal setting. Three remaining role clarification items loaded on a weak Role Clarification factor, and two remaining goal setting items loaded on a weak Goal Setting factor. The results from this study were used to further revise the questionnaire. The primary objective of this revision was to strengthen factors found in the first two studies and achieve a sharper discrimination among factors. No new aspects of leadership behavior were added at this revision.

In the first two studies we used heterogeneous samples containing subordinates of many different kinds of supervisors, managers, and administrators. At this point it seemed appropriate to try the questionnaire with some homogeneous samples in which all managers being described had similar work units.

Production Supervisor Study

The first homogeneous sample consisted of 146 employees in 26 production departments of a paint factory in a large multinational corporation. For this sample, it was only possible to use a shortened version of the questionnaire with fewer items for each of the major scales, and not items on rewarding performance or criticism-discipline. The questionnaire had two item formats (frequency adverbs and magnitude choices) and all items

were positively worded. Several subordinates of each production supervisor were randomly selected to fill out the leader behavior questionnaire.
The questionnaire was administered to groups of employees by a personnel manager from corporate headquarters, and respondents were not
anonymous.

The questionnaire data were factor analyzed using the same procedure as in the first two studies. Ten orthogonal factors were found, and
they accounted for 70 percent of the common variance. One of these
factors was meaningless, because it had only a single item with a large
factor loading. The remaining nine factors were mostly similar to factors
found in the second study. The only important difference is that Planning
emerged as a separate factor by itself rather than in combination with
Coordination. There were only two coordination items in the questionnaire, and they loaded on Direction and Work Facilitation. In addition to
the coordination item, Direction had two role-clarification items, a goal-
setting item and a training item. Since there were no items on rewarding
performance, it is not surprising that no separate factor emerged for
Positive Reinforcement. There were two items on praise, but they loaded
on Consideration and Decision Participation.

Beauty Salon Managers Study

Around the same time as the study on production supervisors, another
study was conducted on a second homogeneous sample. The leaders in this
study were the managers of 18 beauty salons belonging to a national chain
of salons. Some of the nonsupervisory employees in each salon were randomly selected to participate in a questionnaire survey. These employees
were mailed the third version of the leadership questionnaire and asked to
describe the behavior of their salon manager. The questionnaire had three
different item formats (frequency adverbs, magnitude choices, and incident counting items), with only positively worded items. Respondents were
anonymous, although the salon in which the employee worked was identified on the questionnaire. A total of 82 employees (48 percent response
rate) returned completed questionnaires in self-addressed envelopes to a
university address. Even though the sample was quite small for a factor
analysis, one was conducted to see if the factors found in the other studies
would also be found for this different kind of leadership situation. The
factor analysis was conducted using the same procedure as before.

The factor analysis yielded 16 orthogonal factors which accounted for
73 percent of the common variance. However, the last six factors had only
one or two items with strong factor loadings and these factors were essentially meaningless. The remaining ten factors were mostly similar to factors

found in the earlier studies. The only important difference was the combination of Interaction Facilitation and Conflict Management into a composite "team building" factor similar to Integration in the LBDQ-XII. A Positive Reinforcement factor was found, as in the first study, but only the rewarding performance items had high factor loadings on it. The praise and recognition items in the questionnaire loaded primarily on Consideration. A weak Criticism-Discipline factor was found, but only four items loaded on it. The Direction factor for this sample had some items with high factor loadings representing all three major components (i.e., role clarification, goal setting, training). No separate factors were found for any of these components. Items on planning and coordination formed a Planning-Coordination factor, as in the second study.

Discussion of Factor Analysis Studies

The results for the four factor analysis studies are summarized in Table 11. The results were remarkably consistent, considering the changes in the structure and content of the questionnaire from study to study. The few differences that were found appear to be caused by the difficulty subordinates sometimes have in differentiating between Planning and Coordination, between Consideration and Positive Reinforcement, between Interaction Facilitation and Conflict Management, and between the major components of Direction (i.e., role clarification, goal setting, and training). Even though each of these samples was relatively small for a factor analysis, the consistency of results across samples gives us confidence in the accuracy of the results.

In the process of developing a useful typology of leadership behavior, it is necessary to decide whether commonly associated aspects of leader behavior should be treated as separate categories or as a broader composite category. We believe that the perception of subordinates, as reflected in the factor analyses, should not be the only basis for making this difficult decision. It is important to consider other kinds of empirical evidence and theoretical arguments. A strong case can be made for treating all of the above factors as distinct aspects of leader behavior.

With respect to Consideration and Positive Reinforcement, it is possible for a leader to be friendly and supportive without offering praise and rewards for superior performance by a subordinate. Judging from the success of some positive reinforcement programs in industry, there are probably many leaders around who are considerate but who seldom use positive reinforcement. It is also possible for a leader to make extensive use of praise and incentives, but in a very manipulative manner without much consideration for the needs and feelings of subordinates. Other leaders

TABLE 11

Summary of Factor Analysis Results in Four Samples with Eigenvalues for Each Factor after Orthogonal Rotation

Leader Behavior	Heterogeneous Sample 1	Heterogeneous Sample 2	Production Sample	Salon Sample 1
Consideration	12.0	9.2	4.7	9.6
Direction	8.9	2.5	5.5	6.2
Production Emphasis	5.1	3.0	3.2	4.2
Decision Participation	4.6	2.5	5.1	3.6
Work Facilitation	4.3	4.3	4.4	4.1
Autonomy-Delegation	4.1	4.8	2.7	3.0
Conflict Management	4.5	3.4	2.3	6.9
Interaction Facilitation	1.4	3.5	3.4	
Positive Reinforcement	2.2	NF	NF	3.1
Planning-Coordination	NF	3.6	2.3	3.3
Criticism-Discipline	NF	3.1	NI	2.3
Sample Size	202	212	146	82
Items Analyzed	70	80	50	80
Cumulative explained variance for these factors prior to their rotation	70%	54%	68%	62%

Note. NF means no separate factor; NI means to scale items included in questionnaire.

may be high in use of both aspects of behavior, or low in use of both aspects. Since the two aspects of behavior can be varied independently, and since they do not always occur together, it is reasonable to treat them as distinct behavior categories.

The same kind of case can be made for treating planning and coordination as separate aspects of leader behavior. A manager can sometimes achieve coordination by carefully planning in advance how the work should be organized. Yet in other situations, the manager is unable to forecast events with enough accuracy to plan ahead, and he must achieve coordination on a day-to-day basis by dealing with immediate crises. For still other managers, very little coordination is required, either because subordinates work alone at independent tasks, or because coordination is achieved largely through the technology itself. These managers may or may not have to plan ahead extensively in dealing with other aspects of the work besides the coordination of subordinates. Thus, in studying different situations we would expect to find managers with all possible combinations of high and low coordination behavior and high and low planning behavior.

A good case can also be made for separate classification of role clarification, goal setting, and training. A manager can set specific goals for subordinates without providing skill training, and training can be carried out without goal setting. A manager can clarify a subordinate's duties and responsibilities and explain rules and regulations without setting specific performance goals or without providing any explicit instruction in how to do the work. On the other hand, it is likely that goal setting or training will necessarily involve some role clarification. It is apparent that the three components are somewhat interrelated, yet independent enough to be measured separately.

The factor analysis studies demonstrated that subordinates are able to describe their supervisors' behavior in terms of meaningful and widely applicable categories of leadership behavior. This was a promising beginning, but some major measurement problems remained to be solved. The first problem was how to improve discrimination among those aspects of behavior that were sometimes confounded when subordinates described their supervisors. A related problem was the high degree of multi-collinearity among scale scores, even when the scales are based on orthogonal factors. This problem is common to leadership questionnaires, and it limits their usefulness in research on leader effectiveness. One source of multi-collinearity is response tendencies such as halo and leniency. In the second factor analysis study, we attempted to reduce this source of multi-collinearity by including a warning in the instructions. The response tendencies were described, and respondents were asked to make an effort to avoid them. A similar warning was used in the beauty salon study. The warnings appeared to reduce halo and leniency a little, but they were still at an unacceptably high level. Other efforts to reduce multi-collinearity by eliminating or revising items loading on more than one factor also failed to solve the problem. When working with a large number of behavior categories, some of which will be interrelated in any given situation, it is difficult to find items for one aspect of behavior that do not relate to other behavior categories as well. We finally decided to try a completely different approach to facilitate discrimination among categories and reduce multi-collinearity. The next section of this chapter describes how this approach was used in some follow-up studies to improve the leadership questionnaire and verify our proposed typology of leadership behavior.

Follow-up Studies

The approach used for reducing multi-collinearity was to group scale items together in the questionnaire instead of scrambling them into random positions as was done in the earlier versions. Each scale was also labeled with the name of the behavior category to help clarify its meaning for the respondents. Respondents were asked in the instructions to differentiate carefully between the types of leadership behavior, and were again warned to avoid making halo, leniency, and central tendency errors. This fourth version of the questionnaire had separate scales to measure each of the 13 aspects of leadership behavior shown in Table 12. Criticism-Discipline was not included in most of the follow-up research, because its discriminant validity was readily apparent in the earlier studies, and it was not regarded as an important determinant of leader effectiveness for the kinds of leaders studied in our research.

Multiscale-Multimethod Study

The practice of grouping items by scale probably makes the questionnaire unsuitable for a factor analysis, because some potential bias may be introduced by the grouping itself. Since the major objective of the follow-up research was to evaluate the discriminant validity of the 13 behavior scales in the grouped version of the questionnaire, a multiscale-multimethod approach (Campbell & Fiske, 1959) seemed more appropriate for analyzing the data.

This approach has been used before in two studies (Yukl, Wexley, & Nemeroff, 1974; Yunker & Hunt, 1976) to assess the convergent and discriminant validity for comparable leadership scales in the LBDQ-XII and the Survey of Organizations. In the Yukl et al. study, in which hospital

TABLE 12
Definitions of Revised Leader Behavior Scales

Consideration: the extent to which a leader is friendly, supportive, considerate, open, and honest in his or her behavior toward subordinates and tries to be fair and objective.

Positive Reinforcement: the extent to which a leader provides praise and recognition to subordinates who perform effectively, bases recommendations for pay increases and promotions on subordinate performance, and tries to provide supplementary rewards or benefits for subordinates with superior performance.

Decision Participation: the extent to which a leader consults with subordinates and otherwise allows them to participate in making decisions, and the amount of subordinate influence over the leader's decisions that results from this participation.

Production Emphasis: the extent to which a leader emphasizes the importance of subordinate performance, tries to improve productivity and efficiency, tries to keep subordinates working up to their capacity, checks on their performance, and lets them know when it is not up to expectations.

Work Facilitation: the extent to which a leader obtains for subordinates any necessary supplies, equipment, support services, or other resources, eliminates any problems in the work environment, and removes other obstacles that interfere with the work.

Autonomy-Delegation: the extent to which a leader delegates responsibility and authority to subordinates and allows them to determine how to do their work.

Interaction Facilitation: the extent to which a leader tries to get subordinates to be friendly with each other, cooperate, share information and ideas, and help each other.

Conflict Management: the extent to which a leader helps subordinates settle conflicts and disagreements, restrains them from insulting each other, and encourages them to resolve conflicts in a constructive manner.

Planning: the extent to which a leader plans and schedules the work in advance, plans how to efficiently organize the work, plans for future manpower and resource needs, and makes contingency plans for potential problems.

Coordination: the extent to which a leader coordinates the work of subordinates, emphasizes the importance of coordination, and encourages subordinates to coordinate their activities.

Role Clarification: the extent to which a leader informs subordinates about their duties and responsibilities, specifies the rules and policies subordinates must observe, and lets subordinates know what is expected of them.

Goal Setting: the extent to which a leader sets specific performance goals for each important aspect of a subordinate's job, measures progress toward the goals, and provides feedback to subordinates.

Training: the extent to which a leader determines training needs and provides adequate skill training to subordinates.

---

employees described the behavior of their supervisors, Consideration correlated .50 with Supervisory Support, Production Emphasis correlated .52 with Goal Emphasis, Integration correlated .60 with Interaction Facilitation, and Initiating Structure correlated .49 with Work Facilitation. In the study by Yunker and Hunt, in which fraternity members described the behavior of their leaders, Consideration correlated .70 with Supervisory Support, Production Emphasis correlated .66 with Goal Emphasis, and Initiating Structure correlated .64 with Work Facilitation. These results indicate only a moderate degree of convergent validity for most scales, and discriminant validity was much worse.

Our first follow-up study used the same approach. Two parallel versions of the leadership questionnaire were developed, one with frequency choice items (as in the LBDQ-XII), and one with magnitude choice items (as in the Michigan leadership scales). In order to have enough different items to create two versions of each scale, some new items had to be written for most of the scales, especially the newly partitioned scales. The fourth edition of our leadership questionnaire had 95 items, with at least three items in each format version.

The sample for this study consisted of 99 night MBA students who hold regular jobs during the day in a large variety of organizations. The order of the two versions of the questionnaire was counterbalanced so that half of them answered the magnitude format version first. The correlations obtained for the multiscale-multimethod matrix are shown in Table 13. Convergent validity was quite good for all scales except Coordination, for which it was only fair. Discriminant validity was very good for most of the scales and was substantially better than that found in the two earlier studies using the LBDQ-XII and the Michigan questionnaire. The only scale with low discriminant validity was Coordination.

The results from this first study suggested that the new questionnaire was successful in reducing multi-collinearity to acceptable levels. Apparently, grouping items into separate scales helped respondents differentiate among different types of leadership behavior.[1] Two additional studies were conducted next to evaluate further the discriminant validity of the questionnaire scales for homogeneous leaders, as opposed to the heterogeneous leaders in this sample.

---

[1] Editors' Note: This is not always the case, however. A study by Schriesheim and DeNisi (1978a) showed a lower degree of convergent and discriminant validity for grouped as compared with ungrouped leadership items. Unpublished work by J. G. Hunt and R. N. Osborn, Southern Illinois University at Carbondale, also raises a question about the superiority of grouped versus ungrouped leadership items.

TABLE 13

Multiscale-Multimethod Matrix for the Frequency and Magnitude Versions of the Leadership Behavior Questionnaire

Scale Identity	1	2	3	4	5	6	7	8	9	10	11	12	13	14	15	16	17	18	19	20	21	22	23	24	25
Frequency Format																									
1. Consideration																									
2. Pos. Reinforc.	31																								
3. Decis. Partic.	31	51																							
4. Prod. Emphasis	−21	18	19																						
5. Work Facil.	24	14	12	19																					
6. Autonomy-Del.	35	30	31	−10	01																				
7. Planning	02	32	11	34	20	13																			
8. Coordination	10	27	30	40	24	−01	59																		
9. Inter. Facil.	30	36	44	08	13	30	26	36																	
10. Conflict Mgt.	18	23	22	09	20	15	24	25	56																
11. Role Clarif.	16	39	28	38	38	18	43	43	32	19															
12. Training	15	16	06	27	34	−03	28	47	23	21	42														
13. Goal Setting	12	37	24	47	13	22	43	51	39	17	62	46													
Magnitude Format																									
14. Consideration	*63*	38	31	−12	23	42	22	13	44	37	32	23	29												
15. Pos. Reinforc.	28	*77*	33	02	15	34	28	17	28	25	36	12	36	45											
16. Decis. Partic.	35	49	*72*	−02	07	49	05	19	39	16	30	11	26	36	36										
17. Prod. Emphasis	−12	34	33	*76*	17	03	26	42	34	20	31	24	48	02	26	17									
18. Work Facil.	24	29	18	20	*76*	18	26	17	16	38	39	29	19	37	37	16	27								
19. Autonomy-Del.	33	26	42	−07	01	*77*	10	13	44	20	13	04	21	39	25	49	13	15							
20. Planning	06	23	18	27	28	07	*69*	65	24	15	53	41	42	31	25	18	28	28	02						
21. Coordination	17	32	33	27	17	−01	49	58	49	34	42	20	44	24	27	25	43	25	19	50					
22. Inter. Facil.	21	40	32	17	16	10	39	43	75	60	34	28	36	32	33	27	39	26	27	35	65				
23. Conflict Mgt.	20	21	14	07	22	15	20	22	41	77	20	18	21	40	27	11	22	38	13	26	34	53			
24. Role Clarif.	20	54	37	37	34	08	30	42	36	21	69	35	53	29	49	28	48	43	17	34	46	49	28		
25. Training	16	37	19	16	31	12	28	33	37	31	41	71	40	37	39	24	29	49	17	42	24	40	35	44	
26. Goal Setting	17	39	27	37	22	21	41	56	33	16	54	45	71	26	43	26	51	36	30	40	54	37	16	55	52

Note. Decimal points in correlations are omitted; sample size is 99.

Salon Managers and Student Leaders

One sample consisted of 69 employees responding to a questionnaire survey of an additional 13 beauty salons in the same organization used in our earlier study. The other sample consisted of 40 subordinates in eight campus organizations run by undergraduates in a large university. These were not social clubs; each organization had a relatively complex and important function to perform (e.g., student newspaper, concert board, yearbook staff, radio station, etc.), and the members met frequently to administer and conduct the operations of their organization.

The leadership questionnaire used for both samples was the frequency format version of the questionnaire developed for the first follow-up study. The magnitude format version was omitted to shorten the questionnaire and make room for the addition of a questionnaire measuring intervening variables and criterion variables. The correlations among the 13 leadership behavior scales for each sample can be found in Table 14. In evaluating discriminant validity, it is helpful to compare corresponding correlations for the two samples and for the frequency format version used in the first follow-up study (see Table 13, top heteroscale-monomethod triangle). The correlations varied across the three samples for most pairs of scales, as would be expected from differences in the leadership situations. Inadequate discriminant validity would be indicated by consistently high correlations between any two scales across samples. Examination of the data suggests that discriminant validity was generally adequate. Out of the 234 correlations in the three matrices, only 14 percent were greater than or equal to .50. Only two of the 78 pairs of scales (Planning and Coordination, Goal Setting and Coordination) had intercorrelations this large in all three samples, and only two of the remaining pairs of scales (Goal Setting and Training, Interaction Facilitation and Conflict Management) had intercorrelations this large for two out of three samples. The pairs of scales for which discrimination was the lowest were usually the same ones with discrimination problems in the factor analysis studies.

In summary, the three follow-up studies showed that the practice of grouping scale items greatly improved discrimination among most of the scales. Multi-collinearity was reduced to the point where the behavior categories can be studied as separate predictors by using a procedure such as multiple regression or partial correlation to deal with the remaining shared variance among scales. The scales with the lowest discriminant validity have been further modified in the latest version of the questionnaire in an effort to improve discrimination in respondent perception of these behavior categories.

TABLE 14

Correlations among Leader Behavior Scales for the Student Leaders and Second Salon Sample (in parentheses)

Scale Identification	1	2	3	4	5	6	7	8	9	10	11	12
1. Consideration												
2. Positive Reinforcement	39 (59)											
3. Decision Participation	40 (60)	35 (45)										
4. Production Emphasis	01 (44)	42 (40)	15 (35)									
5. Work Facilitation	-16 (50)	17 (43)	18 (20)	29 (56)								
6. Autonomy-Delegation	12 (31)	18 (29)	22 (26)	03 (08)	-14 (30)							
7. Planning	-17 (35)	-01 (29)	11 (19)	40 (29)	38 (48)	10 (17)						
8. Coordination	03 (45)	36 (49)	47 (29)	44 (43)	41 (53)	14 (22)	59 (60)					
9. Interaction Facilitation	33 (51)	67 (44)	39 (46)	55 (41)	16 (61)	28 (28)	26 (49)	50 (49)				
10. Conflict Management	-05 (56)	29 (45)	43 (40)	04 (35)	15 (57)	28 (20)	30 (49)	50 (43)	45 (69)			
11. Role Clarification	17 (53)	25 (42)	32 (34)	25 (62)	16 (58)	-01 (19)	33 (44)	39 (62)	49 (56)	38 (48)		
12. Training	16 (46)	17 (36)	15 (23)	20 (42)	46 (48)	-12 (06)	37 (54)	26 (45)	22 (56)	25 (43)	34 (46)	
13. Goal Setting	32 (39)	28 (41)	49 (16)	32 (52)	25 (53)	27 (18)	45 (34)	54 (59)	43 (34)	30 (30)	39 (68)	35 (42)

Comparison of the Behavior Typology to Earlier Ones

The approximate correspondence between our behavior categories and those proposed by other theorists and researchers is described in Table 15. A certain degree of continuity with the earlier findings is evident. We have succeeded in differentiating a greater number of specific categories, but the content of each category bears some similarity to the content of at least one factor found in earlier research. This similarity is the reason we chose to use earlier scale names whenever feasible rather than coining new names.

Our Consideration scale is very similar to factors found in the Ohio State and Michigan leadership research, although it is more narrowly defined than most of them. The Production Emphasis scale is similar to the Production Emphasis factor in LBDQ-XII, the Goal Emphasis factor in the Michigan questionnaire, and the Pressure for Production scale in the early University of Southern California research (Comrey, Pfiffner, & High, 1954). Our Work Facilitation scale shares some content with the Work Facilitation factor in the Michigan questionnaire, although the latter scale includes training in addition to provision of resources. Our Interaction Facilitation scale corresponds closely to the Interaction Facilitation scale in the Michigan questionnaire. The combination of Interaction Facilitation and Conflict Management is similar to Integration in the LBDQ-XII. The Autonomy-Delegation scale is comparable to the Delegation scale in the leadership questionnaire developed by Bass, Valenzi, Farrow, and Soloman (1975) and the Tolerance of Freedom scale in the LBDQ-XII.

Positive Reinforcement shares some content with Manipulation in the Bass et al. questionnaire, although the latter scale is more broadly defined. The Criticism-Discipline factor found in our research is similar to the Discipline scale in the University of Southern California leadership studies. Positive Reinforcement and Criticism-Discipline also correspond roughly to the Positive Reward Behavior and Punitive Behavior scales used in the leadership research by Sims and Szilagyi (1975). Our Planning scale is comparable to the Planning and Advance Planning scales in the University of Southern California leadership studies, and our Role Clarification scale shares some content with their Formalization scale. There are no direct counterparts in the other studies for our scales on Goal Setting and Coordination, but one or two items on these aspects of leadership behavior are sometimes included in the broadly defined scales on task-oriented behavior found in some of the other studies.

TABLE 15

Comparison of New Leader Behavior Categories to Ones Proposed by Other Researchers

Yukl & Nemeroff (This Volume)	Halpin & Winer (1957)	Fleishman (1953)	Stogdill et al. (1962)	Bowers & Seashore (1966)	House & Dessler (1974)	Bass et al. (1975	Comrey et al. (1954)
Planning							Advance Planning
Coordination	Initiating Structure						
Role Clarification		Initiating Structure	Initiating Structure		Instrumental Leadership	Direction	Formalization
Goal Setting							
Production Emphasis	Production Emphasis		Production Emphasis	Goal Emphasis			Production Pressure
Training							
Work Facilitation				Work Facilitation			
Consideration	Consideration	Consideration	Consideration	Supervisor Support	Supportive Leadership		Helpfulness, Sympathy
Decision Participation					Participative Leadership	Consultation, Participation	Lack of Arbitrariness
Positive Reinforcement						Manipulation	
Autonomy-Delegation			Tolerance of Freedom			Delegation	
Interaction Facilitation			Integration	Interaction Facilitation			
Conflict Management							

Psychometric Properties of the Leader Behavior Scales

In addition to identifying relevant leader behavior categories in our research, we also attempted to evaluate the adequacy of the separate scales for each behavior category. That is, we examined relevant psychometric properties of the scales, and compared the findings to those reported for the Ohio State and Michigan leadership scales. The psychometric properties that appear most relevant for evaluating leader behavior scales include: 1) item response distributions, 2) internal consistency, 3) scale score stability, 4) inter-rater agreement, 5) convergent validity, and 6) criterion-related validity. Discriminant validity has already been discussed.

Item Response Distributions

A major weakness of the Ohio State and Michigan leadership scales is the susceptibility of their items to response tendencies (e.g., leniency, social desirability, halo). One possible indicator of these response tendencies is a highly skewed response distribution for most of the items. If one assumes that the leaders who are being described actually differ with respect to the behaviors in a manner that should generate a normal or relatively flat distribution, then highly skewed distributions suggest that responses are distorted by systematic response tendencies. In reviewing data on item distributions for the Ohio State leadership scales, Schriesheim and Kerr (1974) found that they were highly skewed toward favorable description of the leaders. Seriously skewed item distributions were also found for the Michigan leadership scales by Taylor and Bowers (1972). Approximately 40 percent of respondents selected the To a Very Great Extent response, 35 percent selected the To a Great Extent, 15 percent selected To Some Extent, and 10 percent selected the remaining two responses (To a Little Extent and To a Very Little Extent).

The item response distributions for the leader behavior scales in the scrambled-item version of the questionnaire were determined for each scale, using the second heterogeneous sample and the first salon sample. Both of these samples had a version of the questionnaire with instructions warning respondents to avoid leniency, central tendency, and halo errors. Item distributions were not determined for the first heterogeneous sample and the production sample, because these samples received shorter, less refined versions of the questionnaire, without response error instructions, and without a Don't Know or not Applicable response choice.

The response distributions for the second heterogeneous sample are shown in Table 16, and those for the first salon sample in Table 17. Results

TABLE 16

Mean Response Frequencies in Percents for Each Response Choice and Each Scale (Heterogeneous Sample 2)

Leader Behavior	Not at All	Limited Extent	Some Extent	Considerable Extent	Very Great Extent	Don't Know
1. Consideration	7	20	20	27	26	0
2. Decision Participation	15	35	27	16	5	2
3. Production Emphasis	5	13	22	26	33	1
4. Work Facilitation	3	21	16	29	20	11
5. Autonomy-Delegation	9	16	22	25	25	3
6. Planning-Coordination	8	23	25	21	11	11
7. Interaction Facilitation	9	22	23	23	16	7
8. Conflict Management	9	26	18	16	7	24
9. Direction	7	28	26	22	9	8

Leader Behavior	Never	Seldom	Sometimes	Usually	Always	Don't Know
1. Consideration	7	11	17	30	34	1
2. Decision Participation	19	25	29	17	6	4
3. Production Emphasis	6	13	22	27	27	5
4. Work Facilitation	6	11	17	31	23	12
5. Autonomy Delegation	8	13	16	35	27	1
6. Planning-Coordination	8	14	30	27	10	11
7. Interaction Facilitation	4	24	28	22	14	8
8. Conflict Management	9	19	20	16	9	27
9. Direction	8	16	25	28	15	8

TABLE 17

Mean Response Frequencies in Percents for Each Response Choice and Each Scale (Salom Sample 1)

Leader Behavior	Not at All	Limited Extent	Some Extent	Considerable Extent	Very Great Extent	Don't Know
1. Consideration	11	23	20	25	21	1
2. Decision Participation	24	29	20	17	7	3
3. Production Emphasis	10	24	21	21	24	0
4. Work Facilitation	5	21	21	29	22	2
5. Autonomy-Delegation	5	23	17	24	27	4
6. Planning-Coordination	12	24	24	21	17	2
7. Team Building	11	24	24	20	21	0
8. Direction	10	22	24	20	23	1

Leader Behavior	Never	Seldom	Sometimes	Usually	Always	Don't Know
1. Consideration	8	15	21	28	27	1
2. Decision Participation	28	23	25	14	9	1
3. Production Emphasis	3	14	19	26	37	1
4. Work Facilitation	7	13	13	41	24	2
5. Autonomy-Delegation	2	5	11	40	42	0
6. Planning-Coordination	8	14	22	35	12	9
7. Team Building	12	15	19	27	23	4
8. Direction	8	16	23	29	21	3

are in terms of average frequencies for items in a given scale and format. Only the positively worded items in the frequency and magnitude formats were analyzed. The incident-counting items typically had lower factor loadings and are no longer being used in the questionnaire. The negatively worded items were also dropped because they had less consistent factor loadings and they turned out to be politically unacceptable to management in two organizations.

The results suggest that response tendencies were not a serious problem. The item distributions for the magnitude items were relatively flat for most of the scales in both samples. Some skewness is evident for the frequency items, but the degree varied from scale to scale and across samples, suggesting that no systematic response bias was operating. The only prominent aberration in the response distributions was a low frequency of Never and Not at All responses. This pattern may be evidence that subordinate descriptions were accurate rather than evidence of a response tendency, because most of the behaviors are likely to be exhibited at least some of the time by the kind of managers being described by these two samples of subordinates. Moreover, the Don't Know or Not Applicable option probably competed with the Never and Not at All options, thereby further reducing their response frequencies. In other words, when a behavior is never exhibited, it is likely to be because it is not appropriate (i.e., Not Applicable) for the leader in his or her situation. Certain kinds of leader behavior (i.e., Conflict Management, Planning-Coordination) are likely to be less observable by subordinates than other kinds (i.e., Consideration, Production Emphasis, Autonomy-Delegation). The higher frequency of Don't Know responses for the less observable behaviors suggests that subordinates were using this option when it was appropriate.

An analysis of item response distributions was also conducted for the grouped item version of the questionnaire, using the only sample in the followup studies to receive both item formats. The results are shown in Table 18. The item distributions varied greatly from scale to scale, providing further evidence that respondents were discriminating among the different aspects of leadership behavior. There was no indication of widespread leniency or central tendency errors. Conflict Management and Work Facilitation had the highest frequency of Don't Know or Not Applicable responses.

Internal Consistency

The internal consistency of a scale is the extent to which its items are inter-correlated with each other. In reviewing research on the internal

Leader Behavior	Not at All	Limited Extent	Moderate Extent	Considerable Extent	Very Great Extent	Don't Know
1. Consideration	5	28	27	29	10	1
2. Positive Reinforcement	22	26	18	17	8	9
3. Decision Participation	14	40	22	17	7	0
4. Production Emphasis	12	31	22	18	17	0
5. Work Facilitation	7	21	23	23	13	13
6. Autonomy-Delegation	4	19	24	29	24	0
7. Planning	21	32	16	15	6	10
8. Coordination	15	34	27	15	4	5
9. Interaction Facilitation	27	23	18	19	9	4
10. Conflict Management	27	23	16	12	5	17
11. Role Clarification	14	40	25	13	8	0
12. Training	22	32	18	19	4	5
13. Goal Setting	22	33	21	13	9	2

Leader Behavior	Never	Seldom	Sometimes	Usually	Always	Don't Know
1. Consideration	4	17	31	35	12	1
2. Positive Reinforcement	20	27	27	16	5	5
3. Decision Participation	15	34	31	16	4	0
4. Production Emphasis	7	21	23	26	20	3
5. Work Facilitation	8	13	19	30	16	14
6. Autonomy-Delegation	2	8	22	47	21	0
7. Planning	21	31	18	17	6	7
8. Coordination	15	29	26	17	5	8
9. Interaction Facilitation	17	18	18	30	16	1
10. Conflict Management	21	26	14	16	5	18
11. Role Clarification	10	30	26	23	9	2
12. Training	15	28	24	21	6	6
13. Goal Setting	17	33	21	20	4	5

TABLE 19

Internal Consistency of MBS Scales (Number of Scale Items in Parentheses)

Leadership Behavior	Salon Sample 1	Production Sample	Salon Sample 2	Student Leaders	Heterogeneous Sample 3
Consideration	.93	.89	.80	.77	.86
	(9)	(5)	(5)	(5)	(9)
Positive Reinforcement	.79	NF	.69	.70	.88
	(4)		(4)	(4)	(8)
Decision Participation	.77	.82	.80	.77	.90
	(7)	(4)	(5)	(5)	(10)
Production Emphasis	.86	.55	.77	.72	.90
	(9)	(3)	(4)	(4)	(8)
Work Facilitation	.89	.76	.77	.76	.90
	(8)	(3)	(5)	(5)	(9)
Autonomy-Delegation	.76	.75	.61	.72	.91
	(6)	(4)	(4)	(4)	(8)
Planning	⎰ .83	.83	.72	.67	.80
	⎱ (7)	(2)	(3)	(3)	(6)
Coordination		NF	.67	.65	.80
			(3)	(3)	(6)
Interaction Facilitation	⎰ .90	.89	.89	.93	.91
	⎱ (11)	(4)	(3)	(3)	(6)
Conflict Management		.81	.93	.83	.89
		(3)	(3)	(3)	(6)
Role Clarification			.78	.70	.86
			(4)	(4)	(7)
Training	⎰ .87	⎰ .78	.78	.82	.86
	⎱ (8)	⎱ (4)	(3)	(3)	(6)
Goal Setting			.80	.76	.88
			(3)	(3)	(6)
Sample Size	74	146	69	40	99

Note. NF means no separate factor.

consistency of leadership scales, Schriesheim and Kerr (1977) report that internal consistency coefficients range from .60 upward for the Ohio State leadership questionnaires, with most values in the .80s. Taylor and Bowers (1972) report reliability coefficients for the Michigan leadership scales in excess of .80 for several samples of respondents. In the University of Southern California studies, reliability coefficients were usually in the .60 to .90 range.

The internal consistency of the scales in our earlier, scrambled-item version of the questionnaire was determined for the production sample and the first salon sample. Internal consistency was estimated by Cronbach's alpha coefficient rather than by the split-half method used in most of the earlier studies. The alpha coefficient was computed during an item analysis of each scale, using the items that had strong factor loadings on that scale and fit the scale definition. The results are shown in Table 19. For the first salon sample, internal consistency was high for all the scales except Criticism-Discipline ($r = .67$). In the production sample, internal consistency was adequate for all scales except Production Emphasis, despite the use of a shorter questionnaire with fewer items per scale.

The internal consistency for the grouped-scale version of the questionnaire was determined for three different samples, and the results can also be found in Table 19. Reliability was typically higher for the heterogeneous sample that received both the frequency and magnitude versions of the questionnaire than for the two samples receiving only the shorter frequency version. In Heterogeneous Sample 3, internal consistency was quite good for every scale. For the other two samples, internal consistency ranged from fair to good. It is interesting to note that scales with about the same number of items in the scrambled-item and grouped-item versions of the questionnaire did not differ noticeably in internal consistency. If the grouping had introduced a strong bias to answer all items in a scale the same way, internal consistency should have been much higher for the grouped-item version of the questionnaire than for the scrambled-item version.

In general, the results indicated that internal consistency is adequate for all of our scales as long as the number of items per scale is maintained at reasonable levels. In light of the results, we have included six items per scale in the latest version of the questionnaire.

Scale Score Stability

Stability, sometimes referred to as test-retest reliability, is the degree to which scores on a measure remain constant over a period of time if the construct being measured does not change. It is usually estimated by administering the same measure to the same persons at two or more points in time, with the time interval varying from a few weeks to several years.

In a review of research on the stability of the Michigan leadership questionnaire, Schriesheim and Kerr (1977) report that stability coefficients ranged from .04 to .78 for composite scores for all four leadership scales (data on separate scales were not available). In most cases, the stability of the measures appeared to be unsatisfactory. Stability coefficients ranging from .63 to .87 have been reported for Consideration and Initiating Structure, as measured by the SBDQ and LBDQ-XII, and stability for these measures seems satisfactory.

The stability of our leader behavior scales has been determined for only one sample of respondents, so not much evidence is available. In this study, the 95-item version of the grouped-item questionnaire was readministered to 40 persons in the third heterogeneous sample after an interval of from five to ten weeks. Test-retest correlations were computed for each scale, and the results were as follows: Consideration (.71), Positive Reinforcement (.82), Decision Participation (.64), Production Emphasis (.79), Work Facilitation (.81), Autonomy-Delegation (.85), Role Clarification (.80), Goal Setting (.74), Training (.70), Interaction Facilitation (.66), Conflict Management (.61), Planning (.55), and Coordination (.57). The results indicated satisfactory stability for all scales except Planning, Coordination, and Conflict Management, which were a little below preferred levels. The lower stability for these scales may stem from the fact that it is harder for subordinates to observe and identify these aspects of leader behavior. Some additional studies will be conducted with homogeneous leader samples to assess further scale score stability.

Inter-rater Agreement

Different methods have been used to compute inter-rater agreement. Fleishman (1957) used the Horst coefficient (Horst, 1949) and found values of .50 for Initiating Structure and .55 for Consideration in a sample of workers describing 59 foremen with the SBDQ. In another sample, Fleishman used the unbiased correlation ratio derived from a one-way analysis of variance (across work groups) and found values of .64 for Initiating Structure and .72 for Consideration for workers describing 31 foremen, and values of .47 for Initiating Structure and .65 for Consideration for foremen describing 60 general foremen. Bass et al. (1975) used the unbiased correlation ratio to estimate inter-rater agreement in three samples (middle managers, upper-level managers, and library directors), and obtained values ranging from .46 to .70, with a median value of .54. Hammer (1977) used average inter-rater correlations within work groups and found values ranging from .05 to .54, with a median value of .28.

Inter-rater agreement is sometimes used as an indicator of measurement accuracy. If different subordinates describe the same leader's behavior in the same way, it is more likely that their descriptions are accurate than if they do not agree. There are some potential problems with this approach, however. The use of inter-rater agreement as an indicator of measurement accuracy assumes that the leader behaves in the same way toward each subordinate. As proponents of the Vertical Dyad Linkage Theory have pointed out, there is evidence that leaders do not establish the same kind of relationship with all of their subordinates (Cashman, Dansereau, Graen, & Haga, 1976; Dansereau, Graen, & Haga, 1975). If each leader behaves differently with different subordinates, inter-rater agreement will tend to be low, even if subordinates accurately describe the leader's behavior.

Another problem noted in Bass et al. (1975) is that procedures which are based on a comparison of between group variability to within group variability will not be a very sensitive indicator of inter-rater agreement if there is actually very little between-group variability. Use of such procedures, in effect, rests on the assumption that there is substantial difference between leaders in their behavior and that this difference occurs for each behavior category. The previous studies of inter-rater agreement for leader behavior measures suggest that a moderate amount of agreement is likely to be found. We would expect agreement to be higher for some kinds of leader behavior than for others. Agreement should be lowest for behavior that is likely to be tailored to individual subordinates, such as Autonomy-Delegation and Decision Participation.

Inter-rater agreement was tested by computing a one-way analysis of variance across groups of respondents for each sample in which we had multiple descriptions of the same leader. In conducting this analysis, we used only those work units with at least four respondents. The F-values for each scale in each sample are shown in Table 20. There was some evidence of inter-rater agreement for all of the scales, but some had stronger and more consistent results than others. Inter-rater agreement was determined for Criticism-Discipline only in the first salon sample, because this scale was not used in any of the other homogeneous samples. The F-value for Criticism-Discipline indicated high rater agreement ($F = 3.60$, $P < .01$). Horst r values for the scales with significant F-values ranged from .35 to .82, and they were usually in the .50 to .70 range. As expected, the degree of agreement among respondents was lowest for Autonomy-Delegation and Decision-Participation. We considered analyzing the results separately for individually worded items and collectively worded items in these scales, but the inter-correlation among the two kinds of items was so high that such an analysis did not seem worthwhile. The form of wording did not seem to have much effect on respondents' answers.

It was not evident why inter-rater agreement varied so much from sample to sample. This may have been due in part to the small sample sizes, the highly discrepant group sizes, and perhaps to differences in variability of actual leader behavior across situations. We will continue to explore the question of inter-rater agreement with more adequate samples in an attempt to determine the meaning of the inconsistencies. We will also try to determine whether respondents are answering the questions from an individual or collective perspective for each of the scales, and we will investigate

TABLE 20
Inter-rater Agreement as Indicated by One-way Analysis of Variance

Leadership Behavior	Salon Sample 1	Production Sample	Salon Sample 2	Student Leaders
Consideration	4.01***	3.31***	1.29	4.44***
Positive Reinforcement	11.73***		2.13**	4.35***
Decision Participation	1.56	0.91	0.84	2.14*
Production Emphasis	2.39**	2.06***	2.43**	2.72**
Work Facilitation	1.78*	1.72**	1.75*	3.73***
Autonomy-Delegation	0.92	1.28	1.91*	1.33
Planning	{ 1.05	{ 2.59***	3.16***	1.04
Coordination	{	{	2.74***	2.20*
Interaction Facilitation	{ 3.02***	1.98***	1.14	4.91***
Conflict Management	{	2.08***	1.04	1.71
Role Clarification			1.42	0.37
Training	{ 2.86***	{ 1.80**	2.37**	0.63
Goal Setting	{	{	3.42***	0.48
Number of Groups	10	21	10	8
Number of Respondents	58	135	63	40

*p < .10 for F
**p < .05 for F
***p < .01 for F

the extent to which leaders are varying their behavior in dealing with different subordinates.

Convergent Validity

Convergent validity is demonstrated for a measure when scores obtained by the measure correlate highly with scores on a different measure of the same variable. Earlier in this chapter we found that convergent validity was very good for most scales when tested by the multiscale-multimethod analysis. However, that study provided only a weak test of convergent validity, because two versions of a questionnaire with different item formats do not represent substantially different measurement methods. In order to obtain stronger evidence of convergent validity, it is necessary to conduct a study using more discrepant methods of measuring leader behavior. One such attempt was made by Ilgen and Fujii (1976) for LBDQ-XII Consideration and Initiating Structure. In a laboratory experiment, very little agreement was found between individual subordinates' descriptions of their leaders' behavior and the corresponding descriptions of leader behavior obtained from observers. There was moderate agreement between observers' descriptions and composite group scores for leader behavior. It is questionable whether the results can be readily generalized to a realistic leadership situation where subordinates interact with their leaders frequently over a long period of time.

In an effort to make a realistic early assessment of convergent validity for our questionnaire scales, we used real employees and two different methods of having them describe their supervisors' behavior. The subordinates were 18 of the subordinates in the second heterogeneous sample. They were night students in a class in managerial effectiveness, and they had fulltime jobs during the day in a variety of different organizations. The students filled out the second version of the leader behavior questionnaire during the first class session. As part of their term project, the students were asked to observe their supervisors' behavior over a ten week period and fill out a weekly checklist. The checklist had specific examples of each behavior category measured by the questionnaire. Students were required to turn in the completed checklist each week, and these were scored and returned to them after the ten week observation period was over, so that the data could be used in making a report on their supervisors' leadership effectiveness. The scale scores from the questionnaire were correlated with the composite frequency scores for corresponding behavior items on the observational checklist, and the correlations that were obtained are shown in Table 21. Despite the fact that each behavior category was represented by only a couple of behavior incidents in the checklist and observed only during a relatively short period of time, the degree of convergence was substantial. The results provide evidence of convergent validity for all of the scales except Work Facilitation. More rigorous observational studies are planned to obtain further evidence about the convergent validity of the scales, especially for the latest version of the questionnaire.

Criterion-Related Validity

The criterion-related validity of a leader behavior measure is usually assessed by correlating scale scores with measures of subordinate satisfaction with the leader or with measures of leader effectiveness, such as work unit productivity and performance ratings of the leaders made by superiors. Fairly large correlations are usually found between leader behavior and subordinate satisfaction when they are both measured by questionnaires, but in many cases the correlations could be inflated by method variance. Significant correlations between leader behavior and independent criterion measures have been found in some studies, but the magnitude of these correlations tends to be quite low.

TABLE 21

Convergent Validity of Questionnaire Scales and Observational Checklist Items

Leader Behavior	Correlation	Number of Checklist Items
Consideration	.77**	2
Production Emphasis	.55**	2
Decision Participation	.69**	2
Autonomy-Delegation	.56*	2
Direction	.40*	3
Work Facilitation	.01	2
Interaction Facilitation	.55**	2
Conflict Management	.53**	1
Planning-Coordinating	.54**	2

*p < .05, df = 16, one-tail test
**p < .01

The principal focus of our early research has been on scale development rather than on criterion-related validity. Nevertheless, some evidence on criterion-related validity is available for one sample, and it appears to be very promising. Data on profit margins were obtained for the 26 beauty salons in which at least three subordinates returned the leadership questionnaire. When the leader effectiveness criterion was profit margin for a time period subsequent to the administration of the questionnaire, significant predictive validities were found for Production Emphasis ($r = .49$, $p < .01$) and Direction ($r = .47$, $p < .01$). Percentage increase in sales was also determined, and this supplementary criterion was predicted by Positive Reinforcement ($r = .56$, $p < .01$). The same three leader behavior scales also correlated significantly with a composite performance evaluation for each salon manager based on independent ratings by two raters. Additional information about the procedure and results for this study will be reported in a paper by Yukl and Kanuk. Other studies will be conducted with different samples of leaders to obtain more information about the criterion-related validity of the scales. These studies will include use of alternative methods of data collection so that more detailed information can be obtained about the behavior patterns accounting for leader effectiveness in a given situation.

Conclusions

The research on leader behavior categories suggests that much of the inconsistency between typologies found in earlier factor analytic studies can be eliminated by use of a more carefully developed measure. The 14 behavior categories that we have found to date are meaningful ones, and they are the product of a midrange approach to the description of leader behavior. That is, they are narrower in scope than the early Consideration and Initiating Structure scales, yet they are still general enough to be applicable to most supervisors, managers, and administrators.

With respect to psychometric properties of the scales, the preliminary assessment yielded generally satisfactory results. We are optimistic that the scales emerging from our research will fill the urgent need for a better measure of specific leader behaviors, and we are hopeful that the new questionnaire will prove more useful than earlier ones for determining what makes some leaders more effective than others. Nevertheless, in light of recent studies on sources of bias in questionnaire descriptions of leaders (Eden & Leviatan, 1975; Lord, Binning, Rush, & Thomas, 1978; Mitchell, Larson, & Green, 1977; Rush, Thomas, & Lord, 1977) it is important to point out that our leadership scales still require further validation. None of the psychometric evidence reported in this chapter rules out the possibility that respondents are describing a distorted stereotype of their supervisor instead of his or her actual behavior. Some of the scales in the questionnaire are likely to have greater validity than others, and a few may even prove to be completely invalid. We will be investigating these issues in further research using multiple methods of data collection such as observation of leaders by the researchers, self-report diaries and checklists filled out by the managers, and interviews with managers, peers, superiors, and subordinates. Meanwhile, researchers who desire to use our questionnaire (or any other leadership questionnaire) before validation is completed are advised to use the same kind of multiple-method approach in their own research, rather than depending entirely on questionnaire data.

The latest version of our leadership questionnaire, named the Managerial Behavior Survey (MBS), has 14 scales with six items per scale. It may be possible to subdivide further some of the existing scales, but at the present time, we think it is more important to carry out further validation of the scales and to develop measures of important aspects of managerial behavior not already included in the questionnaire. In the initial development of the questionnaire, we have emphasized aspects of leadership behavior involving relations with subordinates and direct facilitation of subordinate effort. Lateral relations and upward relations have been deemphasized, in part because these aspects of leadership behavior are not easily observed by subordinates. Items on some representation and liaison behaviors were included in the second version of the questionnaire, but they did not cluster together and had a high incidence of Don't Know responses. It may be necessary to measure such behaviors by questioning superiors, peers, and the managers themselves rather than by asking subordinates. Other important aspects of managerial behavior not presently found in the questionnaire include: innovative behavior, strategic planning and policy formation, charismatic leadership, conference leadership behavior, and so forth. Most of these behaviors are more relevant to upperlevel managers than to the lower-level managers and leaders in our first six samples, which is a major reason why these behaviors were not included in the early version of the questionnaire. Research is now in progress to study these aspects of managerial behavior and develop measures of them.

11

Leadership: A Proposal for a Social Learning Theory Base and Observational and Functional Analysis Techniques to Measure Leader Behavior

FRED LUTHANS

When asked to prepare this chapter, I visualized my role as that of resident behaviorist and anticipated taking pot shots at the cognitively based leadership theories and the indirect questionnaire methods of measurement. While becoming reacquainted myself with the leadership literature it was soon evident that the prevailing theme was to be highly critical of existing leadership theory and express the need to get away from the old standardized questionnaire approach to measurement. I also noted that with a few exceptions, such as House's revitalization of charismatic theory (House, 1977) and Scott's (1977) important formulation of an operant based theory of leadership, most of the critics did not attempt to suggest any new theories. The same is true of those who derided questionnaire research; no alternative methods were offered. For example, after Schriescheim and Kerr's (1977) comprehensive analysis of the standardized questionnaires used in leadership research uncovered little or no construct validity, they called for new questionnaire development that pays closer attention to construct validity. This same approach is taken by Yukl and Nemeroff in chapter 10. They are attempting to *improve* questionnaires rather than provide alternative methods of measurement.

Although a bit surprising, it is pleasing to see that so many leadership scholars are seriously questioning existing theory and research methods.

We appear to be at a critical point in the leadership field and must either put up or shut up. If we can not put up, and soon, then I think we should rally behind self-proclaimed heretic John Miner (1975) who stated that the concept of leadership has outlived its usefulness. However, I think there is still time. Unlike Miner, I think we need some fresh, methodologically clean bath water and should not be so quick to throw out the baby.

The purpose here is to propose a new theoretical basis for leadership and suggest some additional techniques to measure leadership behavior. I want to stress from the very beginning that my comments are only preliminary. I am not yet able to put up. But I am also not going to shut up, at least not yet. I am going to depart from a restrictive, behaviorist role and instead take a proactive stance by propsoing new theory and measurement techniques for leadership.

Proposal: Let's Concentrate on Leader Behaviors

Before assuming a proactive role, allow me to slip into a reactive, behaviorist role for just a moment. I strongly feel that the biggest problem with existing leadership theories and measurement techniques is that they have strayed too far away from leadership *behaviors*. Too often theorists forget that "leadership" or "influence" are merely labels that are attached to hypothetical constructs. Too often, the hypothetical construct is treated as the empirical reality. It must be remembered that leadership *behavior* is the empirical reality. Theory building that ignores this behavioral reality would seem to lead up to many nonparsimonious blind alleys.

The same is true of the measurement techniques. The widely used behavioral measurement techniques such as the Ohio State, Fiedler, and Michigan questionnaires are not really measuring leadership behaviors. At best they are measuring the questionnaire respondent's behavior and perceptions/attitudes, not leadership behaviors. They require the respondent to reconstruct a leadership event within the predefined set of responses contained on the instrument. They have nothing to do with the actual leadership situation where leaders affect subordinates and subordinates affect leaders and a whole host of internal cognitive processes and external environmental contingencies in turn affect this interaction. In addition, because the instruments are administered to groups rather than individuals and the scores represent averages, actual leadership behavior may never be described.

What we need is a return back to leadership *behavior* as the unit of analysis for our theory building and measurement techniques. To be helpful in the goals of understanding and prediction, leadership theory should be grounded in the empirical reality of behavior and not in some hypothetical construct that has become an end in itself. We also need better measures of leader behavior than are currently offered by the standard questionnaires. As Korman (1974) pointed out:

> The need for better measurement in leadership theory is a matter of prime necessity. Measurement and theory go hand-in-hand and the development of one without the other is a waste of time for all concerned. . . . The point is *not* that adequate measurement is "nice." It is *necessary, crucial*, etc. Without it, we have nothing. [p. 194]

Our questionnaires need construct validity but we also need to develop other indirect measurement methods as well as place much more emphasis on direct, observational methods of measuring leadership behaviors.

Proposal: A Social Learning Theory of Leadership

Traditional theories viewed leadership as a unilateral influence process flowing from leader to subordinate. The currently popular contingency theories bring in the importance of the situation in the leadership process but then proceed to largely treat the leader, the subordinate, and the environment as independent inputs into leader behavior. Only recently has it been emphasized that leadership is an interactional process. For example, Stogdill has astutely observed the need to investigate leadership variables "in interaction" (1973, p. 103) and Greene (1977) has called for theory building that recognized the "social exchange" and reciprocal relationship between leader and subordinate behaviors. In addition, the few operant-based papers on leadership (Mawhinney & Ford, 1977; Scott, 1977; and Sims, 1977) stress the interaction between leader behaviors and environmental contingencies. What these various approaches suggest is that there are a number of interacting variables that determine leadership behavior.

The interactive idea seems to be a major breakthrough for theory building in leadership. But any of the conceptions offered so far—whether they be Fiedler's suggested interaction between situational factors and personality attributes (Fiedler, 1973, p. 42) or Graen's (1975) concentration on the functional interdependence between the leader and a follower in his dyad linkages or Greene's social exchange between leader and subordinate or even Scott's interaction between leader behaviors and environmental contingencies—all seem too limiting and, at best, partial theories for explaining the complexities of leadership. What is needed is a comprehensive theory that incorporates the *interactive* nature of *all* the variables of leadership behavior—the behavior itself, the environment (including subordinates and macro organization variables) and the leader himself. Social learning theory seems best to meet this challenge.

Albert Bandura is most closely associated with social learning theory. He takes the position that the best explanation of human behavior is in terms of a continuous reciprocal interaction between cognitive, behavioral, and environmental determinants (1977). In a unidirectional conception of interaction (e.g., the Fiedler approach), leaders and situations are considered to be independent entities that somehow combine to determine leadership behavior. A social learning approach would say that the leader and the situation do not function as independent units but instead determine each other in a reciprocal manner—in other words, under social learning theory the conception that leader behavior $= f(P, E)$ is rejected.

The same is true of more one sided cognitive views of leadership (e.g., trait or charismatic approaches) which suggest that leaders be considered causal determinants independent of their behaviors. A social learning theory approach would explain that, "It is largely through their actions that [leaders] produce the environmental conditions that affect their behavior in a reciprocal fashion. The experiences generated by behavior also partly determine what a [leader] becomes and can do which, in turn, affects subsequent behavior" (Bandura, 1977, p. 9).

Even those leadership theorists who would argue they are taking a bidirectional approach (either in an exchange sense between leader and subordinate or between leader and situation) still retain a unidirectional view toward leadership behavior. The causal input into the leader's behavior is the result of the interdependent exchange, but the behavior itself is ignored as an interacting determinant. In other words, under social learning theory the conception that leader behavior $= f(P \rightarrow E)$ is rejected.

A social learning theory of leadership could be depicted by Figure 10 (adapted from Bandura, 1977). It should be noted that by including the leader him/herself, specific recognition is given to cognitive variables. It has been previously argued (Luthans, 1979, in press) that we should concentrate on observable contingencies as the best way to make a diagnostic evaluation of organizational behavior and I still believe that. On the other hand, neither Skinner himself nor I have ever denied the existence of cognitive processes. And to the extent that these processes aid in the clarification of our understanding of the complexities of leadership, they should be included (Skinner, 1963; Luthans, 1979, in press; Luthans & Kreitner, 1975). A social learning theory of leadership says that a leader's behavior is

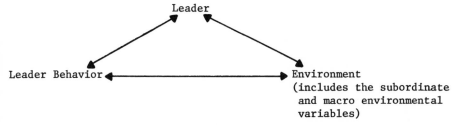

Fig. 10. A social learning theory of leadership

explained as a reciprocal interaction of personal, environmental, and behavioral determinants. Anything less than this seems too limiting for a sound theoretical basis for leadership.

Proposal: Observational and Functional Analysis Approaches to Measurement

As the earlier quote by Korman pointed out, measurement goes hand-in-hand with theory building. There is an interactive relationship—without good theory we can not have good measures and without good measures we can not have good theory. I think this interactive notion between theory and measures explains many of the problems we are having in leadership today. The widely used questionnaires are easy targets as Schriesheim and Kerr (1977) found out, but in all fairness, the existing questionnaires do a good job of reflecting the inadequate theories upon which they are based. However, based on a social learning theory that posits a reciprocal inter-action between the leader, the environment, and the behavior, the traditional questionnaire measures become totally inadequate. In no uncertain terms Kerlinger (1973) states that "observations must be used when the variables of research studies are interactive and interpersonal in nature" (p. 554). Because social learning theory is based on interactive variables it follows that observational techniques take on central importance.

Please allow me to slip into my reactive, behaviorist role one more time. I would say that regardless of the social learning base, one of the biggest problems with leadership research over the years has been the almost total void of observational measures of leadership behaviors in naturalistic settings. In our rush to respectability we have bypassed the widely recognized first stage of any scientific developoment—observation of naturally occurring events. For example, the development of instruments such as the

LBDQ started with terms that were not based on actual observations of leadership behaviors *in situ* (see Fleishman, 1973, for a discussion of how the questionnaires were developed). Obviously, it is much easier to ask than to observe, and this path of least resistance is the one we have taken in the development of leadership.

Back to the proactive role, what is proposed here is to first observe leadership behavior *in situ*. Instead of quickly dismissing observation as having more problems than questionnaires, it must be remembered that these techniques are being perfected in other areas such as ethology and eco-behavioral science (Barker, 1965; Willems & Raush, 1969). As Kerlinger (1973) and Weick (1968) point out, there are definitely problems with observational methods but not as many as most researchers commonly believe and certainly these problems are not insurmountable. Weick (1968) goes on to offer some specific guidelines that can lead to reliable and valid observations of leadership behaviors. The few researchers in management that have attempted to use observational techniques have been quite pleased with the results. For example, Mintzberg (1973) noted that organization members do not change their routine of operations just because an observer is present. Telephones are answered, meetings are attended, and events take place just as they normally would.

Although unstructured observation *in situ* is desperately needed, especially in the initial stages of leadership research, realistically, more generalizable structured observational techniques need to be developed for leadership. In the manner that Bales (1950) developed his technique to observe interactions of group members, and researchers have developed structured observational techniques to measure a variety of human dynamics in education settings (see Simon and Boyer, 1970, for an anthology of 79 observation systems), there is a need for an observational system to measure leadership behaviors. In order to be able to put up in the future, we (Luthans & Maris) are in the very early stages of developing such an approach which we call the leadership Behavior Observation System (LBOS).

Besides the need to develop specific observational techniques for measurement in leadership research, there is also a need for a systematic way of analyzing leadership behaviors that can be used in both research and practice. For example, Bandura (1977) calls for a methodology that "specifies the conditional probabilities that the interacting factors will affect the likelihood of the occurrence of each other in an on-going sequence" (p. 198). What is proposed here is the use of an expanded functional analysis (Davis & Luthans, 1979, in press). In an operant approach to leadership (e.g., Scott, 1977; Sims, 1977) a three-term contingency analysis of antecedent cues (or discriminative stimuli)—behaviors—and consequences is proposed. However, when the person/leader variable is included, as in a social learning theory approach, a four-term contingency analysis is needed.

I have earlier (Luthans, 1977) proposed such a four-term contingency analysis which incorporates environmental (Stimulus [S] and Consequence [C]), person (Organism [O]), and behavioral (Behavior [B]) variables. This is depicted as: Stimulus → Organism → Behavior → Consequence. (Note: There are implicit feedback loops to all variables.) Unlike a more limited A-B-C functional analysis which stresses the need to identify observable environmental contingencies (A and C) for the prediction and control of behavior (B), the expanded $S \rightarrow O \rightarrow B \rightarrow C$ functional analysis recognizes the mediating role of cognitive processes (O) and would go so far as to say that the antecedent cues or discriminative stimuli (S), the behavior itself (B), and/or the contingent consequences (C) can be overt or covert. This represents a significant departure from traditional operant approaches that at least implicitly only recognize overt contingencies and behaviors. Significantly, this expanded functional analysis does not abandon the emphasis on behavior or the principles of operant learning theory; it merely expands the variables to include covert as well as the overt contingencies and behaviors. I still would maintain that the A-B-C functional analysis is better for prediction and control of leadership behaviors but the $S \rightarrow O \rightarrow B \rightarrow C$ certainly leads to better understanding. I will quickly add, however, that as self-control techniques and procedures become better understood and applied in leadership situations, the expanded functional analysis will take on increasing value in prediction and control.

The $S \rightarrow O \rightarrow B \rightarrow C$ functional analysis of leadership covers all the variables in social learning theory and gives specific recognition to self-regulatory processes. By recognizing covert contingencies (for example an expectation may be a covert S and a satisfying feeling may be a covert C) and behaviors (for example, a thought may be a covert behavior), there is a need to develop indirect measures. Bandura (1977) feels comfortable with the present status of such indirect measures of covert processes. He states: "A large body of research now exists in which cognitions are activated instructionally, their presence is assessed indirectly, and their functional relationship to behavior is carefully examined" (p. 10). Applied to leadership behaviors, indirect techniques such as self-reports may prove to be valuable measures of covert variables. Johnston, Duncan, Monroe, Stephenson, and Stoerzinger (1978) have recently provided specific guidelines to help improve the self-report method's reliability and validity in business settings.

In order to put up in the area of self-control we have undertaken a field study to assess the ability of practicing managers to use self-control techniques (mainly based on those suggested by Thoresen & Mahoney, 1974) to improve their performance (see Davis & Luthans, 1979, in press). A laboratory experiment that will attempt to test the impact that extrinsic versus intrinsic versus self-reinforcement has on task performance is also under way. We hope that these and other studies will help us better understand and use the expanded functional analysis technique in leadership research and practice.

In brief summary, three major proposals concerning leadership have been made: 1) We need to get back to behavior as the unit of analysis. 2) We need a social learning theory base that recognizes that leadership is a reciprocal, interactive process that involves the leader, the environment, and the behavior. 3) We need alternatives to questionnaire methods of measurement. In particular, observational systems and an expanded functional analysis are suggested. Only time will tell whether these proposals are enough to put up and, if not, then at least I will shut up about leadership.

12

Limitations and Extensions to Questionnaires in Leadership Research

HENRY P. SIMS, JR.

Shall we ring the death knell for the use of questionnaires in leadership research? In his overview in the 1977 symposium volume, John Campbell said, "We are in very grave danger of transforming the study of leadership to a study of self-report questionnaire behavior, if indeed, the transformation has not already occurred" (Campbell, 1977, p. 229). In addition, it is indeed apparent from the comments in this volume and elsewhere that questionnaire based research is certainly not the darling of current leadership researchers.

Yet, the fact remains that questionnaire research has been the predominant methodology in leadership research for many years. Why? There are at least a couple of reasons. First, questionnaires are a convenient data collection method. Relatively large sample sizes can be garnered with a reasonable investment of time and trouble. Second, questionnaires are useful vehicles for operationalizing concepts (variables) that are generalizable across many different organizational situations. Variables measured by questionnaire are typically not constrained to specific aspects of any single organization. Questionnaires thus lend themselves very easily to research efforts directed at the recent "contingency" approaches to leadership research. In summary, many scholars have found questionnaires to have utility in constructing more general theories that are applicable across many organizational situations. But any research methodology, philosophy, or paradigm is indeed a double-edged sword, and measurement by questionnaire is no exception. There is no question that many contemporary organizational behavior scholars share a common frustration at the current limits and boundaries of questionnaire research.

In the viewpoint here, the use of questionnaires is still in a "childhood" stage. Although questionnaires can be used without computers, there is no question that the widespread diffusion of questionnaire techniques has been inextricably entwined with the development and utilization of computers—a relatively recent technological phenomenon. Our challenge as organizational behavior scholars is to find a way to overcome and transcend the boundaries of current questionnaire research practice. Overall, I believe that abandoning questionnaire research would be a case of throwing out the baby with the bathwater. Questionnaire methodology can have utility for gaining insight into organizational behavior phenomena, but several new directions will be necessary to achieve a higher potential. The purpose of this chapter is to attempt to provide some tangible suggestions as to the nature of those new directions. For purposes of explication, the chapter is separated into four parts: 1) antecedents of questionnaire measures, 2) a perspective on discovering leadership constructs, 3) internal psychometric adequacy of questionnaire measures, and 4) the issue of objective reality versus subjective reality.

Antecedents of Questionnaire Measures

Where do questionnaires come from? The scholarly idealist would reply: "Questionnaires are carefully constructed to operationalize and measure variables that have been derived from a well developed theory of behavioral science. They are the pragmatic specifications of the theoretical constructs about the cause and effect relationships in nature. They are the end-product of a carefully thought-out system of logic." A cynic would provide a dramatically contrary viewpoint: "Questionnaires reflect the way one or two individuals *think* about the way the world should be. They measure constructs that are typically derived from philosophical ramblings that result in a priori notions that often have no foundation in reality. Questionnaires are typically slopped together with little or no consideration of previous findings nor to the state of objective reality."

Truth is probably somewhere between these two extremes. It is indeed true that questionnaires have often been used with virtually no consideration as to the theoretical reasons as to why certain variables should be salient in a particular organizational situation. Those who use off-the-shelf instruments with little consideration of the underlying theory and historical development of the instrument are particularly guilty. Yet, some questionnaires are based on serious and substantial effort to derive the measures from objective reality. The original Ohio State Leadership Studies, for example (which have recently undergone so much reexamination—

e.g., Schriesheim & Kerr, 1974), were derived from extensive interviews with individuals actively engaged in leader-follower situations.

The major point is this: Questionnaires should not be thought of as an end point in themselves. Perhaps more precisely, questionnaires should be regarded as an intermediate point in a long cycle of the process of research. Currently, I believe that we need to provide greater attention to the antecedents of questionnaires. In particular, questionnaires should be well grounded in phenomenological investigation of reality, and should be preceded by substantial development of meta-theory and construct formation. The meta-theory should at least possess internal logical consistency before a questionnaire is derived to explore that theory. Figure 11 shows a representation of a time-oriented process of meta-theory and construct development, *followed by* the questionnaire specification.

In the process shown in Figure 11, a critical antecedent of meta-theory and construct development is some phenomenological investigation of reality. Webster describes phenomenology as "The description of the formal structure of phenomena in abstraction. . . ." That is, theory and constructs should not be drawn from the air, but should be substantially based on *in vivo* explorations of the world as it exists.

Next, specification of the questionnaire should proceed only after the theory has met substantial tests of internal logic. Also, no theory should depend entirely on questionnaire methods, or it is in danger of becoming a method-bound theory. A questionnaire, then, becomes an end-product in a theory-construction process, but is only an intermediate step in the total research cycle.

Note the deliberate use of the term *cycle*. This word implies a series of events of a *recurring* nature. That is, for the process to reach maturity, the series of events must take place again and again. With the process shown in Figure 11, perhaps the most important parts are the feedback loops. As the series of events proceeds over time, each event in turn, causes a reevaluation of the adequacy and completeness of preceding events. In addition, the process is never-ending. Interpretation of data, the end-product of a single cycle, should invariably cause a reevaluation and reconsideration of both the meta-theory and the constructs, and many times should cause a reopening of the phenomenological investigation of reality.

In leadership research, the usefulness of the feedback loops has been sadly lacking. Overall, construct development has remained relatively static since the initial development of the Ohio State Leadership scales. Research projects have created tests and more tests using these constructs, but a serious reevaluation of the scales and their relation to reality has been lacking. Most advances in leadership meta-theory have generally been constructed around these (and a few other) relatively unchanging and some-

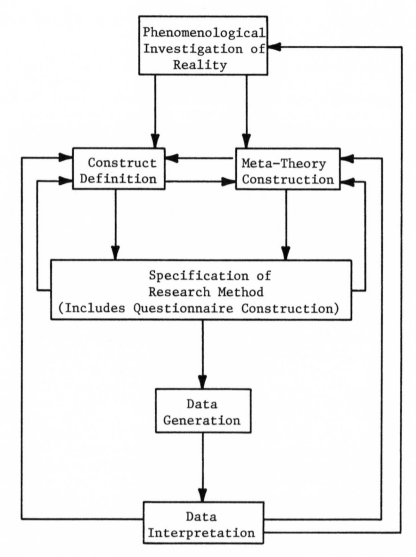

Fig. 11. A process of theory and questionnaire construction

times misunderstood sets of leadership constructs. Only recently has the adequacy of these highly used constructs been reevaluated.

In summary, it is argued that the advancement of leadership construct development has remained static for several years. If this conclusion is correct, then where do we look for the next advances in the development of leadership constructs and meta-theory? Following is one perspective that might be useful in answering this question.

A Perspective on Discovering Leadership Constructs

Virtually every theory about leadership makes certain simplifying assumptions about the interaction between the leader and the follower. I wish to propose a perspective that directly addresses some of these implicit assumptions that have occurred in most previous leadership constructs and theories. Figure 12 is a representation of the first part of that perspective. It begins by asking what are the sources of learning for individuals in organizations? In other words, what are the elements that influence a change or a maintenance of organizationally relevant behaviors?

Any source of learning can be classified according to whether it occurs *before* the follower undertakes an organizational task versus whether the source of learning occurs *after* the follower completes the task. This aspect of learning considers the time element. In addition a source of learning can be classified as to whether it originates *externally* to the follower, or whether it occurs *internally* to the follower. Leader behavior, of course, is one kind of learning source that takes place externally to the individual. Figure 12 shows these two notions in diagrammatic form. Along one dimension is the time element—whether the source of learning occurs prior or subsequent to the task. The vertical dimension addresses the issue of internal sources of learning versus external sources of learning. In this case, external sources are labeled as leader control, and internal sources of learning are labeled as self-control.

Several dimensions from meta-theories of leadership can be located on this diagram. Initiating structure refers to a set of leader behaviors that stem from the leader and occur prior to the task. Analysis of the behaviors within the initiating structure concept includes giving directions, setting goals, and/or objectives, and providing rules and policies. Consideration is also a leader behavior that occurs prior to follower task achievement, and refers to friendly and supportive interpersonal behaviors. Leaders also influence followers before the task through modeling (Bandura, 1977). That is, they personally exhibit the kind of behaviors that can influence subsequent behavior of the follower.

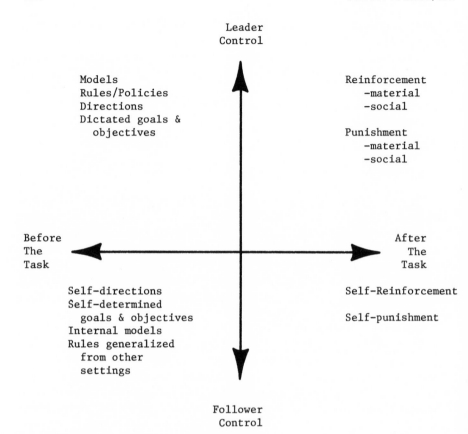

Fig. 12. Sources of follower learning

Several sources of learning occur before the task is undertaken, but stem from *within* the follower rather than from the leader. The follower can provide directions and covert goals and objectives. In addition, internal models can be generated by the follower through the use of imagery.

After the task has been accomplished by the follower, the leader has several behavioral options. First, the leader can seek to encourage the subordinate behavior through the administration of contingent reinforcers. Reinforcers may be material in the form of money, leisure time, or fringe benefits. Reinforcers can also be social in nature. A very important class of reinforcers is the contingent personal verbal recognition that a leader can provide when a task is done well. In a recent review, House and Baetz (1979, in press) have concluded that contingent positive leader reward behavior has shown larger and more consistent predictive relationships with employee performance than any other single leader behavior dimension. The leader also has the option of using aversive contingent behavior in an effort to decrease undesirable follower behaviors. Like reinforcing events, aversive events can be material (e.g., demotion, disciplinary layoff) or social in nature. Verbal reprimands are a frequently encountered supervisory behavior in many organizations. Like the leader, the follower has several options in terms of self-controlling behavior after the task. A follower can reinforce himself through self-recognition and self-praise, either verbal or covert. A follower can also invoke self-punishment subsequent to the task.

Figure 12 is incomplete in that all sources of follower learning are not represented according to this perspective. Kerr (1977) has coined the phrase "substitutes for leadership" in order to refer to non-leader sources of learning that impact on follower behavior. In a similar vein, Hunt (1975) has referred to "non-leader sources of clarity." Interestingly, these sources of learning that emanate from outside the leader-follower dyad can also be categorized as occurring before follower task achievement or after follower task achievement. Some examples might be: professional norms and practices, organizational policies and rules, non-leader behavioral models, and routine task demands. Other sources of learning can occur after the task: incentive pay systems, executive bonus systems, verbal recognition from clients and other employees, merit awards, and verbal sanctions for "rate busting" from fellow employees.

Learning from non-leader sources is important for two reasons. First, they potentially have a "main effect." That is, these factors may influence follower behavior and performance in and of themselves. But second, and of greater relevance to theories of leadership, they may have an interaction effect with both leader sources of learning, and follower sources of learning. A common way of viewing such interaction in the past has been the "contingency" approach to leadership. A contingency theory, in fact, posits some type of interaction effect, where the presence of a third non-leader variable has some moderating influence on the relationship between a first and a second variable, typically between a leader behavior and a subordinate outcome. In House's (House & Dessler, 1974) path-goal theory of leadership, for example, Initiating Structure (instrumental leadership) (a leader source of subordinate learning) is hypothesized to have a lesser effect on follower satisfaction when rules or directions for completing the task are well known. Also, role conflict is a classic case that can occur when leader-specified goals are contradictory to goals specified from non-leader sources.

What ramification does the perspective shown in Figure 12 have for theory construction in leadership? First, I would content that the perspective points out that most theories of leadership are indeed meta-theories, or middle range theories, as opposed to full theories. They typically deal with only a part of the total picture covered in Figure 12. Both House's path-goal theory of leadership and the Vroom and Yetton (1973) model deal with the interactive effects of leader sources of learning, non-leader sources of learning, and follower sources of learning. Yet, these theories do not include behaviors that occur *after* follower task achievement. Conversely, operant approaches to leadership (Sims, 1977) tend to provide an over-focus on leader-reinforcing behavior, but typically have difficulty in dealing with the question of internal sources of learning (e.g., covert goal-setting, self-reinforcement). With the exception of social learning theory (Bandura, 1977; Luthans, this volume) virtually no leadership theory directly addresses the important influence of modeling on follower behavior and performance.

What is the connection with questionnaire construction? I believe that the inadequacies of questionnaires in leadership can be traced, at least in part, to inadequacies of theory construction and to an overly narrow scope of construct development. If theories of leadership have been incomplete, if leadership constructs have been lacking, should more be expected of questionnaires? A questionnaire always reflects the adequacy, completeness, and relevancy of the theoretical antecedents. Before abandoning questionnaires as a methodology, we need to reexamine the adequacy of existing theory and leadership constructs. Questionnaires are bounded by the completeness of the theory. They can test that theory, but no more, because that is all they look for. Thus, one reason for the frustration with the boundaries of existing questionnaire methodology stems from the inadequacies of current theoretical and construct development in leadership research. For questionnaire methodology to advance and overcome this boundary, significant advancements in leadership theory and construct development must be achieved.

Internal Psychometric Adequacy of Questionnaire Measures

My theme on this issue is short and to the point. A researcher who uses questionnaire methodology must provide careful attention to the development and assessment of the internal psychometric qualities of the instrument. The recent series of reports by Schriesheim, Kerr, and colleagues (e.g., Schriesheim & Kerr, 1977), on the Ohio State leadership scales, points out the fallacy of blind acceptance of a questionnaire. Questionnaires need to be evaluated and reevaluated in many different settings by many different researchers before we can gain sufficient confidence to use these measures without a reevaluation.

Currently, I believe that no leadership questionnaire has met this test of evaluation and reevaluation, although Yukl and Nemeroff (this volume) and Sheridan (1979) have projects underway to accomplish this objective. At this time, each leadership researcher who chooses to use questionnaires must take the time to evaluate psychometric qualities such as internal validity and reliability. This evaluation is a base-line prerequisite for the use of any questionnaire in leadership research.

Objective Reality Versus Subjective Reality

Questionnaires deal with perceptual reality. Variables measured by this method have been filtered by a perceptual process. They are a viewpoint of reality from within an individual. In leadership research, questionnaires typically attempt to describe the behavior of the leader as interpreted by the follower. Let's pose some interesting questions. Do follower perceptions of leader behavior accurately reflect the objective reality of leader behavior? Are perceptual leader behavior measures more a reflection of the follower than a reflection of the leader? Does it matter? That is, is not subjective reality a more important determinant of follower behavior than objective reality? In changing leader behavior, should we focus on objective leader behavior, or should we focus on subjective perceptions of leader behavior? Just what is the connection, if any, between objective leader behavior and the follower's subjective perception of that behavior?

Murray (1938) has proposed a conceptual framework that may be useful in examining these questions. First, examine Figure 13. This simple model represents what Mahoney (1974) calls a "mediated" model of behavior. The variable X refers to some objective entity in reality. Variable Y is a cognition, a "mediating" variable. It represents the subjective representation of that objective reality. Variable Z is some end-result or outcome variable of interest.

This model has a more specific counterpart in leadership research. Variable X is some objective leader behavior. Variable Y is the follower's subjective perception of that behavior. In leadership research the value of variable Y typically is inferred through some questionnaire-based measure. Variable Z is an outcome variable—typically follower performance, follower satisfaction, or, more recently, perhaps some specific measurable follower behavior.

Murray proposed the idea of a "press" from the environment that im-

where:

    X = ..."Objective"reality
        ..."True"entity
        ..."Alpha"press

    Y = ..."Subjective"reality
        ..."Perceived"entity
        ..."Beta"press

    Z = ...End-Result
        ...Outcome

Fig. 13. Relations between Alpha press, Beta press, and End-Result variables

pacts on the individual and influences the behavior of that individual. He called the press from the *objective* reality of the environment an "Alpha" press. Murray called the *subjective* perception of that reality the "Beta" press. The idea behind Beta press is that the subjective perception of the environment is the more important antecedent of the end-result variable.

Scholars have engaged in philosophical arguments from time to time as to the relative values of Alpha press versus Beta press. For example, in organizational behavior, expectancy theory is clearly derived from the Beta press school. Conversely, operant theory is undeniably focused on Alpha press. This issue is certainly an ongoing controversy, both in general psychology and in organizational behavior, and the issue will not be resolved here. It is clear, however, that some scholars prefer to operate in the Alpha press realm, while other scholars prefer to operate in the Beta press realm. These preferences appear to be based in philosophical differences rather than any convergent objective evidence. Also, though the trend of Alpha press lines of research remaining distinct from Beta press lines of research has been unfortunate it will probably continue for some time into the future.

Figure 14a
TRADITIONAL MODEL

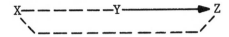

Figure 14b
LUTHANS' MODEL

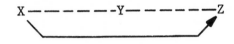

Figure 14c
FULL (OBJECTIVE/SUBJECTIVE) MODEL

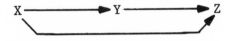

Fig. 14. Different kinds of objective/subjective leader behavior models

What about leadership research? What are the Alpha press trends and Beta press trends regarding the issue of leader-follower interactions? It is abundantly clear that questionnaire research has been well grounded in the Beta press tradition (Figure 14a). It is equally clear the empirical links between Alpha press and Beta press are obscure and have remained largely unexplored. An unfortunate neglect of the questionnaire-based leadership research is the general inattention given to external validity of questionnaire-leader behavior measures. Leadership researchers have focused almost exclusively on the Beta press/outcome relationships, and have virtually ignored the Alpha press/Beta press relationship (i.e., the external validity question).

In chapter 11, Luthans suggests that we focus entirely on the X to Z relationships (Figure 14b)—the direct connections between objective reality and the end-result variables. The rationale for this suggestion, which has some merit, is that a leader who wishes to influence the end-result variables can accomplish this end more effectively by focusing on changing the Alpha press, his own leader behavior.

I believe in a more balanced perspective. We *have made* some advances in knowledge through questionnaire research. Despite problems, the advantages of data collection convenience and generalizability are substantial and should not be ignored. Nevertheless, we do need to give much greater attention to the Alpha press aspect of leader behavior. Perhaps Luthans is correct when he suggests that the more important emphasis now should be on objective reality. Our research efforts have been out of balance. The pendulum should swing towards the Alpha press. Most of all, I believe that we should begin to investigate both *objective and subjective* aspects of leader behavior together. We need more insight about the full "X to Y to Z" (Figure 14c) model rather than more and more marginal extensions of limited parts of this model.

Conclusion

In summary, I believe that questionnaire-based methodology in leadership is neither dead nor dying. It is apparent, however, that many scholars share a frustration at the limitations and boundaries that questionnaire research has currently encountered. In order to overcome these boundaries, future leadership research that utilizes questionnaires should follow these trends.

First, the internal psychometric adequacy of any current instrument should never be accepted on faith. A base-line necessity is that the researcher must evaluate reliability and construct validity in each sample. In addition, researchers should be encouraged both to originate new measurement instruments, and to extend and develop existing instruments.

Second, questionnaires must be more adequately tied to some meta-theory, and the range of leadership constructs must be extended. The blind use of off-the-shelf leader behavior instruments without reconsideration of the underlying theoretical logic is clearly unacceptable. Questionnaire construction should parallel extensions of leadership theory and construct development.

Finally, perceptual measures of leader behavior need substantially more attention devoted to issues of external validity. Perceptual measures will *always* be a reflection of the individual follower, but to make valid prescriptive inferences, we must have greater confidence that these inferred measures of subjective reality are indeed firmly based in objective reality. In order to accomplish this end, we must institute leadership investigations that concurrently focus on *both* subjective and objective measures of leader behavior. The use of observational methods to measure leader behavior holds some potential in the pursuit of this objective.

If these trends are followed, then the use of questionnaire methodology in leadership has the potential to reemerge as a viable tool leading to further insight about leader/follower interaction. If these trends are ignored, then questionnaire methodology will continue to produce results of marginal utility for gaining new knowledge.

Part 5

Overview and Epilog

Introduction

JAMES G. HUNT AND LARS L. LARSON

This part consists first of an overview by a knowledgeable outsider with a perspective different than those in the mainstream of leadership research. Second, it includes an epilog by the editors which covers material not included in previous chapters or treated in a little different way in those chapters. The attempt is to highlight new and perhaps interesting approaches to the field and to encourage collaboration and sharing of work among researchers.

Robert Dubin provides the knowledgeable outsider's perspective in chapter 13. In addition to critiquing, from his perspective, the general directions of much of the current leadership work, he provides an intriguing list of topics that he suggests should be studied by those interested in leadership.

The overview begins with a few observations on the crosscurrents present at the symposium, in particular, the Leader/Manager distinction. His concern is with a lack of such a distinction being made by researchers. Dubin, like Moses earlier, suggests that leadership is a "rare phenomenon." He then indicates that even observational studies of managers will conclude that much of what is observed is management, not leadership.

Dubin is highly critical of the present narrow focus of leadership research. In his own words, "There may be many significant findings among the studies, but in the broad span of human affairs they are largely trivial findings because they fail to address leadership *of* organizations." He suggests that researchers need to step back and ask the question, "What are the circumstances for the enactment of leadership behaviors?" Dubin maintains that if we do that, we will find that leadership of organizations is leadership "at a distance" and that our current preoccupation with face-to-face interpersonal relationships misses much of the nature of leadership.

In his suggestions for the future development of the field of leadership, Dubin suggests that we build on some of the fundamental traditions of the past. He suggests that we examine such basic organizational problems as coordination, adaptation, conflict resolution, and organizational goals and explore the relationship of these problems to leadership behavior. To aid our understanding of what he means by the conditions under which leadership in organizations is exercised, Dubin provides eleven metaphors of leadership and suggests ways in which these metaphors can prove useful in understanding leadership behavior.

It is interesting to contrast the thrust of Dubin's overview with the research directions that are highlighted in the epilog. While many of these appear to be genuinely new, would Dubin consider them to be a continuation of the triviality he condemns? Our view is that the overview and epilog together may be seen as providing some suggestions that could move us toward the next stage of development as suggested by Levinson.

13

Metaphors of Leadership: An Overview

ROBERT DUBIN

I am not an expert on leadership. However, some knowledge of organizations and organizational behavior is claimed. It is from this perspective that I will engage in an *over*-view, not a *re*-view of the contents of this volume. One way to interpret an overview is to think of it as looking over—literally as looking beyond. It is in this sense that this overview is prepared.

Initial Observations

Two initial observations have struck me. 1) Leadership must surely mean followership. 2) Leadership is interesting to us because it occurs within organizations. Of clearly secondary importance for students of organizations is leadership expressed in informal groups, in natural groups, and in temporary groups. Yet, in this volume these simple points seem to slide by unnoticed and ignored to the peril of clarity in presenting and interpreting results.

Another observation: 3) The ease with which the concept of *leadership* is treated as a synonym for *management* and *supervision*. This is amazing. My knowledge of organizational behavior has led me to the conclusion that effective organizations can be managed and supervised and *not* led, while some ineffective organizations can be led into their difficulties without the benefit of management and supervision. Moses's observation in chapter 3 that *only* 20 to 25 percent of the 200,000 people who have gone through the A.T.&T. assessment centers had leadership potential is delightful. I asked him privately, "Of those with the potential for leadership, what proportion actually utilized this potential in their work?" Moses grinned in response, and it is not hard to understand why.

This leads to my first conclusion. Leadership is a rare phenomenon, not a common one in organizational behavior. Those who propose to *observe* leadership behavior as their methodology for study to gain knowledge (an orientation I applaud), will find that tracking managers to record their every behavior will produce relatively little data on leadership. If one records everything observable, one will be overwhelmed by data, as Argyris remarked earlier. The first cut at such data mass will consist of sorting it into two piles: the small stack of leadership acts, and the very large pile of acts of managing and supervising.

Dimensionality of Leadership Phenomena

I would like to begin my "looking beyond" by invoking the style of the late great practitioner, philosopher, and theorist of organizations, Chester Barnard (who, by the way, is never once mentioned in the previous chapters). In the mode he adopted (*The Functions of the Executive*) I want to ask, What are the circumstances for the enactment of leadership behaviors? Another way to state this issue is to follow Luthans's proposal which is to analyze the *functions* of leadership.

I agree with Argyris that there is a major problem in developing our knowledge about leadership. In chapter 4, he focuses this problem on the limitations of the research methodologies we employ. In my view, the central problem has to do with the reluctance, or inability, to specify the dimensionality of the leadership phenomena. We have even succeeded in confusing "leadership" with other social behaviors as my predecessor in this "overview" role, Miner, did when he boldly proposed to substitute "control" for the concept of leadership (Miner, 1975). We have failed in handling the dimensionality problem by focusing on some of the wrong dimensions of leadership, and ignoring others. Let me provide examples of both kinds of failures.

One major problem that has preoccupied American social science has been the formulation of leadership as an interpersonal phenomenon. This has been a major shortcoming in the study of leadership. This should become clear in what follows. There are face-to-face relations between a leader and followers. But it should also be evident that there are situations of leadership which do not involve face-to-face relations with followers. In the modern world these are by far the most frequent leadership situations. Furthermore, there are many face-to-face relations between superiors and subordinates that *do not* involve leadership in the ongoing interaction.

The study of leadership has been so overwhelmingly concerned with a leader in personal relationship with *some* followers that we simply have ignored a broad range of very important leadership phenomena. Incidentally, it should also be pointed out that it is now old fashioned to talk about leadership and followership since the leader in some idealistic formulations is expected to be a follower of his followers in the spirit of democratic governance. If this conclusion causes puzzlement I must refer one to practitioners of the arcane art of organizational development for an explanation. In my limited understanding, some organizational change efforts tend to be directed at an image of the leader as an authoritarian personality, following the influential work of Adorno (1950).

When we distinguish between leader behaviors in social relations (including voluntary groups) and leadership in formal organizations (with special emphasis on work organizations), quite different models emerge. The classic studies of Bales (1950) on interaction process analysis, and of Moreno (1951) on sociometric structure, are relevant to small, face-to-face groups. Most of the subsequent work on the interpersonal aspects of leadership behaviors can be traced to their influences. On the other hand, Machiavelli advising the Prince on the governance of states, made many recommendations for leadership acts that ignore, or lie outside, the range of face-to-face relations.

I believe that the primary emphasis of the work in this volume is on leadership in face-to-face relationships. I will boldly propose: there may be many significant findings among the studies, but in the broad span of human affairs they are largely trivial findings because they fail to address leadership *of* organizations.

The leadership *of* organizations is first and foremost leadership at a distance. Any sizable modern organization, and the significant ones are large, have functionaries called leaders who are never in face-to-face contact with the vast majority of the remaining members. At best, such leaders are symbolically known to the members of the organization. This dimension of the leadership phenomenon is scarcely explored in the vast literature on the subject, with notable exceptions, for example, Selznick (1957) and House (1977). By focusing on leaders' interpersonal relations with followers we have simply chosen a relatively trivial dimension while ignoring a major dimension of "leadership at a distance."

To take an example where we have worked with an important dimension of leadership but chose the wrong aspect upon which to focus, we need only look at the vast array of studies of leaders as individuals. Most of us would agree that trait analysis has not produced much enlightenment. It is, therefore, startling and heartening to see that Fiedler's Stogdill Award presentation in chapter 2 examines how intelligence relates to leadership behavior. This informal announcement was particularly notable since Fiedler is the father of a contingency model of leader behavior which concludes that "it takes different blokes to turn the spokes," and hence we should not be surprised to find little consistency in the personal traits of leaders. Fiedler reports correlations in his presentation. I can only draw upon crude impressions of a relatively small sample of leaders to suggest other traits that seem to characterize leadership behaviors. Leaders are persons of far above average energy level. I have never encountered a lazy, lethargic, or lugubrious leader. Leaders can concentrate personal attention with extraordinary intensity when considering an issue or topic. These may be worthy aspects of leader traits to examine along with Fiedler's reexamination of intelligence. (It should be understood I am not saying that a high energy individual who can concentrate attention will be a leader. I am only asserting that these may be characteristics that appear in a much higher than chance proportion of leaders.)

These examples should at least illustrate some of the issues in determining the dimensionality of leadership of organizations. Before we conclude that there is nothing we can do about improving our efforts to understand leadership, it should be added that there is a substantial set of problems to be examined.

The Universal Problems of Organizations

As a setting for understanding leadership behavior let us turn to a brief examination of "universal" problems of organizational systems. In this I follow the scheme proposed by Parsons (1951) which he developed to analyze social systems in general. These problems are endemic in all organizations. They emerge in the life history of the organization singly or in combination. They are problems in the sense that the functioning organization devotes organizational energy to their solution, in addition to the energy expended in the direct production of goods and services.

The first problem is a very simple and obvious one—it is the coordination and integration of the parts of an organization. Coordination and integration is evident in all work-flow systems, in recruiting to fill vacancies, in inventory management, and in production planning, just to mention a few obvious examples. We pride ourselves on the applied science revealed in the rational divisions of labor in our organizational systems. We are always mindful of the fact that as the functions of an organization are divided and segregated from each other in sections and departments, there is automatically created a need to coordinate the relations among these parts and insure their respective integration within the total system.

Coordination and integration is an endemic feature of all organizations. However detailed the control systems, and however willing the participants, there is need on behalf of the organization as a whole, that the functions of coordination and integration be fulfilled as a central activity of management. I would urge that it is one of the characteristics of leadership constantly to evaluate the coordinating and integrating functions and mechanisms of an organization and to introduce the necessary changes that will improve their outcomes.

A second area that requires attention as a problem of organizations is that of adaptation. This is to be understood as adaptation to changes that are generated within the organization as well as changes generated in what we now fashionably call the turbulent environment. We have come to recognize this adaptive function under the heading of "contingency management" or "contingency leadership." The fact of the matter is that all organizations, but particularly work organizations, are systems attempting to maintain stability under conditions where stability is at best short-lived or a myth. I would urge that it is one of the functions of leadership to recognize the conditions affecting the organization that require adaptation on its part, and then to provide or at least select and/or approve the kinds of viable alternatives that will make the adaptations effective.

A third general characteristic of all organizations is that they are the arena of repeated conflict. This conflict is, in only a minority of circumstances, the consequence of deliberate individual behavior with the intent to produce conflict. Organizations are not typically composed of malevolent persons out to defeat less virile individuals in mortal conflict while carrying out the business of the organization. Conflict is far more "natural" than that. It is conflict that arises from differential points of view and differential objectives of those who collectively engage in a complex division of labor. Industry executives need hardly be told that sales personnel and manufacturing specialists very seldom see eye to eye—stability and long runs in manufacturing are an operational desideratum, while special delivery schedules and meeting customer specifications are what make selling easier. These expectations are antithetical—they need resolution. But what is most important in the resolution is that the losing party be willing to return to the battle the very next time with the same vigor in pursuing its functional objectives. Leadership skills are required in resolving such functional conflicts so that the losers do not feel permanently defeated, and can, therefore, retain their belief in their own special functional perspective. This example is only illustrative of a wide range of such conflicts that are built into all organizations having a significant division of labor among their system parts.

Again I would urge that it is one of the functions of leadership to recognize conflict for what it is. Further, it is one of the continual demands on leaders that they resolve such functionally grounded conflicts by taking decisions that bring the conflict to a halt for the time being. In addition, it is part of the wisdom of leadership to recognize that the same or similar conflict will arise again and that the resolving decision may fly in the face of precedent—consistency in resolving functional conflicts may not be a virtue (does this suggest another meaning for "contingency leadership"?).

The fourth universal organizational problem is to keep the goal(s) of the organization clear for its participants, and where necessary, select and legitimate new goals. For example, a professor may easily fail to give a clear answer to the query about the goals of the university. Are they to pass on the collective wisdom and knowledge of the past, are they to add new knowledge, are they to socialize the young, or are they simply to amuse and bemuse healthy young adults who might very well be spending their time more profitably at work? From time to time it becomes a very central function of organizational leaders to mark out clearly the goals of the organization for all participants to recognize as meaningful for their own organizationally relevant behaviors. When new goals become functionally necessary it is often the signal for the replacement of present leaders.

The skills of leading organizations have to be related to the system problems with which leaders deal in order that we may understand leadership. Very few studies of leaders of organizations seem to deal with these central problems as their analytical focus for understanding leadership. Does leadership really have anything to do with the management of coordination and integration, with the adaptation of the system to its internal and external environments, with the resolution of functional conflict, and with the clarification of goals? One will have to search long and hard in the literature of modern social science to find examples of studies dealing with these issues. A person is often better served by going to biographies and autobiographies of those who have occupied positions of organization leadership to discover what a leader does in handling these four systems problems. Much of the time the leadership behaviors in resolving these endemic systems problems do *not* involve a face-to-face social relationship with subordinates.

Some Metaphors of Leadership

I now shift attention to some of the characteristic conditions under which leadership of organizations is exercised. This is an illustrative rather than an exhaustive listing. The format for presenting these circumstances of leadership is distinctive. They are chosen to set them forth in the form of metaphors. Popular metaphors often grasp a truth that initially eludes a more dispassionate and scientific approach. Perhaps these metaphors might move us toward extracting their underlying truth to the benefit of our knowledge about leaders. The following eleven metaphors (and there are many more that readily come to mind) seem to probe significant dimensions of leadership.

"The Buck Stops Here" Metaphor. This metaphor asserts that somewhere within the organization there will be found a point of final decision, that this organizational position is well known, and that the individual occupying that position is willing to grasp the buck and do something with it. We have increasingly attempted in modern American organizations to make the stopping place for the buck a committee rather than an individual. But even a committee needs its conclusions legitimized by an appropriate authority holder. It has always interested me to discover that the stopping place for the buck is not always the top position in an organization. Indeed, one way to know that leadership is being exercised is to find those positions within an organization where bucks do stop. There I am confident you will find someone who is exercising leadership on behalf of the organization. By the same token, of course, the buck passer, whose passing of the buck onward may be perfectly legitimate, is clearly avoiding the opportunity to exercise leadership.

"Batting a Thousand" Metaphor. It is one of the implicit expectations, to which leaders often subscribe themselves, that they will "bat a 1,000" on the decisions they make. Clearly, this is a humanly impossible self-expectation, and one that is seldom believed, although widely held by followers. For the leader, this can generate deceptive behavior designed to ensure the appearance of having a batting average of 1,000. For a highly respected leader, or one who is loved by his followers, there is the fascinating phenomenon of followers who willingly make the "boss look good," even when he has fouled out. What greater accolade could a leader desire or receive from his followers than this kind of sub rosa correction of his errors? This is a widespread phenomenon in organizations and represents what may be called the "Silent Conspiracy for Good" that is one of the most profoundly effective mechanisms for making an organization run well. We know almost nothing systematically about this feature of leadership.

"Wisdom versus Expertise" Metaphor. In our sophisticated technological era we seem, on the surface, more readily to honor expertise than wisdom. It was the British political scientist Laski (1930) who long ago pointed out that wisdom and expertise are complementary necessities in organizations. In his analysis it turned out that organizational leaders were more likely to possess wisdom than expertise. Does this tell us something about the role of leadership in organizations and about the limitations of experts? Does this illuminate the probability or improbability of converting experts into wise leaders as they move up the promotion ladders of organizations, progress-

ing within areas of narrow specialization until they need to be promoted into general management, if they are to be promoted any further? These issues are intriguing since the crisis of recruitment for senior management seems to be a shortage of individuals with wisdom.

"The N of One" Metaphor. Still another feature of leaders is that this individual has a self-perception, and is so viewed by others, as occupying a class whose membership is exactly one. It is the burden of the chapter in this volume by Stein et al. (chapter 8) that there is an emergent process by which the leader of a group comes to be distinguished from the other group members, and comes to be the sole occupant of the leadership class. Their study is an important attempt to tease out the processes by which this happens. Surely, this exclusivity, when acknowledged both by the leader and the organizational members, must generate significant barriers to the process and substance of interaction between leader and followers. The barrier exists from both sides. The barrier may lead to deferential behavior toward the leader. It may also generate arrogance and authoritarianism on the part of the leader, but not necessarily inevitably. A search of the leadership literature reveals a paucity of analysis and insight about the barrier phenomenon in leadership behaviors (Barnard, 1948, dealt with this phenomenon in another of his contributions).

"The Lone Ranger" Metaphor. There is perhaps greater recognition today than ever before of the lonesomeness surrounding leadership positions in organizations. The awesome burden and remoteness of the United States presidency has often been noted. We have almost no studies of this phenomenon. Jackson (1977) has given a very insightful introspective account of the loneliness of his own experience as a leader (this autobiographical methodology strongly recommends itself for precisely these kinds of analytical problems). What are the conditions that create the lone-ranger status of the leader? Is it that the leader fails to seek out advice and counsel of others? Or could we mean that the leader becomes the lone ranger because what the leader must do on significant occasions is assume responsibility for decisions made, or at least legitimated in his/her name? There is always accompanying a decision a nagging concern that it may be wrong, or mediocre, and sometimes even brilliant. Is the lonesomeness of the leader the need ultimately to satisfy the severest critic of all—the self?

"The Confidant" Metaphor. We know of key individuals associated with historic leaders who played the role of confidant to the leader. Colonel House in relation to President Wilson and Harry Hopkins in the entourage of President Roosevelt come to mind immediately as examples. Often there is ascribed a sinister role to the confidant as guardian of access to the leader, or perhaps even wielding Rasputin-like control over the leader. A search of the leadership literature provides almost no insight into the role

of the confidant in the development and maintenance of leaders. It could very well turn out, for example, that the intimate interpersonal world of the leader vis-à-vis other organizational members is severely limited by virtue of the barriers separating them. A confidant, who very often is not in the organization being led, can provide to the leader the opportunities to be wholly human and react emotionally and even irrationally to the exigencies of office without jeopardizing the leader's hold on that office. Thus, the office of leadership may be singularly devoid of opportunities to be "just human," opportunities that are provided by interacting with a confidant.

"The Chosen One" Metaphor. A fair amount of literature seems to support the notion that some groups "make" their own leaders. There emerges a group consensus that selects out a given individual from among its members as the group leader. Such a leader may be the most characteristic member of the group, summarizing in his/her characteristics the features of all the group members. It has been suggested that this quality of being chosen places limitations on the directions in which such a leader can take the group. Presumably a leader who is chosen by group consensus must continually cater to that consensus to retain the leadership position. Within organizations such leaders are often designated "informal leaders" because of their special origin. It is one of the old saws of management lore that informal leaders make good organizational leaders. I have serious doubt that that is an accurate conclusion but its assessment is difficult since there is little literature to illuminate the issue.

"The Charismatic Leader" Metaphor. The charismatic leader, unlike "the chosen one" is accorded the position of leadership by followers because of distinctiveness from, rather than similarity to, the group members. In a small face-to-face group a charismatic leader may be the sociometric "star." In a mass organization the charismatic leader has symbolically attributed to him/her extraordinary abilities or virtues that set apart the individual from the mass. It was precisely this consideration that led Weber (1947) to conclude that leaders with charisma need more than a belief in their own extraordinary character—they also need to have this belief shared by a follower group.

This charisma (literally, the gift of grace) endows the leader with an aura of infallibility, of being above mere mortal error and sin. A charismatic leader of a work organization, with its dedication to rationality in operations, may be most effective under trying circumstances ("the difficult we do immediately, the impossible takes a little longer") by being able to mobilize intense mass emotional energy devoted to the work of the organization. We should not forget, however, that this emotional pitch, and its dedication to the charismatic leader, may prove highly dysfunctional to the organization. Schism in religious organizations results when a charismatic leader disputes the congregation's goals and leads his followers into a new church. Schisms in business organizations have exhibited similar phenomena when a charismatic leader takes his loyal followers out of a parent company and sets up a competitor. House's work on charismatic leadership may be a place to begin (House, 1977).

"The Office Makes the Man" Metaphor. It is one of the delights of organizational participation to discover that an individual thrust into a position turns out to be a leader in that office. Usually there was no previous clue that such would be the case in spite of the *post hoc* "I told you so's." The best we can usually conclude about this phenomenon is to declare that the office has made the man. This seems improbable unless we have an image of the individual as being malleable throughout the active years (a position that is associated with the work of Argyris, for example). If the office really does make the man, then the man must be made over to fit the office. This becomes a profound conclusion about adult socialization that needs significantly more investigation. Dr. Patinka's presentation in chapter 3, although concluding that the individual's background characteristics were the best predictors of success as a manager, also indicated that present managers were the standard against which such success is measured. Copying the role model provided by present managers may well be an important mechanism by which the man is made over to fit the office.

"The Zone of Indifference" Metaphor. It is exceedingly trite to suggest that a leader needs followers. A leader in an organizational setting may have hundreds or thousands of individuals who respond as subordinates or followers without any personal contact with the leader. Our current models of this relationship are polarized around an authoritarian model and a participative leadership model. Both of these models are likely to have rare empirical counterparts. The most common linkage between followers and leaders who are distant from each other is that of compliance, acceptance, and a belief in the legitimacy of what the leader does when leading. Compliance is touched on in chapters 5 and 14. Much of the work dealing with it is directed at establishing that democratic leadership types produce the relatively greatest amount of compliance with a decision and commitment to it on the part of subordinates. Participation in making decisions that affect the individual's subsequent performance in the organization does increase commitment to it, as well as acceptance of it.

However, there is a wide range of decisions that from the standpoint of individuals' working behavior remotely, if at all, affects them. Where then does acceptance or compliance come from whether or not the individual participates in the decision? Perhaps we have to go back to Barnard's great insight about the "zone of indifference" of subordinates, to understand this phenomenon. Barnard concluded that there is a wide range of acceptance and compliance with the decisions of the leader. Because of the broad division of labor within organizations, no single decision is likely to have an immediate impact on the daily operations of more than a small proportion of the total members of the organization. Hence, the vast majority will be compliant because of their relative indifference to the consequences of a given decision.

Their compliance also rests on their belief in the legitimacy of the leader's action, and a belief in the competence of the leader to take such action. This, of course, suggests a corollary metaphor of leadership behavior—divide and conquer. The "divide" part of the metaphor suggests that the leader be aware of the fact that most individual decisions on behalf of the organization impact directly on only a small portion of the total participants. The "conquer" part of the aphorism suggests that no single series of decisions should impact the same segment of the organization, lest it generate possible antagonisms. The zone of indifference, overlapping as it does for the sum of all groups in the organization, will provide a substantial base of compliant and acceptant responses from the organizational participants. We simply have failed to study this phenomenon in the forty years since Barnard called attention to it.

"Power Corrupts" Metaphor. Lord Acton declared that power corrupts, and absolute power corrupts absolutely. One of the great points of consensus in the literature on leadership is that leaders are believed to have power. Was Lord Acton then providing us with the inevitable conclusion that leaders become corrupt as a natural consequence of occupying their positions? The meaning of "corrupt" is not so much the stealing, chicanery, and shady business practices that are daily documented for business leaders in the *Wall Street Journal*. It is moral corruption that is the focus of attention—the exploitation of leadership positions for personal and private aggrandizement, or vindictive attack on subordinates and others who are relatively defenseless. It is a matter of some note that there are corrupt leaders. It is equally notable that there are noncorrupt and even incorruptible leaders. It is worthy of our enterprise that we give some attention to this issue, at least to study the incidence of corruption, and perhaps, even to devise organizational forms and processes to minimize corruption if it is found to be widespread.

We can put these metaphors to use in a way that further illuminates the nature of leadership of organizations. The concluding section of this analysis addresses the ideas underlying these metaphors to universal organizational problems.

Leadership Metaphors and Organizational Problems

Here some bare bones suggestions are made to illustrate how the meta-phoric ideas may prove useful in understanding leadership behaviors. This treatment is intended to be suggestive. It is, therefore, an incomplete and even sketchy discussion designed to encourage more thorough and pene-trating efforts by others.

Integration and Coordination. When discovered, the need to improve in-tegration and coordination usually has limited time horizons. It is a here and now problem. Clearly then, if leadership is exercised to solve such a problem, the buck has to stop and a solution has to be generated. Fur-thermore, the solution is expected to be an effective one since those por-tions of the organization needing better integration and coordination have a high awareness of the present inadequacies in these regards. Hence, the leader's actions may take on the appearance of being appropriate—other-wise the problem may be seen as persisting. Repeated perceptions that suc-ceeding actions by the leader appear to be appropriate may give the per-formance the aura of a batting average of 1,000.

Where integration and coordination is limited to a few segments of the organization, the leader can depend on a wide zone of indifference among most organization members to provide considerable latitude in working out solutions. This very latitude may provide opportunities for corruption of the leader since the solution of integration and coordination problems often involve moving functions from one organizational location to another which is the essence of "empire building" when such moves build the lead-er's particular empire.

An interesting counter to the possibility of power corrupting the lead-er may be the "chosen one" source of the leader. Such a leader may be ac-ceptable precisely because he understands the historic systems of the organization's coordination and integration. Leader actions to resolve problems of coordination and integration would be referenced to the his-torical practices. Consequently, departures from historical precedent would be unlikely, and the leader's resolution of such problems would not be judged corrupt or corrupting.

Adaptation. Two special characteristics of leader skills are related to the adaptations made by organizations: Insight is required to recognize the dis-turbing environmental conditions, and specific knowledge of the organiza-tion is required to know the possible range of adaptive responses of which it is capable. Regardless of the sources of this insight and knowledge, they may come together in a single individual, who, in the very possession of this combination may become an "n of one." When such an individual is a lead-er who seizes the insight and knowledge to propose appropriate adaptations, the responsibility for such proposals may generate a feeling of being isolated and a "lone ranger." This kind of leadership behavior is often more obviously a display of wisdom than the application of expertise. Insofar as there is a significant followership to make the proposed adaptation operative, the leader may have his wisdom acknowledged, and it becomes one basis for charisma.

Conflict Resolution. In the resolution of functional conflict within the organization the recurrent nature of this problem mitigates against the leader forming permanent alliances with any single organizational faction. To do so would inevitably lead to charges of favoritism by the leader in resolving conflicts. Hence, in instances of conflict the leader is driven into a "lone ranger" position in the role of adjudicating the conflicts. In this very isolation will arise the need for a confidant to whom the leader may reveal his private reactions and evaluations of the contending parties and issues in conflict. To reveal these personal evaluations and reactions to the contending parties would undermine their belief in the legitimacy and objectivity of the leader. The resolution of the intra-organizational conflict is a "judgment call," and as with a referee in a ball game, there has to be some position where the conflict comes to rest or the buck stops, and the call is made.

Of particular importance in conflict resolution is its tendency to be shifted upward in the organization. It is not likely then that individuals promoted to higher office may have experience in regularly resolving conflict before attaining that office. Indeed, they are more likely to have more frequently been parties to such conflicts rather than the source of their resolution. A display of skill in conflict resolution at that advanced stage of a career may give rise to the happy conclusion that the office has made the man, solely because he has never before been observed to display such skill.

Finally, it should be observed that parties to intra-organizational conflict may believe they have large stakes involved. The attempt to influence a favorable decision, by whatever means, may become the basis for seeking or succeeding to corrupt the leader.

Goal Clarification. The most abstract and infrequent function of organizational leaders is to clarify present goals and develop new ones. Most organizations can readily continue to operate without goal clarification, although we usually label that condition "muddling through." Organizational goals have the character of being directional rather than end points. ("We will make a profit this year," not necessarily, "We will make a $50,000 profit this year by producing this new product.")

Given these features of organizational goals and leaders' episodic concern with them, there is a large element of choice as to whether the leader will enact the goal clarification role. This very act of choosing to focus on goals, and the choice of particular goals to emphasize, burdens the leader with the lone ranger responsibility of whether it was a good choice, well timed. Since goals are general and tend to be organization-wide in their import, there is likely to be a broad and complementing set of zones of indifference that by their sheer magnitude can kill the effectiveness of the goal clarification, or produce an uncommitted acceptance. Should goal clarification prove to be inspirational for organizational members, the leader may be acclaimed for his/her wisdom, and be anointed with charisma for this display of wisdom.

This chapter is an attempt to be constructively critical in addressing the subject of leadership of organizations. We need a strong infusion of knowledge and understanding of this complex phenomenon. Perhaps among these observations there may be some that spark an interest patiently to contribute to our knowledge of leadership.

14

Toward Transition to a New Stage of Development: An Epilog

JAMES G. HUNT AND LARS L. LARSON

We have argued that the previous chapters in this book address a number of crosscurrents in the field. Now let's go beyond these and look at other current work which may help in moving us toward the transition to the next stage of development in leadership research.

We will do this by taking a brief look at some sixty studies in various stages of development from conception to recently published results. Information concerning these studies was obtained from summary questionnaires completed by those working in the area and from materials available to the authors from presentations at professional meetings, personal solicitations, and the like. While this sampling of work is not exhaustive it is believed to be reasonably representative of much of what is happening in the study of leadership today. Where appropriate, we link this discussion with various aspects of previous chapters. Taken as a whole, the previous portions of the book, along with the discussion presented here should impart the flavor of most of the emerging trends in the field.

That flavor is conveyed by grouping material together which emphasizes a given theme. Of course, many of these studies focus on other themes as well. However, the themes emphasized here are considered to be the most important for our purposes.

It is also important to note that the present treatment, while something more than an annotated bibliography, is not a comprehensive, critical literature review, nor an attempt at theoretical integration. The material is described in just enough detail to convey its general thrust. Findings are emphasized more heavily for some contributions than others, depending upon the extent to which they are reported in the cited material and their contribution to the theme being emphasized.

Since the contributions were obtained to illustrate emerging trends, they are in various stages of development. Some of them are completed studies, others are in-process studies, and some are in the preliminary planning stage. Thus the work reported here has undergone less uniform screening than that typically found in referred journals. While the screening is less uniform, the inclusion of this material allows for earlier communication than would exclusive reliance on journal articles. Where appropriate the material is related back to earlier published material.

With these things in mind we can now look at the general categories which have been used to classify the themes. These are: 1) recent literature reviews, 2) a focus on some conceptual and methodological considerations, 3) congruence or fit approaches, 4) emphasis on process, 5) reinforcement or operant approaches, 6) power influence and attribution, 7) examples of behavioral criterion variables, 8) emergent leadership, and 9) some extensions to currently emphasized approaches.

The first of these topic areas sets the stage for those remaining. The second examines some conceptual and methodological considerations that have implications for the field in general. The remaining topics address specific kinds of models or variables that are receiving attention.

Recent Literature Reviews

The most recent and lengthy review of the leadership literature is by House and Baetz (1979, in press) and was briefly touched upon by Sims (chapter 12). That review, in addition to one by Schriesheim and Kerr (1977), Hunt, Osborn, and Schriesheim (1978), and the content included in a book by McCall and Lombardo (1978a), not only help set the stage for the remaining topics but provide perspective for the earlier chapters. We concentrate on the House and Baetz review here.

That review starts by addressing the importance of leadership as a separate construct from other more general measures of influence. House and Baetz then derive a definition of leadership which justifies its existence as a separate construct. This definition then serves to focus the topics chosen for discussion.

These topics start with a reconsideration of trait theory. And like some of the work reported in this volume House and Baetz emphasize its resurgence and point out some new directions such resurgence might take. They then spend a considerable number of pages on various aspects of leader behavior and some key determinants of leader behavior. Here, experimental findings concerned with task and socio-emotional behaviors and field findings relating to consideration and initiating structure are treated. Also, experimental and field work bearing on participative decision making are reviewed. The authors then review a number of individual and situational determinants of leader behavior. These range from a predisposition toward dominance to the leader's role in the social structure.

The remainder of the review is then devoted to a number of currently discussed theories of leadership. Specifically these are: 1) Hollander's (1960) idiosyncratic theory, 2) Fiedler's contingency theory (Fiedler & Chemers, 1974), 3) path-goal theory (House & Dessler, 1975; House & Mitchell, 1974), 4) Vroom and Yetton's (1973) decision-making theory, 5) House's (1977) charismatic theory, 6) Calder's (1977) attribution theory, 7) operant conditioning theory (Mawhinney & Ford, 1977; Scott, 1977; Sims, 1977), and 8) other theories (including the work of Graen and his associates, e.g., Graen & Cashman, 1975).

While there have been other reviews covering much of this material, the greatest strength of this review appears to lie in the insights which the authors bring in interpreting and integrating the findings. They intersperse suggestions for future research as they discuss the various topic areas. In addition, they devote separate sections to new research directions for trait research, Fiedler's contingency theory and path-goal theory. They also, as does this volume, heavily emphasize research thrusts devoted to additional leader behaviors and emergent leadership.

A Focus on Some Conceptual and Methodological Considerations

The first focus here is on the conceptualization and measurement of the behavior of those occupying a leadership role.[1] It thus echoes the theme so strongly emphasized in part 3 of this volume and also addressed in the previously discussed literature reviews. The second focus is on simulation as a methodology for investigating leadership in complex settings.

Behavior

A review of studies covering managerial work (McCall, Morrison, & Hannan, 1978) serves to lay the groundwork for much of the other material. That review covers diary and observational studies of managerial work

---

[1] As indicated earlier, this perspective focuses on the total range of behavior involved in the leadership role. Thus, it goes beyond simply concentrating on those interpersonal influence variables so often used in studying leadership.

in all its different forms. The authors find that there are ten different characteristics of managerial work that are consistently supported by the studies reviewed (e.g., managers are busy, a manager's work is fragmented, a manager's work is primarily oral, etc.). The relative strengths and weaknesses of interviews, surveys, diaries, and observational data-gathering techniques are also discussed. Finally, several areas requiring more research are highlighted.

Interest leading to McCall and associates' review also lead to the development of a survey instrument to measure managerial work using Mintzberg's (1973) ten managerial roles which were developed observationally. Questionnaires based on 2,655 usable responses from six managerial levels and eight functions in a large manufacturing organization were analyzed. The leader, liaison, monitor, spokesman, entrepreneur, and resource allocator scales showed good convergent and discriminant validity. The other four roles failed to survive the analysis. The final scales were then analyzed as a function of organizational level and function. Not surprisingly, a number of these relationships appeared to be relatively complex, that is, some were curvilinear in nature.

Mintzberg's categories and multiple data gathering techniques also serve as the basis of a study of United States Navy civilian executives (all civil service employees of the Navy in GS 16–18 grades) being conducted by the Navy Personnel Research and Development Center in San Diego (Broedling & Lau, 1979). Interviewing, observation, diaries, and survey instruments are being used to obtain the data. In addition to role behaviors, data covering a number of other job related aspects are being obtained.

The use of Mintzberg's categories and modifications of his observational technique are also reported by Larson, Bussom, and Vicars (1978) and Vicars, Bussom, and Larson (1979) in an in-depth study of 7 school superintendents and 10 police executives representing over 800 hours of observation.

Two other contributions of considerable interest here come from the political science area and are concerned with what they call "at a distance techniques." These are techniques which involve analysis without interpersonal interaction with the individual being studied. The first of these contributions (Frank, 1978) is a concept paper on studying political or quasi-political elites. In a discussion of measurement, the author treats a number of different content analysis approaches which can be used on speeches, videotapes, and documents to provide measures of personality, behaviors, and "psychopolitical state" data. While the major emphasis here is on measurement, Frank's paper is also interesting because of its emphasis on the importance of developing situational paradigms and models of political behavior in studying political leaders. In this, then, he reflects views consistent with those of current organizational behavior leadership researchers.

The second political science paper (Hermann, 1978) assessed the personal characteristics of the current Soviet decision-making Politburo. Fifty 250-word units of each of these individuals were selected from speeches/interviews during the 1970–76 period. These were content analyzed to assess eight personal characteristics (e.g., ethnocentrism, need for power, conceptual complexity, task vs. interpersonal leadership orientation, etc.). Comparisons were then made with other heads of state for a number of these variables.

There are at least a couple of points worth emphasizing from these two contributions. First, is their application of quantifiable and relatively rigorous techniques to the study of leaders of great public interest (heads of state and the like). This provides the potential for adding much to the clinical analyses of those such as Barber (1977) and Burns (1978). Second, is the potential extension of this approach to the study of other kinds of organizational leaders.

Still another contribution concerns the SYMLOG (SYstematic Multiple Level Observation of Groups) technique developed by Bales and his associates (Bales, Cohen, & Williamson, 1979, in press). It integrates elements from Lewinian field theory, psychoanalytic theory, social interaction theory (including Bales, 1950, 1970), earlier interaction process analysis, social psychological cognitive consistency theory, and the like. These serve as the base for observational and questionnaire approaches to tapping behaviors of group members including leaders. These have been developed using laboratory groups and small group organizational work teams. The authors indicate potential applicability of this work to a broad range of settings. In its combination of observation and questionnaire techniques, and theoretical grounding, SYMLOG appears to be consistent with a number of points emphasized in part 4 of this book.

A final contribution here is an investigation of Fiedler's LPC measure (Downey, Kirkeide, & Shiflett, 1978). While there have been many of these, this investigation is especially timely in that it attempts to deal with a number of issues raised in earlier work and in recent reviews. Essentially it was found that LPC was multidimensional with from four to five subdimensions. It was also found that in selecting a least preferred co-worker some subsets of items were more relevant in that selection than others. The authors interpret their findings as calling into question Fiedler's theoretical interpretation of LPC and argue that alternative measures for classifying leader types are needed.

Simulations

It may be argued that if we are to understand leadership within a complex organizational context, simulation may be necessary to provide a means for establishing and unraveling the myriad potential relationships. With this concern and the advent of computer based management games and the like, it is surprising that more leadership work based on complex simulations is not reported in the literature. Two contributions which do emphasize a complex simulation are considered here. The first of these (McCall & Lombardo, 1978b) treats the development of a simulation called Looking Glass along with some preliminary results. That simulation is designed to provide a vehicle for the study of managers/leaders as they function in a complex organizational setting. Unlike most simulations, which are used almost exclusively for training purposes, this one is designed for research purposes as well. Its developers are now using it for hypothesis generation concerning what managers do. These data are being placed in a data bank so that the simulation can be used for hypothesis-testing purposes in the future.

The second study involving a complex simulation is reported by Storm (1978). That simulation is designed to investigate the impact of leader behavior, decision-making style, and group strategy over several time periods on gross profit, market share, and decision-making consistency. Moderators are size, group composition, participation, and previous-period profit and market share. The subjects are managers representing a number of different industries in the Netherlands.

The potential contributions which simulations can make to the study of leadership in dynamic, complex organizations have been emphasized. A different type of simulation such as one done more than a decade ago (Kaczka & Kirk, 1967) also appears to have much to offer. That simulation used a large-scale computer model which integrated an empirically based model of work groups and managers with a behavioral theory of the firm. The model was then used to investigate a number of organizational and leadership hypotheses. The trick in a simulation such as this is to be able to generate mathematical relationships upon which to base a model. Kaczka and Kirk show some ways in which this might be done using previously gathered real world data from a data bank. The data base now being generated in the Looking Glass simulation also offers the potential for this kind of hypothesis testing.

Congruence or Fit Approaches

The notion of congruence or fit among variables has been heavily emphasized in previous symposium books and implicitly underlies contingency organization and leadership approaches (Osborn, Hunt, & Jauch, 1980, in press). The contributions in this section explicitly treat such a fit as an important consideration. The first of these consists of two papers based on laboratory studies conducted in Australia (O'Brien & Harary, 1977; O'Brien & Kabanoff, 1978). These authors hypothesize that leader satisfaction and group performance are a function of the fit between leader need for control and participation and the opportunity for satisfying these needs within the group structure. The rationale is that, as the discrepancy between needs and structure increases, leader motivation will decrease and there will be an increase in the leader's effort to change his role to get a better fit. These efforts should divert the leader from concentration on group productivity and hence such productivity should suffer. Some support was found for this hypothesis from a number of experimental small-group studies. Of particular interest is the way in which group structure is operationalized and the way in which the fit or discrepancy index is calculated.

The authors argue that even though there was some support for their hypothesis these results and those of a related study (Kabanoff & O'Brien, 1978) suggest that structural variables (conceptualized in terms of such requirements as cooperation/collaboration and coordination) alone account for most of the productivity variance. Thus, a particularly effective leadership strategy will be one where the leader is taught how to modify group structure after consideration of task demands and member abilities. This approach is briefly contrasted with some of Fiedler's recent work (Fiedler & Leister, 1977).

A somewhat similar model developed from a different literature base is that of Griffin (1979, in press). That model considers congruence between the level of individual growth needs and task scope using a four-cell matrix. The higher the congruence, the higher satisfaction and performance are hypothesized to be. Leader behavior is considered to be a moderator variable such that each of the four conditions calls for a different kind of behavior. Specifically, achievement-oriented and participative behaviors are considered most relevant where there is high growth need–high task scope, directive where there is high scope–low growth, supportive where there is low scope–high growth, and maintenance where there is low scope–low growth. The model has so far been presented in conceptual form only and is considered to be an extension of House's path-goal model (House & Mitchell, 1974).

Another, not dissimilar, model is one developed by Halal and discussed conceptually in a 1974 article (Halal, 1974). The author now reports some empirical testing. Essentially, the model is based on leadership, technology, and subordinate need structure. Each of these lies along a continuum with leadership varying from directiveness to permissiveness, technology varying from simple to complex, and subordinate motivation from materialistic to idealistic. One proposition is that subordinate job satisfaction and performance will be positively related to congruence among leadership permissiveness, complexity of task technology, and idealness of subordinate motivation.

Finally, recent work by Hunt, Osborn, and Schuler (1978), Osborn and Hunt (1977), Hunt and Osborn (1979, in press) has led to a multiple influence approach. One key aspect of that approach involves fits between and among environmental, organizational, technological, and group variables, and the interactions of these fits with leader behavior to influence outputs. The latest treatment of this approach is in Osborn, Hunt, and Jauch (1980, in press). Empirical testing has been started but results are not available as of this writing.

Emphasis on Process

An important trend in the literature is to consider process and role aspects of the supervisor-subordinate relationship. The Vertical Dyad Linkage (VDL) work of Graen and his associates discussed earlier by Sashkin and Garland (chapter 5) and emphasized in the House and Baetz literature review, has this as a central focus, Graen's theory (Graen & Cashman, 1975; Graen, Cashman, Ginsburgh, & Schiemann, 1977) postulates that each dyadic leader-subordinate relationship develops through the role-making process, with leader exchanges (resources, support, trust) and subordinate exchanges (job-related behaviors, commitment) resulting in a set of interlocked behaviors (activity levels, communication) expressive of their relationship. The theory argues that both leader and subordinate play an active role in the interactive process as the exchange develops.

This model has recently been extended to focus on the leader-subordinate communication process (Schiemann & Graen, 1978). The communication process is hypothesized to be affected by the interpersonal processes in the model and by structural variables. Longitudinal data from 108 leader-subordinate dyads in three organizations wee utilized to examine this hypothesis. Structural measures included eight different variables ranging from job type to type of organization. Six interpersonal measures were used covering such variables as leader behavior, dyadic exchange, and dyadic agreement. Six different aspects of communication were used covering areas ranging from content to directionality. Both interpersonal and structural variables were found to be antecedents of various aspects of communication.

A related study (Bruning & Cashman, 1978) examined the developmental process for leader-subordinate dyads within newly structured student task groups. Previous studies have examined this process within formal organizations. However, the authors argue that part of the developmental process was obscured because of organizational constraints. Hence, less structured organizations should make the developmental process more visible. The task groups were formed from undergraduate organizational behavior students assigned to perform various projects. The developmental process was monitored at three different time periods. During the first several weeks of new working relationships more than three quarters of the groups showed differential development of vertical dyadic relationships. This differentiation was found to be related to early interpersonal attraction between members of leader-member dyads.

In a related paper (Cashman & Bruning, 1978) the authors used this sample to examine the leader behavior–performance ordering (does behavior cause performance or vice versa?). Interestingly, they found that subordinates perceived a leader behavior–performance ordering but leaders perceived a performance–behavior relationship. They argue that studying the developmental process is the most appropriate way to provide further insight into findings such as this. These findings may be considered in attributional terms as are those in a later part of this chapter.

Additional work using the dyadic development approach is reported by Larwood (1978). She used the VDL model to examine the impact of manager sex on dyadic linkages. She found among other things, that managers of either sex will discriminate against potential leaders of the opposite sex because those persons are less likely to be members of their ingroup. She concludes that her data provide support for the Graen approach and that that approach helps provide additional insights into discrimination.

Still another extension (and a most ambitious one) of the Graen approach is reported by Dansereau. While he uses variations of the Graen theory and methodology, his major focus is on the unit of analysis. He is conducting empirical work in a number of organizations with samples covering different functional areas, managerial levels, and technologies over five time periods. The major thrust of his work is to test the unit of analysis notions set forth in a contribution in the 1977 symposium book (Danse-

reau & Dumas, 1977). Essentially, it is argued that different variables operate at different levels of analysis and that there are a number of issues
which have to be dealt with as one moves from one level of analysis to
another. See Dansereau, Dumas, and Alutto (1978a, b) and Dansereau and
Dumas (1978) for extensions to the above symposium contribution.

A quite different treatment of the leadership process is involved in the
"psychological isotope technique" developed by Chemers, Goza, and Plumer (1978). It is essentially a technique which involves planting identifiable
units of information with specific group members. The movement of the
traceable bits provides data on the flow of information in the group, the
relative impact of specific group members, and the sources of conflict. The
authors used the approach to clarify effects of the Least Preferred Co-
worker leadership style variable on group process and to examine various
aspects of group conflict in laboratory groups. While the general approach
itself is not new, its development by Chemers and associates appears to
have potential for examining a wide range of process variables, especially
as they relate to leadership.

Reinforcement or Operant Approaches

A key thrust here is the work of Mawhinney (1978). He develops a
laboratory design to study reciprocal causality in leader-subordinate relations. That thrust is consistent with the work of Scott and Sims from the
previous symposium book as well as the earlier Luthans contribution and
that of individuals such as Greene (1975), and Graen and his associates
(e.g., Cashman & Bruning, 1978) interested in reciprocal causality. Mawhinney's approach, though, is different from any of these. In the present
paper he describes an operant laboratory research design that will allow for
a much more systematic investigation of reciprocal causality than has previously been done in lab and field work. He also reports some preliminary
results concerning reward contingencies.

Two other papers rely on survey field research. The first (Curran &
Curran, 1978) is of interest primarily because it replicates results previously found using what is now becoming a frequently used questionnaire instrument to measure contingent leader reward behavior. The instrument
taps leader contingent reward and punishment behaviors and leader contingent advancement behavior. Earlier work of Sims and Szilagyi (1975),
among others, has suggested that this instrument or variations based on it
appears to be associated with a number of subordinate criteria.

The final paper is a conceptual one by Ashour (1978). It emphasizes questionnaire measurement of the incentive value of a leader's behavior, the degree to which that behavior is contingent upon subordinate task performance, and the reinforcement schedule employed by the leader. Its thrust appears similar to that of other reinforcement approaches.

Power, Influence, and Attribution

Not all the studies here deal with power and not all deal with attribution. A number of studies do treat the two together, though, and thus form the basis for the grouping in this section. An appropriate place to start is with a recent review of the power, influence, and authority literature by McCall (1978). In it McCall considers the various meanings, sources, uses, and impacts of organizational power. The review is useful for familiarizing oneself with much of the power and influence literature which is closely related to leadership. Indeed two recently published studies (Lord, 1977; Sheridan & Vredenburgh, 1978) empirically link social power and leadership. Martin and Hunt (1979) formulate and test a path-analytic process model suggesting that social power affects leader behavior which in turn is hypothesized to operate through group cohesiveness and satisfaction to affect subordinate intent to leave. While not all these linkages were confirmed, there was evidence linking social power to leader behavior.

The earlier power work of Kipnis (1976) serves as the genesis for later work by him as well as others. His work has evolved over a period of years. Its major focus has been on the personal and situational factors associated with the choice of influence tactics, and the consequences for the power user of these choices in terms of self-perceptions and perceptions (attributions) of the target of influence. The current thrust involves the development of factored instruments to measure influence tactics directed toward superiors, peers, and subordinates.

A recent study (Brief, Aldag, & Russell, 1978) reports results of a constructive replication and extension of the findings of Kipnis, Castell, Gergen, and Mauch (1976). There relationships between leaders' perceptions of their own power and attributions regarding causes of subordinate job behavior or evaluations of subordinate job performance, and relationships between powerful leaders and social distance from subordinates were reported. The Brief et al. findings generally were not found to confirm those of Kipnis et al. obtained in a different setting with different instruments. Further, perceived superior power was not found to be associated with subordinate attributions of their own behavior, social distance, or job satisfaction. Another extension of Kipnis's work was conducted by Fodor and

Farrow (1978) using an industrial simulation. They found that supervisors high on the power need evaluated ingratiators more favorably than leaders with a lower need for power.

A final study which intertwines power with attribution is a laboratory investigation by McFillen (1978). Here forty subjects were randomly assigned to a supervisory role in either a reward-power only or penalty-power only condition. The subjects then supervised two unsuccessful subordinates, one closely and one generally. Only subordinate performance consistently affected leader perceptions of subordinate performance as well as the allocation of incentives and later supervision. Power and closeness of supervision had no direct measurable effect on the supervisor's attributions or behaviors concerning subordinates, though there were some interactive effects.

Two recent works concentrating on power are those by Mowday (1978) and Grimes (1978). Mowday's work again used the work of Kipnis as a base. It was designed to direct greater attention to the exercise of influence as an integral part of the leadership role. More specifically, it was concerned with relating influence activity to various characteristics of the person exercising influence and the person's perception of the influence situation. The choice of a method of influence was related to both leader characteristics and characteristics of the influence situation. Influence effectiveness was most consistently related to the use of manipulation as a method of influence.

In a conceptual piece, Grimes conceives of power as influence and social control with influence reducing authority and social control reinforcing authority. He argues that these constructs permit reexamination of authority and leadership. He is now in the process of empirically testing a number of the relations postulated in this conceptual article.

Two works which focus on attributional issues but do not consider power are by Lundberg (1978) and Mitchell and Green (1978). The Lundberg investigation, conducted in a laboratory setting, examines the effect of leader self-expectations on perceived leadership. It was found that individuals previously informed by the experimenter that they possessed leadership ability were seen by their cohorts (who did not know of the information conveyed by the experimenter) as higher on exhibited leadership than others in the group. Interestingly, though, the individuals so evaluated by their cohorts did not see themselves as higher than their cohorts in terms of leadership.

The Mitchell and Green piece is a conceptual one which develops an attributional model of leader role behavior concerning subordinate performance. It uses attribution theory as an explanation of leader responses to poor subordinate performance. The authors indicate that they are in the process of empirically testing the model.

Implicit Leadership

A special case of attribution theory involves what have come to be called implicit leadership theories (Hunt & Larson, 1977). Simply put, it is argued that raters are likely to rely heavily on stereotypes and implicit theories of what a "good" leader should be to reduce the amount of information processing required in perceiving the behavior of others. Thus stimuli other than an individual's "real" behavior may have a substantial impact on the descriptions of those describing that person's behavior. Rush, Thomas, and Lord (1977) and Lord, Binning, Rush, and Thomas (1978) report evidence in support of this argument and are quite pessimistic concerning the use of questionnaires as a result of their findings. On the other hand, Schriesheim and DeNisi (1978) and DeNisi and Schriesheim (1978) find a minor role for implicit theories in their field studies when appropriate information is made available to the describers.

Examples of Behavioral Criterion Variables

One of the points made by J. P. Campbell (1977) in an incisive overview, is that we need to be investigating "the observable behavior of the followers that could 'reasonably' be expected to be influenced by the leader in a face-to-face situation" (p. 233). One example of this appears to be subordinate compliance, and it has recently received attention in both field and laboratory investigations.

The field study (Greene, 1978) is a longitudinal one which examined, among other things, the impact of leader role-clarifying behavior, leader supportiveness, leader participativeness, and leader-reinforcement behavior on subordinate compliance to work-related and non-work-related norms and vice versa under high and low structured tasks. While the findings were complex, in general they suggested that leader behavior was strongly influenced by subordinate compliance. While compliance was emphasized here, the study can also be considered an extension of House's path-goal model (House & Mitchell, 1974) and has something to say about reciprocal causation and reinforcement.

The laboratory work on compliance consists of a series of investigations conducted by Price and Garland (1976a, b, 1978 a, b). In general, the studies indicate that leader competence is strongly related to subordinate endorsement of leaders. Leader competence is not by itself, however, related to subordinate compliance in terms of leader suggestions for problem solution and leader suggestions regarding work methods. Subordinates' perceptions of their own incompetence is a necessary condition for subordinate compliance with the suggestions of competent leaders. Taken together, this lab and field work suggests that compliance may be a particularly important dependent variable in the study of leadership. We should also note that its importance was emphasized in Dubin's overview chapter.

Emergent Leadership

Emergent leadership was emphasized in the House and Baetz review and one approach to emergent leadership was emphasized in the earlier chapter by Stein and his associates. Other recent work looks at a number of additional considerations. First is a series of papers which examine what Sashkin and Garland earlier called the "babble hypothesis"—that is, leadership status is a function of verbal participation. In carefully reviewing this literature Heller and Stein (1978) found that this hypothesis though strongly supported was an oversimplification. They found that 63 percent of the variance of the leadership status-participation rate correlations reported in the literature could be accounted for by: 1) the type of leadership measure used (task vs. socio-emotional), 2) how general the leadership measure is, 3) if the groups contain mixed or same sex members, and 4) if the leadership ratings are made by observers or group members. The authors argue that these results show the limits of the experimental settings in which the research has been done and highlight quite clearly some future research directions to obtain a better understanding of how leadership status is bestowed in informal groups.

A literature review of ongoing non-laboratory groups (Stein, 1978) examines the exemplar hypothesis, "High status group members [those who are: in a leadership role, more esteemed, better liked, etc.] are closer to the normative ideal in their attitudes and behaviors than are lower status members." Findings, contrary to currently accepted views that high status members are more *deviant* than other members, largely confirm the hypothesis. The review sheds light on some effects of leader and non-leader conformity to behavioral and attitudinal expectations. The author suggests a number of future research directions for empirical work in ongoing groups.

Two contributions concern themselves with elected leaders. The first of these (Stein, Childs, Cooley, & Fedota, 1978), proposes an examination of how information concerning candidates for leadership positions is combined when a choice is made. Statements from laboratory subjects on reasons why they prefer a specific leader candidate, ratings of candidates on 11 dimensions (e.g., motivation, task competency, interpersonal skills, etc.), and their impact on ratings and rankings of leadership are being examined. The second study is that of Hollander and Neider (1978), which is briefly treated in Hollander's commentary in chapter 6. It examines "good" and "bad" leader characteristics for non-appointed (emergent or elected) versus appointed leaders. While other details are covered by Hollander in his commentary, the conclusion of the study is worth reiterating: Appointed leaders were found to differ from non-appointed leaders in a number of different ways under the bad but *not* the good leadership condition. In other words, people saw a different set of characteristics describing bad appointed leaders than they did bad non-appointed leaders.

Finally, work (Childs & Stein, 1978) is underway which looks at the importance of nonverbal behavior in leadership analysis. It is hypothesized that nonverbal behavior will be more reliable in predicting socio-emotional leadership, while verbal behavior will be more accurate in predicting task-oriented leadership. The hypothesis is being investigated using undergraduate college students in a laboratory setting.

Some Extensions to Currently Emphasized Approaches

Here we briefly focus on some updates and extensions to the models of Vroom and Yetton (1973), Bass and Valenzi (1974), House (House & Mitchell, 1974), and to Fiedler's contingency model (Fiedler & Chemers, 1974). As has been argued earlier, refinement and extension is a key part of model development which has sometimes not received the attention it deserves.

Vroom and Yetton

This approach is concerned with the effects of seven situational variables on the choice of autocratic versus participative leader behavior using a measure of behavioral intent in hypothetical managerial decision-making problems. It was emphasized in Smith's summary of the Kepner-Tregoe work in chapter 3.

Three recent studies concentrate on refinements to this general approach. The first of these is (Vroom & Jago, 1978) concerned with a more rigorous validation procedure for the model than has been previously employed. A number of methodological issues are addressed in this validation attempt. In general, this more rigorous validation strategy lends support to the model. The authors discuss a number of remaining methodological and theoretical issues relating to the model.

The second study (Jago, 1978) addresses speculation that the use of the behavioral intent instrument produces spurious results attributable to confounded differences in the hierarchical level of the hypothetical decision-making problems. One situation, for example, may describe a problem encountered by a corporate president; another may describe an issue encountered by a first-level manager. Because respondents to the problem set are asked to assume the role of the manager in each problem, it has been argued that the appropriateness of specified leader behaviors for different hierarchical levels may influence the responses to a great extent. Thus, effects attributed by Vroom and Yetton to situational variables (e.g., leaders' information, structure of the problem, etc.) may instead be confounded by hierarchical level. Jago describes the development of a new instrument which is designed to minimize this hierarchical confounding. He shows it to have greater internal reliability than the measure previously used and discusses the implications for previously reported results.

The third study (Jago, 1979, in press) investigates the manner in which managers employ information concerning four fundamental decision-making situations in choosing leadership behaviors deemed appropriate for those situations. It reveals certain similarities and differences between normative and descriptive leadership models. It also highlights a previously undocumented source of individual differences among managers. Finally, it reevaluates conclusions reached in previous research on the Vroom-Yetton and related approaches and discusses training implications.

Bass and Associates

Bass and Valenzi presented a systems model of leadership in the 1974 symposium book (Bass & Valenzi, 1974). The model consists of: system inputs (organizational, work group, task and subordinate personality); within-system relations (subordinate and superior power and information distribution, organization structure, and objectives); within-system leader behavior dimensions (directive, manipulative, consultative, participative, and delegative); and system outputs (effectiveness, and various aspects of satisfaction).

Some previous validation efforts and refinements were reported by Bass (1976) and Bass, Valenzi, Farrow, and Soloman (1975). A current thrust is reported by Bass, Valenzi, and Farrow, 1977. It uses thirty-one variables defined in the systems model and described by a manager and his immediate subordinates to provide an individualized prescription for a manager concerning what he can do to enhance his units' outputs in selected organizational settings. As such it is broader in scope than most of the other approaches treated in this volume. It is also consistent with recent attempts by Bass to bridge the academician/practitioner gap so apparent in part 2 of the book.

House

House, of course, in the House and Baetz review, discusses a number of refinements and suggested extensions to his path-goal model. In addition, a recent study conducted within a police department setting treated some path-goal extensions as a part of its focus (Jermier & Berkes, 1979, in press). In general, it supported earlier research, confirming the importance of task demands as an important component of path-goal models. The study is especially interesting because it found that more participation and task variability had a positive impact on subordinate satisfaction and commitment. This result was interpreted as being contrary to the conventional wisdom that a quasi-military model (impersonal, highly directed, routine tasks, etc.) is most desirable. This is in line with some recent work by Guyot (1977).

House's path-goal model has also been used as the basis for a recent study by Marsh (1979). He essentially applied path-goal hypotheses at the macro-organizational level rather than the individual task level. Type of organization (organic versus mechanistic) rather than task structure was used as a key moderator variable in a large sample of United States Army units.

Fiedler's Contingency Model

A recent thrust of Fiedler's model has been an application to practicing managers. This has led to what Fiedler has termed the leader match concept (Fiedler, Chemers, & Mahar, 1976). Csoka and Bons (1978) report some validation evidence concerning leader match. Hosking and Schriesheim (1978), in an essay review, consider some theoretical and empirical considerations relating to leader match. They are generally quite critical of it.

Conclusions

In reviewing the studies for this epilog we drew a number of conclusions. First, we were struck by the interest in measuring what it is that leaders do and the breadth with which these activities were conceived. While earlier literature lamented the heavy reliance on questionnaire instruments such as the Leader Behavior Description Questionnaire, it looks as if an effort is finally being made to do something about it. That effort extends beyond face-to-face influence measures and extends to role behaviors of managers.

Second, there is the emphasis on laboratory investigations and causal investigations of leadership. The proportion of laboratory studies reported in a recent review by Hunt, Osborn, and Schriesheim (1978) as well as in the Sashkin and Garland chapter was relatively small. Since the Hunt and associates' review concentrated on six scholarly journals such as *Administrative Science Quarterly*, *Journal of Applied Psychology*, and *Academy of Management Journal*, it is possible that the results reflect a sampling difference. We suspect, though, that they go beyond that and may really reflect an emerging trend. Much the same can be said concerning causal field studies. They appear much more prevalent here than in the earlier review.

Third, there is the emphasis on attribution. This trend was beginning to become apparent in the previous symposium and has picked up considerably since then. Attribution cuts across a wide range of leadership studies and in addition to being important in its own right seems to have especially important implications in terms of questionnaire measures of leader behavior.

Fourth, there is the focus on leadership-related variables such as power and various forms of influence. While these have always been with us, a number of attempts at integration within the leadership literature seem to be emerging.

Fifth, there are the followups and extensions to what have now become well-known leadership approaches. This was perhaps most clearly illustrated with the Graen, Vroom-Yetton, and House approaches but also carried over to Fiedler and Bass. A substantial amount of effort is being devoted to these paradigms.

Finally, we were struck by a couple of additional points. First, there did not seem to be as heavy a reliance on survey designs involving predictor (leadership), moderator, criterion (performance, satisfaction, etc.) relations as in the past. In the earlier Hunt and associates' review, this was the predominant thrust in the literature. Here this focus seems to have been sharply diffused with a number of additional emphases. Second, there seemed to be a relative lack of emphasis on broad-ranging macro models of leadership which consider a whole host of environmental, structural, and technological variables. While some work such as that by Hunt and Osborn (1979, in press) and Bass et al. (1977) emphasizes this, it does not yet appear to be a strong trend. In virtually all of the previous symposium volumes we have lamented this lack of emphasis. One might speculate as to why this trend does not seem to be evolving faster than it is. Will the emphasis on simulation by those such as McCall and Lombardo encourage a heavier macro thrust? Or will the field largely ignore the use of simulations for research purposes as it did the work of Bass and his colleagues (Bass, 1963) in the early sixties?

References
Name Index
Subject Index

References

Adorno, T. W., Brunswik, F., Levinson, D. J., & Sanford, N. R. *The authoritarian personality.* New York: Harper, 1950.

Allen, W. R., & Ruhe, J. A. Verbal behavior by black and white leaders of biracial groups in two different environments. *Journal of Applied Psychology,* 1976, *61,* 441–45.

Argyris, C. *Executive Leadership.* New York: Harper, 1953.

Argyris, C. *Understanding organizational behavior.* Homewood, IL: Irwin-Dorsey, 1960.

Argyris, C. *Organization and innovation.* Homewood, IL: Irwin-Dorsey, 1965.

Argyris, C. Some unintended consequences of rigorous research. *Psychological Bulletin,* 1968, *70,* 185–97.

Argyris, C. The incompleteness of social psychological theory. *American Psychologist,* 1969, *24,* 893–908.

Argyris, C. *The applicability of organizational sociology.* Cambridge, MA: Harvard University Press, 1972.

Argyris, C. Dangers in applying results from experimental social psychology. *American Psychologist,* 1975, *30,* 469–85.

Argyris, C. Theories of action that inhibit individual learning. *American Psychologist,* 1976, *31,* 638–54.

Argyris, C. Organizational learning and management information systems. *Accounting, Organizations and Society,* 1977, *2*(2), 113–23.

Argyris, C. The inner contradictions of rigorous research. Unpublished manuscript, Graduate School of Education, Harvard University, 1978.

Argyris, C., & Schön, D. *Theory in practice.* San Francisco: Jossey-Bass, 1974.

Argyris, C., & Schön, D. *Organizational learning.* Reading, MA: Addison-Wesley, 1978.

Aronson, E. *The social animal.* San Francisco: W. H. Freeman, 1972.

Ashour, A. S. A reinforcement model of leadership effectiveness. Unpublished manuscript, Faculty of Commerce, Alexandria University, 1978.

Ashour, A. S., & England, G. Subordinate's assigned level of discretion as a function of leader's personality and situational variables. *Journal of Applied Psychology,* 1972, *56,* 120–23.

Back, R. F. Influence through social communication. *Journal of Abnormal and Social Psychology*, 1951, *46*, 190–207.

Bales, R. F. *Interaction process analysis: A method for the study of small groups.* Cambridge, MA: Addison-Wesley, 1950.

Bales, R. F. The equilibrium problem in small groups. In T. Parsons, R. F. Bales, and E. A. Shils (Eds.), *Working papers on the theory of action.* Glencoe, IL: Free Press, 1953.

Bales, R. F. In conference. *Harvard Business Review*, 1954, *32*(2), 44–50.

Bales, R. F. Task roles and social roles in problem-solving groups. In E. E. MacCoby, T. M. Newcomb, and E. L. Hartley (Eds.), *Readings in social psychology* (3rd ed.). New York: Holt, Rinehart, and Winston, 1958.

Bales, R. F. *Personality and interpersonal behavior.* New York: Holt, Rinehart, and Winston, 1970.

Bales, R. F., Cohen, S. P., & Williamson, S. A. *Symlog—A system for the multiple level observation of groups.* New York: Macmillan, Free Press, 1979, In press.

Bales, R. F., & Strodtbeck, F. L. Phases in group problem solving. *Journal of Abnormal and Social Psychology*, 1951, *46*, 485–95.

Bandura, A. *Social learning theory.* Englewood Cliffs, NJ: Prentice-Hall, 1977.

Barber, J. D. *The presidential character: Predicting performance in the White House* (2nd ed.). Englewood Cliffs, NJ: Prentice-Hall, 1977.

Barker, R. G. Explorations in ecological psychology. *American Psychologist*, 1965, *20*, 1–14.

Barnard, C. I. *Organization and management.* Cambridge, MA: Harvard University Press, 1948.

Barrow, J. C. Worker performance and task complexity as causal determinants of leader behavior style and flexibility: *Journal of Applied Psychology*, 1976, *61*, 433–40.

Bass, B. M. An analysis of the leaderless group discussion. *Journal of Applied Psychology*, 1949, *33*, 527–33.

Bass, B. M. Effects of the nature of the problem on LGD performance. *Journal of Applied Psychology*, 1953, *37*, 96–99.

Bass, B. M. The leaderless group discussion. *Psychological Bulletin*, 1954, *51*, 465–92.

Bass, B. M. Experimenting with simulated manufacturing organizations. In S. B. Sells (Ed.), *Stimulus determinants of behavior.* New York: Ronald Press, 1963, 117–96.

Bass, B. M. A systems survey research feedback for management and organizational development. *Journal of Applied Behavioral Science*, 1976, *12*, 215–19.

Bass, B. M., Cascio, W. F., & O'Connor, E. J. Magnitude estimations of expressions of frequency and amount. *Journal of Applied Psychology*, 1974, *59*, 313–20.

Bass, B. M., & Coates, C. H. Forecasting officer potential using the leaderless group discussion. *Journal of Abnormal and Social Psychology*, 1952, *47*, 321–25.

Bass, B. M., & Valenzi, E. R. Contingent aspects of effective management styles. In J. G. Hunt and L. L. Larson (Eds.), *Contingency approaches to leadership.* Carbondale, IL: Southern Illinois University Press, 1974.

Bass, B. M., Valenzi, E. R., & Farrow, D. L. Discriminant functions to identify ways to increase leadership effectiveness. Technical Report 77-3, School of Management, State University of New York at Binghamton, 1977.

Bass, B. M., Valenzi, E. R., Farrow, D. L., & Soloman, R. J. Management styles associated with organizational, task, personal, and interpersonal contingencies. *Journal of Applied Psychology*, 1975, *60*, 720–29.

Bateson, G. *Steps to an ecology of mind*. New York: Ballantine, 1972.

Bavelas, A., Hastorf, A. H., Gross, A. D., & Kite, W. R. Experiments on the alteration of group structure. *Journal of Experimental Social Psychology*, 1965, *1*, 55–70.

Beer, M., & Kleisath, S. The effects of the managerial grid on organizational and leadership dimensions. In S. S. Zalkind (Chairman), Research on the Impact of Using Different Laboratory Methods for Interpersonal and Organizational Change. Symposium presented at the annual meeting of the American Psychological Association, Washington, D.C., September 1967.

Bennis, W. *Changing organizations*. New York: McGraw-Hill, 1966.

Berger, J., Cohen, B. F., & Zelditch, M., Jr. Status characteristics and social interaction. *American Sociological Review*, 1972, *37*, 241–55.

Berkowitz, L. Sharing leadership in small decision-making groups. *Journal of Abnormal and Social Psychology*, 1953, *48*, 231–38.

Berkowitz, L. Personality and group position. *Sociometry*, 1956, *19*, 210–22.

Bion, W. R. Experiences in groups: III. *Human Relations*, 1949, *2*, 13–22.

Blake, R. R., & Mouton, J. S. *The managerial grid*. Houston: Gulf, 1964.

Blake, R. R., & Mouton, J. S. *Building a dynamic corporation through grid organization development*. Reading, MA: Addison-Wesley, 1969.

Blake, R. R., & Mouton, J. S. *The new managerial grid*. Houston: Gulf, 1978.

Blalock, H. M. *Causal inference in nonexperimental research*. New York: Norton, 1964.

Blau, P. M., & Scott, W. R. *Formal organizations*. San Francisco: Chandler, 1962.

Blum, M. L., & Naylor, J. C. *Industrial Psychology: Its theoretical and social functions*. New York: Harper and Row, 1968.

Blumenthal, Arthur L. *The process of cognition*. Englewood Cliffs, NJ: Prentice-Hall, 1977.

Bons, P. M. The effect of changes in leadership environment on the behavior of relationship- and task-motivated leaders. Unpublished doctoral dissertation, Department of Psychology, University of Washington, 1974.

Bons, P. M., & Fiedler, F. E. Changes in organizational leadership and the behavior of relationship- and task-motivated leaders. *Administrative Science Quarterly*, 1976, *21*, 433–72.

Bons, P. M., & Fiedler, F. E. Leadership. In L. Bittel (Ed.) *Encyclopedia of professional management*, New York: McGraw-Hill, 1977.

Borgatta, E. F. (Ed.). *Sociological methodology*. San Francisco: Jossey-Bass, 1969.

Borgatta, E. F., & Bales, R. F. Task and accumulation of experience as factors in the interaction of small groups. *Sociometry*, 1953, *16*, 239–52.

Borgatta, E. F., & Bales, R. F. Sociometric status patterns and characteristics of interaction. *Journal of Social Psychology*, 1956, *43*, 289–97.

Bormann, E. G. *Discussion and group methods: Theory and practice*. New York: Harper and Row, 1969.

Bowers, D. G., & Seashore, S. E. Predicting organizational effectiveness with a four-factor theory of leadership. *Administrative Science Quarterly*, 1966, *11*, 238–63.

Bray, D. W., Campbell, R. J., & Grant, D. L. *Formative years in business.* New York: Wiley, 1974.

Bray, D. W., & Grant, D. L. The assessment center in the measurement of potential for business management. *Psychological monographs*, 1966, *80* (17, Whole No. 625).

Bray, D. W., & Moses, J. L. Personnel selection. *Annual Review of Psychology*, 1972, *23*, 545–76.

Brief, A. P., Aldag, R. J., & Russell, C. J. The metamorphic effects of power: Another perspective. Paper presented at the 38th Annual Academy of Management Meeting, San Francisco, August 1978.

Broedling, L. A., & Lau, A. W. Executive summary: Navy civilian executive study. Special Report No. 79–10. San Diego: Navy Personnel Research and Development Center, January 1979.

Bronzo, A. F., Jr. Increased zero defects participation through group discussion and public commitment. *Psychological Reports*, 1968, *23*, 72.

Bruning, N. S., & Cashman, J. Leadership: Studying the developmental process. Paper presented at the 38th Annual Academy of Management Meeting, San Francisco, August 1978.

Burke, P. J. Authority relations and disruptive behavior in small discussion groups. *Sociometry*, 1966, *29*, 237–50.

Burns, J. M. *Leadership.* New York: Harper and Row, 1978.

Butcher, H. J. *Human intelligence: Its nature and assessment.* New York: Harper and Row, Torch Books, 1968.

Butterfield, D. A., & Bartol, K. M. Evaluation of leader behavior: A missing element in leadership theory. In J. G. Hunt and L. L. Larson (Eds.), *Leadership: The cutting edge.* Carbondale, IL: Southern Illinois University Press, 1977.

Calder, B. J. An attribution theory of leadership. In B. M. Staw and G. R. Salancik (Eds.), *New Directions in Organizational Behavior.* Chicago: St. Clair Press, 1977.

Campbell, D. T., & Fiske, D. W. Convergent and discriminant validation by the multitrait-multimethod matrix. *Psychological Bulletin*, 1959, *56*, 81–105.

Campbell, D. T., and Stanley, J. C. *Experimental and quasi-experimental designs for research.* Chicago: Rand McNally, 1963.

Campbell, J. P. Personnel training and development. *Annual Review of Psychology*, 1971, *22*, 565–602.

Campbell, J. P. The cutting edge of leadership: An overview. In J. G. Hunt and L. L. Larson (Eds.), *Leadership: The cutting edge.* Carbondale, IL: Southern Illinois University Press, 1977.

Campbell, J. P., Dunnette, M. D., Lawler, E. E., III, & Weick, K. E., Jr. *Managerial behavior, performance, and effectiveness.* New York: McGraw-Hill, 1970.

Campbell, R. Long range planning committee report. *Industrial-Organizational Psychologist*, 1978, *15*(3), 6–8.

Cappella, J. N. An introduction to the literature of causal modeling. *Human Communication Research*, 1975, *1*, 362–77.

Carter, L. F. Recording and evaluating the performance of individuals as members of small groups. *Personnel Psychology*, 1954, *7*, 477–84.

Carter, L. F., Haythorn, W., Shriver, B., & Lanzetta, J. The behavior of leaders and other group members. *Journal of Abnormal and Social Psychology*, 1950, *46*, 589–95.

Cartwright, D. S. The nature of group cohesiveness. In D. Cartwright and A. Zander (Eds.), *Group dynamics: Research and theory* (3rd ed.). New York: Harper and Row, 1968.

Cartwright, D. S., & Robertson, R. J. Membership in cliques and achievement. *American Journal of Sociology*, 1961, *66*, 441–45.

Cartwright, D. S., & Zander, A. (Eds.). *Group dynamics: Theory and research* (3rd ed.). New York: Harper and Row, 1963.

Cashman, J., & Bruning, N. S. Leader behavior causes performance: A review and longitudinal study. Paper presented at the 86th Annual Convention of the American Psychological Association, Toronto, Ontario, Canada, September 1978.

Cashman, J., Dansereau, F., Jr., Green, G., & Haga, W. J. Organizational understructure and leadership: A longitudinal investigation of the managerial role-making process. *Organizational Behavior and Human Performance*, 1976, *15*, 278–96.

Chemers, M. M., & Fiedler, F. E. The effectiveness of leadership training: A reply to Argyris. *American Psychologist*, 1978, *33*, 391–94.

Chemers, M. M., Goza, B., & Plumer, S. I. Leadership style and communication process: An experiment using the psychological isotope technique. Paper presented at the 86th Annual Convention of the American Psychological Association, Toronto, Ontario, Canada, September 1978.

Childs, L. M., & Stein, R. T. Verbal and nonverbal behavior in leadership analysis. Investigation in progress, Department of Psychology, University of Illinois at Chicago Circle, 1978.

Christner, C. A., & Hemphill, J. K. Leader behavior of B-29 commanders and changes in crew members' attitudes toward the crew. *Sociometry*, 1955, *18*, 82–87.

Coch, L., & French, J. R. P., Jr. Overcoming resistance to change. *Human Relations*, 1948, *1*, 512–32.

Comrey, A. L. Pfiffner, J. M., & High, W. S. Factors influencing organizational effectiveness: A final report. Office of Naval Research, Final Technical Report, Department of Psychology, University of Southern California, 1954.

Cook, T. D., & Campbell, D. T. The design and conduct of quasi-experiments in field settings. In M. D. Dunnette (Ed.), *Handbook of industrial and organizational psychology*. Chicago: Rand McNally, 1976, 223–326.

Crozier, M. *The bureaucratic phenomenon*. London: Tavistock, 1964.

Csoka, L. S., & Bons, P. M. Manipulating the situation to fit the leader's style: Two validation studies. *Journal of Applied Psychology*, 1978, *63*, 295–300.

Cummings, L. L. Assessing the Graen/Cashman model and comparing it with other approaches. In J. G. Hunt and L. L. Larson (Eds.), *Leadership frontiers*. Kent, OH: Comparative Administration Research Institute, Kent State University, 1975.

Curran, K. E., & Curran, M. A. Leader reward behavior and subordinate satisfaction in a health care environment. Paper presented at the 38th Annual Academy of Management Meeting, San Francisco, August 1978.

Dachler, H. P., & Willpert, B. Conceptual dimensions and boundaries of participation in organizations: A critical evaluation. *Administrative Science Quarterly*, 1978, *23*, 1–39.

Dansereau, F., & Dumas, N. S. Pratfalls and pitfalls in drawing inferences about leader behavior in organizations. In J. G. Hunt and L. L. Larson (Eds.), *Leadership: The cutting edge*. Carbondale, IL: Southern Illinois University Press, 1977.

Dansereau, F., & Dumas, N. S. A first step in dealing with aggregation and disaggregation problems in leadership research. Unpublished manuscript, Department of Organization and Human Resources, State University of New York at Buffalo, 1978.

Dansereau, F., Dumas, N. S., & Alutto, J. A. An exploration in methods for reconciling aggregation problems in organizational structure. Paper presented at the 38th Annual Academy of Management Meeting, San Francisco, August 1978. (a)

Dansereau, F., Dumas, N. S., & Alutto, J. A. A first step in empirically assessing the level of analysis at which leadership phenomena occur. Unpublished manuscript, Department of Organization and Human Resources, State University of New York at Buffalo, 1978. (b)

Dansereau, F., Graen, G., & Haga, W. J. A vertical dyad linkage approach to leadership within formal organizations: A longitudinal investigation of the role-making process. *Organizational Behavior and Human Performance*, 1975, *13*, 46–78.

Davis, S. M., & Lawrence, P. R. *Matrix*. Reading, MA: Addison-Wesley, 1977.

Davis, T., & Luthans, F. Leadership reexamined: A behavioral approach. *Academy of Management Review*, 1979, in press.

DeNisi, A. S., & Schriesheim, C. A. Leader behavior and attribution of subordinate satisfaction and performance. Unpublished Manuscript, Graduate School of Business Administration, Kent State University, 1978.

DeNuoy, P. L. *Between knowing and believing*. New York: McKay, 1966.

Downey, R. G., Kirkeide, L., & Shiflett, S. C. Dimensions and dimension relevance in LPC selection and evaluation. Paper presented at the 86th Annual Convention of the American Psychological Association, Toronto, Ontario, Canada, September 1978.

Dubin, R. Supervision and productivity: Empirical findings and theoretical considerations. In R. Dubin, G. C. Homans, F. C. Mann, and D. C. Miller (Eds.), *Leadership and productivity*. San Francisco: Chandler, 1965.

Dubin, R. *Theory building* (rev. ed.). New York: Macmillan, Free Press, 1978.

Dunnette, M. Fads, fashion, and folderol in Psychology. In R. Dubin, *Theory building* (rev. ed.). New York: Macmillan, Free Press, 1978.

Dunnette, M., & Campbell, J. P. Development of the Penney Career Index: Final technical report. Unpublished Manuscript, Department of Psychology, University of Minnesota, 1969.

Eden, D., & Leviatan, U. Implicit leadership theory as a determinant of the factor structure underlying supervisory behavior scales. *Journal of Applied Psychology*, 1975, *60*, 736–41.

Edwards, A. L. Experiments: Their planning and execution. In G. Lindzey (Ed.), *Handbook of Social Psychology*, Cambridge, MA: Addison-Wesley, 1954.

Elkin, F., Halpern, G., & Cooper, A. Leadership in a student mob. *Canadian Journal of Psychology*, 1962, *16*, 199–201.

Erickson, E. H. *Identity: Youth and crisis.* New York: Norton, 1968.

Evan, W. M. *Organizational experiments: Laboratory and field research.* New York: Harper and Row, 1971.

Evans, M. G. Leadership behavior: Demographic factors and agreement between subordinate and self-descriptions. *Personnel Psychology*, 1972, *25*, 649–53.

Exline, R. V. Group climate as a factor in the relevance and accuracy of social perception. *Journal of Abnormal and Social Psychology*, 1957, *55*, 382–88.

Farris, G. F., & Lim, F. G. Effects of performance on leadership, cohesiveness, influence, satisfaction and subsequent performance. *Journal of Applied Psychology*, 1969, *53*, 490–97.

Festinger, L. Informal social communication. *Psychological Review*, 1950, *57*, 271–82.

Festinger, L. Laboratory experiments. In W. M. Evan (Ed.), *Organizational experiments: Laboratory and field research.* New York: Harper and Row, 1971, 9–24.

Fiedler, F. E. Assumed similarity measures as predictors of team effectiveness. *Journal of Abnormal and Social Psychology*, 1954, *49*, 381–88.

Fiedler, F. E. *A theory of leadership effectiveness.* New York: McGraw-Hill, 1967.

Fiedler, F. E. Leadership experience and leader performance—Another hypothesis shot to hell. *Organizational Behavior and Human Performance*, 1970, *5*, 1–14.

Fiedler, F. E. Validation and extension of the contingency model of leadership effectiveness: A review of empirical findings. *Psychological Bulletin*, 1971, *76*, 128–48.

Fiedler, F. E. Personality, motivational systems, and behavior of high and low LPC persons. *Human Relations*, 1972, *25*, 391–412.

Fiedler, F. E. Personality and situational determinants of leader behavior. In E. A. Fleishman and J. G. Hunt (Eds.), *Current developments in the study of leadership.* Carbondale, IL: Southern Illinois University Press, 1973.

Fiedler, F. E., & Chemers, M. M. *Leadership and effective management.* Glenview, IL: Scott, Foresman, 1974.

Fiedler, F. E., Chemers, M. M. & Mahar, L. *Improving leadership effectiveness: The leader match concept.* New York: Wiley, 1976.

Fiedler, F. E., & Leister, A. Intelligence and group performance: A multiple screen model. *Organizational Behavior and Human Performance*, 1977, *20*, 1–14.

Fiedler, F. E., & Meuwese, W. A. T. Leader's contribution to task performance in cohesive and uncohesive groups. *Journals of Abnormal and Social Psychology*, 1963, *67*, 83–87.

Fiedler, F. E., Meuwese, W., and Oonk, S. An exploratory study of group creativity in laboratory tasks. *Acta Psychologica*, 1961, *18*, 100–119.

Fisek, M. H., & Ofshe, R. The process of status evolution. *Sociometry*, 1970, *33*, 327–46.

Fishbein, M., Landy, E., & Hatch, G. Some determinants of an individual's esteem for his least preferred co-worker: An attitudinal analysis. *Human Relations*, 1969, *22*, 173–88.

Fivars, G. *The critical incident technique: A bibliography*. Palo Alto, CA: American Institutes for Research, 1973.

Flanagan, J. C. The critical incident technique. *Psychological Bulletin*, 1954, *51*, 327–58.

Flanagan, J. C. Leadership skills: Their identification, development and evaluation. In L. Petrullo and B. M. Bass (Eds.), *Leadership and interpersonal behavior*. New York: Holt, Rinehart, and Winston, 1961.

Fleishman, E. A. The description of supervisory behavior. *Journal of Applied Psychology*, 1953, *37*, 1–6.

Fleishman, E. A. A leader behavior description for industry. In R. M. Stogdill and A. E. Coons (Eds.), *Leader behavior: Its description and measurement*. Columbus, OH: Bureau of Business Research, The Ohio State University, 1957.

Fleishman, E. A. Overview. In E. A. Fleishman and J. G. Hunt (Eds.), *Current developments in the study of leadership*. Carbondale, IL: Southern Illinois University Press, 1973. (a)

Fleishman, E. A. Twenty years of consideration and structure. In E. A. Fleishman and J. G. Hunt (Eds.), *Current developments in the study of leadership*. Carbondale, IL: Southern Illinois University Press, 1973. (b)

Fleishman, E. A., & Harris, E. F. Patterns of leadership behavior related to employee grievances and turnover. *Personnel Psychology*, 1962, *15*, 43–56.

Fleishman, E. A., Harris, E. F., & Burtt, H. E. *Leadership and supervision in industry*. Columbus, OH: Bureau of Educational Research, Ohio State University, 1955.

Fodor, E. M., & Farrow, D. L. The power motive as an influence on use of power. Paper presented at the 86th Annual Convention of the American Psychological Association, Toronto, Ontario, Canada, September 1978.

Ford, R. N. *Motivation through the work itself*. New York: American Management Association, 1960.

Frank, R. S. Studying political or quasi-political elites using at-a-distance techniques. Unpublished manuscript. Philadelphia: University City Science Center, September 1978.

French, J. R. P., Jr. Organized and unorganized groups under fear and frustration. *University of Iowa Studies in Child Welfare*, 1944, *20*, 231–308.

French, J. R. P., Jr. Field experiments: Changing group productivity. In J. G. Miller (Ed.), *Experiments in social process: A symposium on social psychology*, New York: McGraw-Hill, 1950.

French, J. R. P., Jr. A formal theory of social power. *Psychological Review*, 1956, *63*, 181–94.

French, J. R. P., Jr., & Raven, B. H. The bases of social power. In D. Cartwright (Ed.), *Studies in social power*. Ann Arbor, MI: Institute for Social Research, University of Michigan, 1959.

French, J. R. P., Jr., & Snyder, R. Leadership and interpersonal power. In D. Cartwright (Ed.), *Studies in social power*. Ann Arbor, MI: Institute for Social Research, University of Michigan, 1959.

Frohman, M. A., Sashkin, M., & Kavanagh, M. J. Action research as applied to organization development. *Organization and Administrative Sciences*, 1976, *7*, 129–64.

Fromkin, H. L., & Streufert, S. Laboratory experimentation. In M. D. Dunnette, (Ed.) *Handbook of industrial and organizational psychology*. Chicago: Rand McNally, 1976, 415–65.

Geis, F. Machiavellianism in a semireal world. *Proceedings of the 76th Annual Convention of the American Psychological Association*, 1968, *3*, 407–8.

Gellner, E. Beyond truth and falsehood. *British Journal of the Philosophy of Science*, 1975, *26*, 331–42.

George, C. E. Some determinants of small-group effectiveness. Research Memorandum (Subtask Unifect No. 26). Alexandria, VA: Human Resources Research Office (HumRRO), October 1962.

Georgopoulis, B. S., Mahoney, G. M., & Jones, N. W. A path-goal approach to productivity. *Journal of Applied Psychology*, 1957, *41*, 345–53.

Ghiselli, E. E. The validity of a personnel interview. *Personnel Psychology*, 1966, *19*, 389–95.

Ginter, G., & Lindskold, S. Rate of participation and expertise as factors influencing leader choice. *Journal of Personality and Social Psychology*, 1975, *32*, 1085–89.

Gleason, J. M., Seaman, F. J., and Hollander, E. P. *Social behavior and personality*. 1978, *6*(1), 33–36.

Gomberg, W. The trouble with democratic management. *Trans-action*, 1965, *3*(5), 30–35.

Graen, G. Role making processes within complex organizations. In M. D. Dunnette (Ed.), *Handbook of industrial and organizational psychology*. Chicago: Rand McNally, 1975, chapter 28.

Graen, G., & Cashman, J. F. A role-making model of leadership in formal organizations: A developmental approach. In J. G. Hunt and L. L. Larson (Eds.), *Leadership Frontiers*. Kent, OH: Comparative Administration Research Institute, Kent State University, 1975.

Graen, G., Cashman, J., Ginsburgh, S., & Schiemann, W. Effects of linking-pin quality upon the quality of life of lower participants: A longitudinal investigation of the managerial understructure. *Administrative Science Quarterly*. 1977, *22*, 191–202.

Graen, G., Dansereau, F., Haga, W. J., & Cashman, J. R. Organizational understructure and leadership: A longitudinal investigation of the role-making process. *Organizational Behavior and Human Performance*, 1976, *15*, 278–96.

Graen, G., Dansereau, F., Minami, T., & Cashman, J. Leadership behaviors as cues to performance evaluation. *Academy of Management Journal*, 1973, *16*, 611–23.

Gray, L. N., Richardson, J. T., & Mayhew, B. M., Jr. Influence attempts and effective power: A re-examination of an unsubstantiated hypothesis. *Sociometry*, 1968, *31*, 245–58.

Gray, L. N., & von Broembsen, M. H. The effects of extraneous mass mediated stimuli on power relations: Some preliminary findings. *Human Relations*, 1974, *27*, 793–812.

Greene, C. N. The reciprocal nature of influence between leader and subordinate. *Journal of Applied Psychology*, 1975, *60*, 187–93.

Greene, C. N. Causal connections among cohesion, drive, goal acceptance, and productivity in work groups. Paper presented at the 36th Annual Academy of Management Meeting, Kansas City, MO, August 1976.

Greene, C. N. Disenchantment with leadership research: Some causes, recommendations, and alternative directions. In J. G. Hunt and L. L. Larson (Eds.), *Leadership: The cutting edge.* Carbondale, IL: Southern Illinois University Press, 1977, 57–67.

Greene, C. N. Modifications to a situational model of leadership effectiveness. In C. N. Greene (Chairman), Leadership Research: Nonestablishment Views. Symposium presented at the 38th Annual Academy of Management Meeting, San Francisco, August 1978.

Greene, C. N., & Schriesheim, C. A. Causal paths among dimensions of leadership, group drive, and cohesiveness: A longitudinal field investigation. Paper presented at the 37th Annual Academy of Management Meeting, Orlando, FL, August 1977.

Griffin, R. W. Task design determinants of effective leader behavior. *Academy of Management Review*, 1979, in press.

Grimes, A. J. Authority, power, influence and social control: A theoretical synthesis. *Academy of Management Review*, 1978, *3*, 724–35.

Gross, E. Some functional consequences of primary controls in formal work organizations. *American Sociological Review*, 1953, *18*, 368–73.

Gross, E. Primary functions of the small group. *American Journal of Sociology*, 1954, *60*, 24–30.

Guyot, D. The organization of police departments: Changing the model from the army to the hospital. *Criminal Justice Abstracts*, 1977, *9*, 231–56.

Habermas, J. *Knowledge and human interest.* London: Heinemann, 1972.

Hackman, R. J. Group influences on individuals. In M. D. Dunnette (Ed.), *Handbook of industrial and organizational psychology.* Chicago: Rand McNally, 1976.

Hackman, J. R., Oldham, G., Janson, R., & Purdy, D. A new strategy for job enrichment. *California Management Review*, 1975, *17*(4), 57–71.

Haga, W. J., Graen, G., & Dansereau, F. Professionalism and role-making within a service organization. *American Sociological Review*, 1974, *39*, 122–33.

Halal, W. E. Toward a general theory of leadership. *Human Relations*, 1974, *27*, 401–16.

Hall, J., & Watson, W. The effects of a normative intervention on group decision-making performance. *Human Relations*, 1970, *23*, 299–317.

Halpin, A. W. The leader behavior and combat effectiveness of aircraft commanders. In R. M. Stogdill and A. E. Coons (Eds.), *Leader Behavior: Its description and measurement.* Columbus, OH: Bureau of Business Research, The Ohio State University, 1957. (a)

Halpin, A. W. *Manual for the leader behavior description questionnaire.* Columbus, OH: Bureau of Business Research, The Ohio State University, 1957. (b)

Halpin, A. W., & Winer, B. J. A factorial study of the leader behavior descriptions. In R. R. Stogdill and A. E. Coons (Eds.), *Leader behavior: Its description and measurement.* Columbus, OH: Bureau of Business Research, The Ohio State University, 1957

Hamblin, R. L. Leadership and crises, *Sociometry*, 1958, *21*, 322–35.

Hammer, T. H. Towards an understanding of the leadership concept: Construct validation of a leadership process model. Technical Report, School of Industrial and Labor Relations, Cornell University, 1977.

Hammer, T. H., & Dachler, H. P. A test of some assumptions underlying the Path-goal model of supervision: Some suggested conceptual modifications. *Organizational Behavior and Human Performance*, 1975, *14*, 60–75.

Hamner, W. C., & Hamner, E. Behavior modification on the bottom line. *Organizational Dynamics*, 1976, *4*(4), 2–21.

Hand, H. H., & Slocum, J. W., Jr. A longitudinal study of the effects of a human relations training program on managerial effectiveness. *Journal of Applied Psychology*, 1972, *56*, 412–17.

Hare, A. P. *Handbook of small group research* (2nd ed.) New York: Macmillan, Free Press, 1976.

Havelock, R. G. Dissemination and translation roles. In T. L. Erdell and J. M. Kitchell (Eds.), *Knowledge production and utilization in educational administration.* Eugene, OR: University Council for Educational Administration, and Center for the Advanced Study of Educational Administration, University of Oregon, 1968.

Havelock, R. G., Guskin, A., Frohman, M., Havelock, M., Hill, J., & Huber, J. *Planning for innovation through the dissemination and utilization of knowledge.* Ann Arbor, MI: Institute for Social Research, University of Michigan, 1969.

Havelock, R. G., & Havelock, M. *Training for change agents.* Ann Arbor, MI: Institute for Social Research, University of Michigan, 1970.

Haythorn, W., Couch, A., Haefner, D., Langham, P., & Carter, L. F. The behavior of authoritarian and equalitarian personalities in small groups. *Human Relations*, 1956, *9*, 57–74. (a)

Haythorn, W., Couch, A., Haefner, D., Langham, P., & Carter, L. F. The effects of varying combinations of authoritarian and equalitarian leaders and followers. *Journal of Abnormal and Social Psychology*, 1956, *53*, 210–19. (b)

Heinen, J. S., & Jacobsen, E. A model of task group development in complex organizations and a strategy for implementation. *Academy of Management Review*, 1976, *1*, 98–111.

Heinicke, C. M., & Bales, R. F. Developmental trends in the structure of small groups. *Sociometry*, 1953, *16*, 7–38.

Heller, T., & Stein, R. T. Explaining the relationship of leadership status to high verbal participation. *Personality and Social Psychology Bulletin*, 1978, *4*, 356.

Hemphill, J. K., & Coons, A. E. Development of the Leader Behavior Description Questionnaire. In R. M. Stogdill and A. E. Coons (Eds.), *Leader behavior: Its description and measurement.* Columbus, OH: Bureau of Business Research, The Ohio State University, 1957.

Hemphill, J. K., Siegel, A., & Westie, C. W. An exploratory study of relations between perceptions of leader behavior, group characteristics, and expectations concerning the behavior of ideal leaders. Unpublished manuscript, Personnel Research Board, The Ohio State University, 1951.

Hermann, M. G. Assessing the personalities of political leaders at a distance: The Soviet politburo. Paper presented at the 86th Annual Convention of the American Psychological Association, Toronto, Ontario, Canada, September 1978.

Herold, D. M. Interaction of subordinate and leader characteristics in moderating the consideration-satisfaction relationship. *Journal of Applied Psychology*, 1974, *59*, 649–51.

Herold, D. M. Two-way influence processes in leader-follower dyads. *Academy of Management Journal*, 1977, *20*, 224–37.

Hersey, P., & Blanchard, K. H. Life Cycle Theory of Leadership. *Training and Development Journal*, 1969, *23*(5), 26–34.

Hersey, P., & Blanchard, K. H. *Management of organizational behavior* (3rd ed.). Englewood Cliffs, NJ: Prentice-Hall, 1977.

Heslin, R., & Dunphy, D. Three dimensions of member satisfaction in small groups. *Human Relations*, 1964, *17*, 99–112.

Hilgard, E. R., Sait, E. M., & Margaret, G. A. Level of aspiration as affected by relative standing in an experimental social group. *Journal of Experimental Psychology*, 1940, *27*, 411–21.

Hill, W. A., & Hughes, D. Variations on leader behavior as a function of task type. *Organizational Behavior and Human Performance*, 1974, *11*, 83–96.

Hoffman, L. R. The beginnings of a hierarchical model of group problem solving. In L. R. Hoffman (Ed.), *The group problem-solving process: Studies of a valence model*. New York: Praeger, 1979, in press.

Hoffman, L. R., Bond, G., & Falk, G. Valence for criteria: A preliminary exploration. In L. R. Hoffman (Ed.), *The group problem-solving process: Studies of a valence model*. New York: Praeger, 1979, in press.

Hoffman, L. R., & Clark, M. M. Participation and influence in problem-solving groups. In L. R. Hoffman (Ed.), *The group problem-solving process: Studies of a valence model*. New York: Praeger, 1979, in press.

Hoffman, L. R., Friend, K. E., & Bond, G. Problem differences and the process of adopting group solutions. In L. R. Hoffman (Ed.), *The group problem-solving process: Studies of a valence model*. New York: Praeger, 1979, in press.

Hoffman, L. R., & Maier, N. R. F. Valence in the adoption of solutions by problem-solving groups: Concept, method and results. *Journal of Abnormal and Social Psychology*, 1964, *69*, 264–71.

Hoffman, L. R., & Maier, N. R. F. Valence in the adoption of solutions by problem-solving groups: II. Quality and acceptance as goals of leaders and members. *Journal of Personality and Social Psychology*, 1967, *6*, 175–82.

Hoffman, L. R., & O'Day, R. The process of adopting reasoning and value problems. In L. R. Hoffman (Ed.), *The group problem-solving process: Studies of a valence model*. New York: Praeger, 1979, in press.

Hollander, E. P. Conformity, status, and idiosyncrasy credit. *Psychological Review*, 1958, *65*, 117–27.

Hollander, E. P. Competence and conformity in the acceptance of influence. *Journal of Abnormal and Social Psychology*, 1960, *61*, 365–69.

Hollander, E. P. Emergent leadership and social influence. In L. Petrullo and B. M. Bass (Eds.), *Leadership and interpersonal behavior*. New York: Holt, Rinehart, and Winston, 1961.

Hollander, E. P. *Leaders, groups and influence.* New York: Oxford University Press, 1964.

Hollander, E. P. *Leadership dynamics.* New York: Macmillan, Free Press, 1978.

Hollander, E. P., Fallon, B. J., & Edwards, M. T. Some aspects of influence and acceptability for appointed and elected group leaders. *Journal of Psychology,* 1977, *95,* 289–96.

Hollander, E. P., & Julian, J. W. Contemporary trends in the analysis of leadership processes. *Psychological Bulletin,* 1969, *71,* 387–97.

Hollander, E. P., & Julian, J. W. Studies in leader legitimacy, influence, and innovation. In L. Berkowitz (Ed.), *Advances in Experimental Social Psychology* (Vol. 5). New York: Academic Press, 1970, 33–69.

Hollander, E. P., & Julian, J. W. A further look at leader legitimacy, influence, and innovation. In L. Berkowitz (Ed.), *Group Processes.* New York: Academic Press, 1978.

Hollander, E. P., & Neider, L. L. Critical incidents and rating scales in comparing 'good'-'bad' leadership. Paper presented at the 86th Annual Convention of the American Psychological Association, Toronto, Ontario, Canada, September 1978.

Holton, G. *Science and culture.* Boston: Houghton Mifflin, 1965.

Homans, G. C. The Western Electric researches. In S. D. Hoslett (Ed.), *Human factors in management.* Parkville, MO: Park College Press, 1946.

Homans, G. C. *Social behavior: Its elementary forms.* New York: Harcourt, 1961.

Horst, P. A generalized expression for the reliability of measures. *Psychometrika,* 1949, *14,* 21–31.

Horwitz, M. The recall of interrupted group tasks: An experimental study of individual motivation to group goals. *Human Relations,* 1954, *7,* 3–38.

Hosking, D.-M. A critical evaluation of Fiedler's predictor measures of leadership effectiveness. Unpublished doctoral dissertation, University of Warwick, 1978.

Hosking, D.-M., & Schriesheim, C. A. Improving leadership effectiveness: The leader match concept, *Administrative Science Quarterly,* 1978, *23,* 496–505.

House, R. J. A path-goal theory of leader effectiveness. *Administrative Science Quarterly,* 1971, *16,* 321–38.

House, R. J. A 1976 theory of charismatic leadership. In J. G. Hunt and L. L. Larson (Eds.), *Leadership: The cutting edge.* Carbondale, IL: Southern Illinois University Press, 1977, 189–207.

House, R. J., & Baetz, M. L. Leadership: Some empirical generalizations and new research directions. In B. Staw (Ed.), *Research in Organizational Behavior.* Greenwich, CT: JAI Press, 1979, in press.

House, R. J., & Dessler, G. The path-goal theory of leadership: Some post hoc and a priori tests. In J. G. Hunt & L. L. Larson (Eds.), *Contingency approaches to leadership.* Carbondale, IL: Southern Illinois University Press, 1974.

House, R. J., & Mitchell, T. R. Path-goal theory of leadership. *Journal of Contemporary Business,* 1974, *3*(4), 81–97.

Hovland, C. I. Reconciling conflicting results derived from experimental and survey studies of attitude change. *American Psychologist,* 1959, *14,* 8–17.

Howells, L. T., & Becker, S. W. Seating arrangement and leadership emergence. *Journal of Abnormal and Social Psychology*, 1962, *64*, 148–50.

Huck, J. R. Assessment centers: A review of the external and internal validities. *Personnel Psychology*, 1973, *26*, 191–212.

Hunt, J. G. Different nonleader sources of clarity as alternatives to leadership. In B. J. Kolasa (Ed.), *Proceedings of the 12th annual Eastern Academy of Management Meeting*. Pittsburgh: College of Business Administration, Duquesne University, 1975.

Hunt, J. G., & Larson L. L. Some additional facets of the cutting edge: An epilog. In J. G. Hunt and L. L. Larson (Eds.), *Leadership: The cutting edge*. Carbondale, IL: Southern Illinois University Press, 1977.

Hunt, J. G., & Osborn, R. M. A multiple influence approach to leadership for managers. In J. S. Stinson and P. Hersey (Eds.), *Perspectives in Leader Effectiveness*. Athens, OH: Center for Leadership Studies, Ohio University, 1979, in press.

Hunt, J. G., Osborn, R. N., & Schriesheim, C. A. Some neglected aspects of leadership research. In C. N. Greene and P. H. Birnbaum (Eds.), *Proceedings of the 21st Annual Midwest Academy of Management Conference*. Bloomington/Indianapolis, IN: Graduate School of Business, Indiana University, 1978.

Hunt, J. G., Osborn, R. N., & Schuler, R. S. Relations of discretionary and non-discretionary leadership to performance and satisfaction in a complex organization. *Human Relations*, 1978, *31*, 507–23.

Ilgen, D. R., & Fujii, D. S. An investigation of the validity of leader behavior descriptions obtained from subordinates. *Journal of Applied Psychology*, 1976, *61*, 642–51.

Ingham, A. G., Levinger, G., Graves, J., & Peckham, V. The Ringlemann effect: Studies of group size and group performance. *Journal of Experimental Social Psychology*, 1974, *10*, 371–84.

Ivancevich, J. M. An analysis of control, bases of control, and satisfaction in an organizational setting. *Academy of Management Journal*, 1970, *13*, 427–36.

Ivancevich, J. M., & Donnelly, J. H. Leader influence and performance. *Personnel Psychology*, 1970, *23*, 539–49.

Jackson, J. M. Structural characteristics of norms. In National Society for the Study of Education Yearbook, *The dynamics of instructional groups*. Chicago: University of Chicago Press, 1960.

Jackson, P. W. Other voices. *School Review*, 1977, *85*, 425–32.

Jacobs, T. O. *Leadership and exchange in formal organizations*. Alexandria, VA: Human Resources Research Organization (HumRRO), 1970.

Jaffe, C. L., & Lucas, R. L. Effects of rates of talking and correctness of decision on leader choice in small groups. *Journal of Social Psychology*, 1969, *79*, 247–54.

Jago, A. G. A test of spuriousness in descriptive models of participative leader behavior. *Journal of Applied Psychology*, 1978, *63*, 383–87.

Jago, A. G. Configural cue utilization in implicit models of leader behavior. *Organizational Behavior and Human Performance*, 1979, in press.

Jago, A. G., & Vroom, V. H. Perceptions of leadership style: Superior and subordinate descriptions of decision-making behavior. In J. G. Hunt and L. L.

Larson (Eds.), *Leadership frontiers*. Kent, OH: Comparative Administration Research Institute, Kent State University, 1975.

Janis, I. L. *Victims of Groupthink*. Boston: Houghton Mifflin, 1972.

Jenkins, D. H. Feedback and group self-evaluation. *Journal of Social Issues*, 1948, *4*, 50–60.

Jermier, J. M., & Berkes, L. J. Leader behavior in a police command bureaucracy: A closer look at the quasi-military model. *Administrative Science Quarterly*, 1979, in press.

Johnston, J. M., Duncan, P. K., Monroe, C., Stephenson, H., & Stoerzinger, A. Tactics and benefits of behavioral measurement in business. *Journal of Organizational Behavior Management*, 1978, *1*, 164–78.

Kabanoff, B., & O'Brien, G. E. Cooperation structure and the relationship of leader and member ability to group performance. Unpublished manuscript, School of Social Sciences, University of Flanders, Australia, 1978.

Kaczka, E., & Kirk, R. L. Managerial climate, work groups, and organizational performance. *Administrative Science Quarterly*, 1967, *12*, 253–72.

Kaplan, A. *The conduct of inquiry: Methodology for behavioral science*. San Francisco: Chandler, 1964.

Karmel, B. Leadership: A challenge to traditional research methods and assumptions. *Academy of Management Review*, 1978, *3*, 475–82.

Katzell, R. A., Miller, C. E., Rotter, N. G., & Venet, T. G. Effects of leadership and other inputs on group processes and outputs. *Journal of Social Psychology*, 1970, *80*, 157–59.

Keeler, B. T., & Andrews, J. H. M. Leader behavior of principals, staff morale, and productivity. *Alberta Journal of Educational Research*, 1963, *9*, 179–91.

Kelly, R. W., & Ware, H. F. An experiment in group dynamics. *Advanced Management*, 1947, *12*(3), 116–19.

Kelman, H. C., *A Time to Speak*, San Francisco: Jossey-Bass, 1969.

Kerlinger, F. N. *Foundations of behavioral research*. New York: Holt, Rinehart, and Winston, 1973.

Kerr, S. Ability and willingness-to-leave as moderators of relationships between task and leader variables and satisfaction. *Journal of Business Research*, 1973, *2*, 115–28.

Kerr, S. Substitutes for leadership: Their meaning and measurement. In H. E. Schneider (Ed.), *American Institute of Decision Sciences Proceedings*. San Francisco, 1976.

Kerr, S., & Schriesheim, C. A. Consideration, initiating structure, and organizational criteria—An update of Korman's 1966 review. *Personnel Psychology*, 1974, *27*, 555–68.

Kiessling, R. J., & Kalish, R. A. Correlates of success in leaderless group discussion. *Journal of Social Psychology*, 1961, *54*, 359–65.

Kipnis, D. *The powerholder*. Chicago, University of Chicago Press, 1976.

Kipnis, D., Castell, P. J., Gergen, M., & Mauch, D. Metamorphic effects of power. *Journal of Applied Psychology*, 1976, *61*, 127–35.

Klein, L. *A social scientist in industry*. New York: Wiley, 1976.

Korman, A. K. 'Consideration,' 'initiating structure,' and organizational criteria. *Personnel Psychology*, 1966, *18*, 349–60.

Korman, A. K. Contingency approaches to leadership: An overview. In J. G. Hunt and L. L. Larson (Eds.), *Contingency approaches to leadership*. Carbondale, IL: Southern Illinois University Press, 1974, 189–95.

Kuhn, T., *The Structure of Scientific Revolution*. Chicago: University of Chicago Press, 1970.

Langer, E. J. Rethinking the role of thought in social interaction. Unpublished manuscript, Department of Psychology, Harvard University, 1977.

Larson, L. L., Bussom, R. S., & Vicars, W. M. The nature of a school superintendent's work. Unpublished manuscript, Department of Administrative Sciences, Southern Illinois University at Carbondale, 1978.

Larson, L. L., Hunt, J. G., & Osborn, R. N. The great hi-hi leader behavior myth: A lesson from Occam's razor. *Academy of Management Journal*, 1976, *19*, 628–41.

Larwood, L. Organizational implications of exchange theory. In C. Pinder and L. F. Modre (Eds.), *Middle range theory and the study of organization*. Leiden: Martinus Nijhoff, 1978, in press.

Laski, H. J. The limitations of the expert. *Harper's Magazine*, 1930, *162*, 102–6.

Latham, G. P., & Yukl, G. A. A review of research on the application of goal setting in organizations. *Academy of Management Journal*, 1975, *18*, 824–45.

Lawler, E. E., III. Motivation in work organizations. Belmont, CA: Brooks/Cole, 1973.

Lawrence, L. C., & Smith, P. C. Group decision and employee participation. *Journal of Applied Psychology*, 1955, *39*, 334–37.

Leavitt, H. J. Some effects of certain communication patterns on group performance. *Journal of Abnormal and Social Psychology*, 1951, *46*, 38–50.

Leavitt, H. J. Suppose we took groups seriously. In E. L. Case and F. G. Zimmer (Eds.), *Man and work in society*. New York: Van Nostrand Reinhold, 1975.

Levinson, D. L. *The Seasons of a Man's Life*. New York: Knopf, 1978.

Lewin, K. Frontiers on group dynamics. *Human Relations*, 1947, *1*, 5–42.

Lewin, K. *Resolving social conflicts: Selected papers on group dynamics*. New York: Harper, 1948.

Lewin, K., Lippitt, R., & White, R. K. Patterns of aggressive behavior in experimentally created 'social climates.' *Journal of Social Psychology*, 1939, *10*, 271–99.

Lewis, S. A., Langan, C. J., & Hollander, E. P. Expectation of future interaction and the choice of less desirable alternatives in conformity. *Sociometry*, 1972, *35*, 440–47.

Likert, R. *New Patterns of management*. New York: McGraw-Hill, 1961.

Likert, R. *The human organization*. New York: McGraw-Hill, 1967.

Lippitt, R. An experimental study of the effect of democratic and authoritarian group atmospheres. *University of Iowa Studies in Child Welfare*, 1940, *16*, 43–95.

Litwin, G. H., & Stringer, R. A., Jr. *Motivation and organizational climate*. Cambridge, MA: Graduate School of Business Administration, Harvard University, 1968.

Lombardo, M. M. Looking at leadership: Some neglected issues. Technical Report No. 6. Greensboro, NC: Center for Creative Leadership, January 1978.

Lord, R. G. Functional leadership behavior: Measurement and relation to social power and leadership perceptions. *Administrative Science Quarterly*, 1977, *22*, 114–33.

Lord, R. G., Binning, J. F., Rush, M. C., & Thomas, J. C. The effect of performance cues and leader behavior on questionnaire ratings of leadership behavior. *Organizational Behavior and Human Performance*, 1978, *21*, 27–39.

Lott, A. J., & Lott, B. E. Group cohesiveness as interpersonal attraction: A review of relationships with antecedent and consequent variables. *Psychological Bulletin*, 1965, *64*, 259–302.

Lott, B. E. Cohesiveness: A learning phenomenon. *Journal of Social Psychology*, 1961, *55*, 275–86.

Lowin, A., & Craig, J. R. The influence of level of performance on managerial style: An experimental object-lesson in the ambiguity of correlational data. *Organizational Behavior and Human Performance*, 1968, *3*, 440–58.

Lowin, A., Hrapchek, W. J., & Kavanagh, J. J. Consideration and initiating structure: An experimental investigation of leadership traits. *Administrative Science Quarterly*, 1969, *14*, 238–53.

Lundberg, C. C. The effect of self-expectations on perceived leadership: An experimental inquiry. Paper presented at the 86th Annual Convention of the American Psychological Association, Toronto, Ontario, Canada, September 1978.

Lupton, T. *On the shop floor.* London: Pergamon, 1963.

Luthans, F. *Organizational behavior.* New York: McGraw-Hill, 1977.

Luthans, F. Resolved: Functional analysis is the best way to make a diagnostic evaluation of organizational behavior. In B. Karmel (Ed.), *Point and counterpoint in organizational behavior.* Philadelphia: Saunders, 1979, in press.

Luthans, F., & Kreitner, R. *Organizational behavior modification.* Glenview, IL: Scott, Foresman, 1975.

McCall, M. W., Jr. Leaders and leadership: Of substance and shadow. In J. Hackman, E. E. Lawler, and L. Porter (Eds.), *Perspectives on behavior in organizations.* New York: McGraw-Hill, 1977.

McCall, M. W., Jr. Leadership as a design problem. Technical Report No. 5. Greensboro, N.C.: Center for Creative Leadership, January 1978.

McCall, M. W., Jr. Power, influence and authority: The hazards of carrying a sword. Technical Report No. 10. Greensboro, NC: Center for Creative Leadership, August 1978.

McCall, M. W., Jr. and Lombardo M. M. (Eds.) *Leadership: Where Else Can We Go?* Durham, NC: Duke University Press, 1978.(a)

McCall, M. W., Jr., & Lombardo, M. M. Looking Glass, Inc.: An Organizational simulation. Technical Report No. 12, Operational Manual Vol. 1. Greensboro, NC: Center for Creative Leadership, October 1978.(b)

McCall, M. W., Jr., Morrison, A. M., & Hannan, R. L. Studies of managerial work: Results and methods. Technical Report No. 9. Greensboro, NC: Center for Creative Leadership, May 1978.

McFillen, J. M. Situational determinants of supervisor attributions and behavior. Unpublished manuscript, College of Business administration, Arizona State University, 1978.

McGrath, J. E., & Altman, I. *Small group research.* New York: Holt, 1966.

MacKinnon, D. W. An overview of assessment centers. Technical Report No. 1. Greensboro, NC: Center for Creative Leadership, May 1975.

Mahoney, J. J. *Cognition and behavior modification*. Cambridge, MA: Ballinger, 1974.

Maier, N. R. F. *Psychology in industrial organizations* (4th ed.). Boston: Houghton Mifflin, 1974.

Maier, N. R. F., & Hoffman, L. R. Financial incentives and group decision in motivating change. *Journal of Social Psychology*, 1964, *64*, 369–78.

Maier, N. R. F., & Sashkin, J. Specific leader behaviors that promote problem solving. *Personnel Psychology*, 1971, *24*, 35–44.

Mann, F., & Baumgartel, H. *Absences and employee attitudes in an electric power company*. Ann Arbor, MI: Institute for Social Research, University of Michigan, 1962.

Mann, R. D. A review of the relationships between personality and performance in small groups. *Psychological Bulletin*, 1959, *56*, 241–70.

March, J. G., & Simon, H. A. *Organizations*. New York: Wiley, 1958.

Marquis, D. G., Guetzkow, H., & Heyns, R. W. A social psychological study of the decision-making conference. In H. Guetzkow (Ed.), *Groups, leadership, and men: Research in human relations*. Pittsburgh: Carnegie Press, 1951.

Marsh, M. K. The moderating effect of organizational type on the relationship between leadership style and organizational effectiveness. Doctoral dissertation in progress, Department of Management, University of Oklahoma, 1979.

Martin, T. N., & Hunt, J. G. A path-analytic influence process model of intent to leave. In Miller, E. (Ed.), *Proceedings of the twenty-second annual Midwest Academy of Management Conference*. Ann Arbor, MI: University of Michigan, 1979.

Mawhinney, T. C. Operant terms and concepts in the description of individual work behavior: Some problems of interpretation, application, and evaluation. *Journal of Applied Psychology*, 1975, *60*, 704–12.

Mawhinney, T. C. Contingencies of leadership: A paradigm for causing and analyzing reciprocal causation in the superior-subordinate dyad. Unpublished manuscript, Graduate School of Business, Indiana University, 1978.

Mawhinney, T. C., & Ford, J. D. The path-goal theory of leader effectiveness: An operant interpretation. *Academy of Management Review*, 1977, *2*, 398–411.

Mayhew, B. M., Jr., Gray, L. N., & Richardson, J. T. Behavioral measurement of operating power structures: Characterizations of asymmetrical interaction. *Sociometry*, 1969, *32*, 474–89.

Meichenbaum, Donald. Toward a cognitive theory of self-control. In G. Schwartz and D. Shapiro (Eds.), *Consciousness and Self-regulation: Advances in Research*. New York: Plenum, 1976, 223–60.

Melcher, A. J. Leadership models and research approaches. In J. G. Hunt and L. L. Larson (Eds.), *Leadership: The cutting edge*. Carbondale, IL: Southern Illinois University Press, 1977, 94–108.

Meltzer, H., & Wickert, F. R. *Humanizing organizational behavior*. Springfield, IL: Charles C. Thomas, 1976.

Merton, R. K. *Social theory and social structure*. Glencoe, IL: Free Press, 1957.

Meuwese, W. & Fiedler, F. E. Leadership and group creativity under varying conditions of stress. Cited in Fiedler, F. E., *A theory of leadership effectiveness*. New York: McGraw-Hill, 1967.

Michener, H. A., & Burt, M. R. Components of authority as determinants of compliance. *Journal of Personality and Social Psychology*, 1975, *31*, 606–14.

Mills, C. W. Situated actions and vocabularies of motive. *American Sociological Review*, 1940, *5*, 904–13.

Miner, J. B. The uncertain future of the leadership concept: An overview. In J. G. Hunt and L. L. Larson (Eds.), *Leadership Frontiers*. Kent, OH: Comparative Administration Research Institute, Kent State University, 1975, 197–208.

Mintzberg, H. *The nature of managerial work*. New York: Harper and Row, 1973.

Mitchell, T. R. The construct validity of three dimensions of leadership research. *Journal of Social Psychology*, 1970, *80*, 89–94.

Mitchell, T. R., & Green, S. G. Leader responses to poor performance: An attributional analysis. Paper presented at the 86th Annual Convention of the American Psychological Association, Toronto, Ontario, Canada, September 1978.

Mitchell, T. R., Larson, J. R., & Green, S. G. Leader behavior, situational moderators, and group performance: An attributional analysis. *Organizational Behavior and Human Performance*, 1977, *18*, 254–68.

Moreno, J. L. *Sociometry, Experimental Method and the Science of Society*. Beacon, NY: Beacon House, 1951.

Morris, C. G., & Hackman, J. R. Behavioral correlates of perceived leadership. *Journal of Personality and Social Psychology*, 1969, *13*, 350–61.

Moses, J. L., & Byham, W. C. *Applying the assessment center method*. New York: Pergamon Press, 1977.

Mowday, R. T. The exercise of upward influence in organizations. *Administrative Science Quarterly*, 1978, *23*, 137–56.

Murray, H. *Explorations in personality*. New York: Oxford University Press, 1938.

Nisbett, R. E., & Wilson, T. D. Telling more than we can know: Verbal reports on mental processes. *Psychological Review*, 1977, *84*, 231–59.

Normann, R. *Management for growth*. London: Wiley, 1977.

Nystrom, P. C. Managers and the hi-hi leader myth. *Academy of Management Journal*, 1978, *21*, 325–31.

O'Brien, G. E., & Harary, F. Measurement of the interactive effects of leadership style and group structure upon group performance. *Australian Journal of Psychology*, 1977, *29*, 59–71.

O'Brien, G. E., & Kabanoff, B. The effects of leadership style and group structure upon group performance: Implications for training. Paper presented at the International Congress of Applied Psychology, Munich, August 1978.

Oldham, G. R. The impact of supervisory characteristics on goal acceptance. *Academy of Management Journal*, 1975, *18*, 461–75.

Osborn, R. N., & Hunt, J. G. Environment and leadership: Discretionary and non-discretionary leader behavior and organizational outcomes. Unpublished manuscript, Department of Administrative Sciences, Southern Illinois University at Carbondale, 1977.

Osborn, R. N., Hunt, J. G., & Jauch, L. R. *Organizational theory: An integrated approach*. New York: Wiley, 1980, in press.

Osgood, C. E., & Walker, E. Motivation and language behavior: A content analysis of suicide notes, *Journal of Abnormal and Social Psychology*, 1959, *59*, 58–67.

Palmer, W. J. Management effectiveness as a function of personality traits of the manager. *Personnel Psychology*, 1974, *27*, 283–396.

Parsons, T. *The social system.* Glencoe, IL: Free Press, 1951.

Paul, W. J., Robertson, K. B., & Herzberg, F. Job enrichment pays off. *Harvard Business Review*, 1969, *47*(2), 61–78.

Pepinsky, P. N., Hemphill, J. K., & Shevitz, R. N. Attempts to lead, group productivity, and morale under conditions of acceptance and rejection. *Journal of Abnormal and Social Psychology*, 1958, *57*, 47–54.

Perrow, C. *Organization analysis: A sociological view.* Belmont, CA: Wadsworth, 1970.

Peterson, M. F. A problem-appropriate model of leader behavior determinants. Unpublished manuscript, Department of Psychology, University of Michigan, 1978.

Philip, H., & Dunphy, D. Developmental trends in small groups. *Sociometry*, 1959, *2*, 162–74.

Polanyi, M. *The tacit dimension.* Garden City, NY: Doubleday, 1966.

Pondy, L. R. Leadership is a language game. In M. W. McCall, Jr., and M. M. Lombardo (Eds.), *Leadership: Where else can we go?* Durham, NC: Duke University Press, 1978, 88–99.

Porter, L. W., & Steers, R. M. Organizational, work and personal factors in employee turnover and absenteeism. *Psychological Bulletin*, 1973, *80*, 151–76.

Potter, E., & Fiedler, F. E. Stress and the utilization of staff members' intelligence and experience. Unpublished manuscript, Department of Psychology, University of Washington, 1978.

Price, K. H., & Garland, H. Group member compliance as a function of leader competence, group versus individual decision making and leader monitoring behavior. Unpublished manuscript, Department of Business Administration, University of Texas at Arlington, 1976. (a)

Price, K. H., & Garland, H. Group member compliance as a function of leader endorsement and monitoring behavior of the leader. Unpublished manuscript, Department of Business Administration, University of Texas at Arlington, 1976. (b)

Price, K. H., & Garland, H. Group member endorsement and compliance toward the leader as a function of leader competence and group member competence. Paper presented at the 38th Annual Academy of Management Meeting, San Francisco, August, 1978 (a)

Price, K. H., & Garland, H. Leader interventions to ameliorate the negative consequences of group failure. *Journal of Management*, 1978, *4*, 7–16. (b)

Reason, J. T. Skill and error in everyday life. In J. A. H. Howe (Ed.), *Adult learning: Psychological research and applications.* New York: Wiley, 1977.

Rhenmann, E. *Organization theory for long-range planning.* London: Wiley, 1973.

Richardson, J. T., Dugan, J. R., Gray, L. N., & Mayhew, B. H., Jr. Expert power: A behavioral interpretation. *Sociometry*, 1973, *36*, 302–24.

Roethlisberger, F. J., & Dickinson, W. J. Management and the worker. Cambridge, MA: Harvard University Press, 1939.

Rosenthal, R., & Rosnow, R. (Eds.). *Artifact in behavioral research.* New York: Academic Press, 1969.

Rotter, J. B. Generalized expectancies for internal versus external control of reinforcement. *Psychological Monographs*, 1966, *80*(1, Whole No. 609).

Roy, D. Quota restriction and goldbricking in a machine shop. *American Journal of Sociology*, 1952, *57*, 427–42.

Roy, D. Work satisfaction and social reward in quota achievement: An analysis of piecework incentive. *American Sociological Review*, 1953, *18*, 507–14.

Roy, D. Efficiency and the 'fix': Informal intergroup relations in a piecework machine shop. *American Journal of Sociology*, 1954, *60*, 255–66.

Runyon, K. E. Some interactions between personality and management styles. *Journal of Applied Psychology*, 1973, *57*, 649–51.

Rush, M. C., Thomas, J. C., & Lord, R. G. Implicit leadership theory: A potential threat to the internal validity of leader behavior questionnaires. *Organizational Behavior and Human Performance*, 1977, *20*, 93–110.

Rychlak, J. F. Personality correlates of leadership among first level managers. *Psychological Reports*, 1963, *12*, 43–52.

Rychlak, J. F. *The Psychology of Riborous Humanism.* New York: Wiley, 1977.

Salancik, G. R., & Pfeffer, J. Who gets power—and how they hold on to it. *Organizational Dynamics*, 1977, *5*(3), 3–21.

Sample, J., & Wilson, I. Leader behavior, group productivity, and rating of least preferred coworker. *Journal of Personality and Social Psychology*, 1965, *1*, 266–70.

Sashkin, M., Morris, W. C. & Horst, L. A. A comparison of social and organizational change models. *Psychological Review*, 1973, *80*, 510–26.

Sayles, L. *Behavior of industrial work groups.* New York: Wiley, 1958.

Schachter, S., Ellertson, N., McBride, D., & Gregory, D. An experimental study of cohesiveness and productivity. *Human Relations*, 1951, *4*, 229–39.

Schachter, S., Willerman, B., Festinger, L., & Human, R. Emotional disruption and industrial productivity. *Journal of Applied Psychology*, 1961, *45*, 201–13.

Schiemann, W. A., & Graen, G. The predictability of communication in organizations: An empirical investigation and integration. Unpublished Manuscript, College of Industrial Management, Georgia Institute of Technology, 1978.

Schriesheim, C. A., & DeNisi, A. S. Effects of format variation on the convergent and discriminant validity of two leadership description questionnaires. In C. N. Greene and P. H. Birnbaum (Eds.), *Proceedings of the 21st Annual Midwest Academy of Management Conference.* Bloomington/Indianapolis, IN: Indiana University, 1978. (a)

Schriesheim, C. A., & DeNisi, A. S. The impact of implicit theories on the validity of questionnaires. Unpublished Manuscript, Department of Management, University of Southern California, 1978. (b)

Schriesheim, C. A., & Kerr, S. Psychometric properties of the Ohio State Leadership Scales. *Psychological Bulletin*, 1974, *81*, 756–65.

Schriesheim, C. A., & Kerr, S. Theories and measures of leadership: A critical appraisal of current and future directions. In J. G. Hunt and L. L. Larson

(Eds.), *Leadership: The cutting edge*, Carbondale, IL: Southern Illinois University Press, 1977, 9–45.

Schriesheim, C. A., & Kissler, C. D. Validity of subordinate-provided leader behavior descriptions as measures of objective or perceived group-directed leader behaviors. Unpublished manuscript, Graduate School of Business Administration, Kent State University, 1978.

Schriesheim, C. A., & Schriesheim, J. F. The development and empirical verification of new response categories to increase the validity of multiple response alternative questionnaires. *Educational and Psychological Measurement*, 1974, *34*, 877–84.

Schriesheim, C. A., & Schriesheim, J. F. The effects of group drive and cohesion, and member motivation and satisfaction on objective measures of productivity, turnover, and absenteeism. Unpublished manuscript, Graduate School of Business Administration, Kent State University, 1978.

Schutz, A. The stranger: An essay in social psychology. In A. Schutz, *Collected Papers* (Vol. 2). The Hague: Martinus Nijhoff, 1964, 91–105.

Schutz, W. C. *FIRO: A three-dimensional theory of interpersonal behavior*. New York: Holt, Rinehart, and Winston, 1958.

Scott, W. E., Jr. Leadership: A functional analysis. In J. G. Hunt and L. L. Larson (Eds.), *Leadership: The cutting edge*. Carbondale, IL: Southern Illinois University Press, 1977, 84–93.

Seashore, S. E. *Group cohesiveness in the industrial work group*. Ann Arbor, MI: Institute for Social Research, University of Michigan, 1954.

Seashore, S. E. Field experiments with formal organizations. In W. M. Evan (Ed.), *Organizational experiments: Laboratory and field research*. New York: Harper and Row, 1971, 147–53.

Seashore, S. E., & Bowers, D. G. Durability of organizational change. *American Psychologist*, 1970, *25*, 227–33.

Sellitz, C., Jahoda, M., Deutsch, M., & Cook, S. W. *Research methods in social relations* (rev. ed.). New York: Holt, Rinehart, and Winston, 1965, 236–38.

Selznick, P. *Leadership in administration*. Evanston, IL: Row, Peterson, 1957.

Shaw, M. E. A comparison of two types of leadership in various communication nets. *Journal of Abnormal and Social Psychology*, 1955, *50*, 127–34.

Shaw, M. E. *Group dynamics: The psychology of small group behavior* (2nd ed.). New York: McGraw-Hill, 1976.

Shepard, H. A. Rules of thumb for change agents. *OD Practitioner*, 1975, *7*, 1–5.

Sheridan, J. Profile analysis of leader behavior. Unpublished manuscript, Department of Organizational Behavior, The Pennsylvania State University, 1979.

Sheridan, J. E., & Vredenburgh, D. J. Usefulness of leadership behavior and social power variables in predicting job tension, performance, and turnover of nursing employees. *Journal of Applied Psychology*, 1978, *63*, 89–95.

Sherif, O. J., Harvey, B., White, J., Hood, W., & Sherif, C. *Intergroup conflict and cooperation*. Norman, OK: University of Oklahoma Institute of Intergroup Relations, 1961.

Sherwood, C. E., & Walker, W. S. Role differentiation in real groups: An extrapolation of a laboratory small-group research finding. *Sociology and Social Research*, *45*, 14–17.

Simon, A., & Boyer, E. (Eds.). *Mirrors for behavior, I and II*. Philadelphia: Classroom Interaction Newsletter, 1970.

Sims, H. P., Jr. The leader as a manager of reinforcement contingencies: An empirical example and a model. In J. G. Hunt and L. L. Larson (Eds.), *Leadership: The cutting edge*. Carbondale, IL: Southern Illinois University Press, 1977, 121–37.

Sims, H. P., Jr., & Szilagyi, A. D. Leader reward behavior and subordinate satisfaction and performance. *Organizational Behavior and Human Performance*, 1975, *14*, 426–38.

Skinner, B. F. *Science and human behavior*. New York: Macmillan, 1953.

Skinner, B. F. Behaviorism at fifty. *Science*, 1963, *140*, 951–58.

Skinner, B. F. *About behaviorism*. New York: Basic Books, 1976.

Slater, P. E. Contrasting Correlates of group size. *Sociometry*, 1958, *21*, 129–39.

Smith, E. R., & Miller, F. D. Limits on perception of cognitive processes: A reply to Nisbett and Wilson. *Psychological Review*, 1978, *85*, 355–62.

Smith, K. H. Changes in group structure through individual and group feedback. *Journal of Personality and Social Psychology*, 1972, *24*, 425–28.

Sorrentino, R. M. & Boutillier, R. G. The effect of quantity and quality of verbal interaction on ratings of leadership ability. *Journal of Experimental Social Psychology*, 1975, *1*, 403–11.

Stang, D. J. Effect of interaction rate on ratings of leadership and liking. *Journal of Personality and Social Psychology*, 1973, *27*, 405–8.

Steers, R. M., & Rhodes, S. R. Major influences on employee attendance: A process model. *Journal of Applied Psychology*, 1978, *63*, 391–407.

Stein, R. T. Identifying emergent leaders from verbal and non-verbal communications. *Journal of Personality and Social Psychology*, 1975, *32*, 125–35.

Stein, R. T. The exemplar hypothesis: High status group members as conformers. Unpublished manuscript, Department of Psychology, University of Illinois at Chicago Circle, 1978.

Stein, R. T., Childs, L. M., Cooley, S. H., & Fedota, S. Preferences for leadership candidates. Investigation in progress, Department of Psychology, University of Illinois at Chicago Circle, 1978.

Stein, R. T., & Heller, T. The relationship of emergent leadership status and high verbal participation in small groups: A review of the literature. Unpublished manuscript, Department of Psychology, University of Illinois at Chicago Circle, 1978.

Steiner, I. D. *Group process and productivity*. New York: Academic Press, 1972.

Steiner, I. D. *Task-performing groups*. Morristown, NJ: General Learning Press, 1974.

Stinson, J. E. The measurement of leadership. In J. G. Hunt and L. L. Larson (Eds.), *Leadership: The cutting edge*. Carbondale, IL: Southern Illinois University Press, 1977, 111–16.

Stogdill, R. M. Personal factors associated with leadership: A survey of the literature. *Journal of Psychology*, 1948, *25*, 37–71.

Stogdill, R. M. *Individual behavior and group achievement.* New York: Oxford University Press, 1959.

Stogdill, R. M. *Manual for the Leader Behavior Description Questionnaire—Form XII.* Columbus, OH: Bureau of Business Research, The Ohio State University, 1963. (a)

Stogdill, R. M. *Team achievement under high motivation.* Columbus, OH: Bureau of Business Research, The Ohio State University, 1963. (b)

Stogdill, R. M. *Managers, employees, organizations.* Columbus, OH: Bureau of Business Research, The Ohio State University, 1965.

Stogdill, R. M. Group productivity, drive and cohesiveness. *Organizational Behavior and Human Performance*, 1972, *8*, 26–43.

Stogdill, R. Comments. In E. A. Fleishman and J. G. Hunt (Eds.), *Current developments in the study of leadership.* Carbondale, IL: Southern Illinois University Press, 1973, 102–4.

Stogdill, R. M. *Handbook of leadership.* New York: Macmillan, Free Press, 1974.

Stogdill, R. M., & Coons, A. E. *Leader behavior: Its description and measurement.* Columbus, OH: Bureau of Business Research, The Ohio State University, 1957.

Stogdill, R. M., Goode, O. S., & Day, D. R. New leader behavior description subscales. *Journal of Psychology*, 1962, *54*, 259–69.

Storm, P. M. An organizational simulation of leader behavior, decision-making style and group strategy. Investigation in progress, Faculty of Management, State University of Groningen, Groningen, The Netherlands, 1978.

Student, K. R. Supervisory influence and work-group performance. *Journal of Applied Psychology*, 1968, *52*, 188–94.

Taylor, J. C. An empirical examination of a four-factor theory of leadership using smallest space analysis. *Organizational Behavior and Human Performance*, 1971, *6*, 249–66.

Taylor, J. C., & Bowers, D. G. *Survey of organizations: Toward a machine-scored, standardized questionnaire instrument.* Ann Arbor, MI: Institute for Social research, University of Michigan, 1972.

Thomas, E. J., & Fink, C. F. Effects of group size. *Psychological Bulletin*, 1963, *60*, 371–84.

Thompson, J. D. *Organizations in action.* New York: McGraw-Hill, 1967.

Thoresen, C. E., & Mahoney, M. J. *Behavioral self-control.* New York: Holt, Rinehart, and Winston, 1974.

Thorndike, E. L. *Educational psychology* (Vol. 1). New York: Teachers College, Columbia University, 1913.

Thorngate, W. Must we always think before we act? *Personality and Social Psychology Bulletin*, 1976, *2*, 31–35.

Torrance, E. P. Perception of group functioning as a predictor of group performance. *Journal of Social Psychology*, 1955, *42*, 271–81.

Trieb, S. E., & Marion, B. W. *Managerial leadership and the human capital of the firm.* Columbus, OH: College of Agriculture, The Ohio State University, 1969.

Trist, E. L., & Murray, H. Progressive adaptation of team work organization. *Bulletin de C.E.R.P.*, 1960, *9*, 153–64.

Tuckman, B. W. Developmental sequence in small groups. *Psychological Bulletin*, 1965, *63*, 384–99.

Van Zelst, R. H. Validation of a sociometric regrouping procedure. *Journal of Abnormal and Social Psychology*, 1952, *47*, 299–301.

Varela, J. A. *Psychological solutions to social problems.* New York: Academic Press, 1971.

Vicars, W. M., Bussom, R. S., & Larson, L. L. The nature of a police executive's work. Unpublished manuscript, Department of Administrative Sciences, Southern Illinois University at Carbondale, 1979.

Von Neumann, J. *The computer and the brain.* New Haven, CT: University Press, 1958.

Vroom, V. H. *Some personality determinants of the effects of participation.* Englewood Cliffs, NJ: Prentice-Hall, 1960.

Vroom, V. H., & Jago, A. G. Decision making as a social process: Normative and descriptive models of leader behavior. *Decision Sciences*, 1975, *5*, 743–69.

Vroom, V. H., & Jago, A. G. *On the validity of the Vroom-Yetton model.* Technical Report No. 9. New Haven, CT: Yale University, 1976.

Vroom, V. H., & Jago, A. G. On the validity of the Vroom-Yetton model. *Journal of Applied Psychology*, 1978, *63*, 151–62.

Vroom, V. H., & Yetton, P. W. *Leadership and decision-making.* Pittsburgh: University of Pittsburgh Press, 1973.

Warr, P. Aided experiments in social psychology. *Bulletin of British Psychological Society*, 1977, *30*, 2–8.

Warwick, C. E. Relationship of scholastic aspiration and group cohesiveness to the academic achievement of male freshmen at Cornell University, *Human Relations*, 1964, *17*, 155–68.

Warwick, D. P. *A theory of public bureaucracy.* Cambridge, MA: Harvard University Press, 1975.

Weber, M. *The theory of social and economic organization.* New York: Oxford, 1947.

Weick, K. E. Laboratory experiments with organizations. In J. G. March (Ed.), *Handbook of organizations.* Chicago: Rand McNally, 1965, 194–260.

Weick, K. E. Organizations in the laboratory. In V. Vroom (Ed.), *Methods of Organizational research.* Pittsburgh: University of Pittsburgh Press, 1967.

Weick, K. E. Systematic observational methods. In G. Lindzey and E. Aronson (Eds.), *The handbook of social psychology.* Reading, MA: Addison-Wesley, 1968, 357–451.

Weick, K. E. Social psychology in an era of social change. *American Psychologist.* 1969, *24*, 990–98. (a)

Weick, K. E. *The social psychology of organizing.* Reading, MA: Addison-Wesley, 1969. (b)

Weick, K. E. Enactment processes in organizations. In B. Staw and G. Salancik (Eds.), *New directions in organizational behavior.* Chicago: St. Clair, 1977, 267–300. (a)

Weick, K. E. Laboratory experimentation with organizations: A reappraisal. *Academy of Management Review.* 1977, *2*, 123–218. (b)

Weick, K. E. Spines of leaders. In M. W. McCall, Jr., and M. M. Lombardo (Eds.),

Leadership: Where else can we go? Durham, NC: Duke University Press, 1978, 37–61.

White, R. K., & Lippitt, R. *Autocracy and democracy.* New York: Harper, 1960.

Whitehead, T. N. *The industrial worker.* Cambridge, MA: Harvard University Press, 1938.

Willems, E., & Raush, H. *Naturalistic viewpoints in psychological research.* New York: Holt, Rinehart, and Winston, 1969.

Wonderlic, E. F. *Wonderlic personnel test.* Northfield, IL: Wonderlic, 1977.

Wyatt, S., Frost, L., & Stock, F. G. L. *Incentives in repetitive work.* Technical Report No. 39, Medical Research Council, Industrial Health Research Board. London: H. M. Stationery Office, 1934.

Yukl, G. A. Toward a behavioral theory of leadership. *Organizational Behavior and Human Performance.* 1971, *6*, 414–40.

Yukl, G. A. *Leadership and management.* Reading, MA: Addison-Wesley, 1979.

Yukl, G. A., Wexley, K. N., & Nemeroff, W. F. Evaluation of the equivalence of Leader Behavior Description Questionnaire and Institute for Social Research leadership dimensions by means of multitrait, multimethod analysis. *Catalog of Selected Documents in Psychology.* 1974, *4* (Summer), 94.

Yunker, G. W., & Hunt, J. G. An empirical comparison of the Michigan four-factor and Ohio state LBDQ leadership scales. *Organizational Behavior and Human Performance,* 1976, *17*, 45–65.

Zais, M., & Fiedler, F. E. Intelligence and experience—is more better?: The impact of intelligence and experience on the performance of Army line and staff officers. Unpublished manuscript, Department of psychology, University of Washington, 1978.

Zaleznik, A., Christensen, C. R., & Roethlisberger, F. J. *The motivation, productivity, and satisfaction of workers.* Boston: Graduate School of Business Administration, Harvard University, 1958.

Zander, A. Group aspirations. In D. Cartwright and A. Zander (Eds.), *Group dynamics: Research and theory* (3rd ed.). New York: Harper and Row, 1968.

Zander, A. *Motives and goals in groups.* New York: Academic Press, 1971.

Zander, A. *Groups at work.* San Francisco: Jossey-Bass, 1977.

Zander, A., & Armstrong, W. Working for group pride in a slipper factory. *Journal of Applied Social Psychology,* 1972, *2*, 193–207.

Zander, A., Forward, J., & Albert, R. Adaptation of board members to repeated success and failure by their organizations. *Organizational Behavior and Human Performance,* 1969, *4*, 56–76.

Zander, A., & Medow, H. Individual and group levels of aspiration. *Human Relations,* 1963, *16*, 89–105.

Zander, A., Medow, H., & Dustin, D. Social influences on group aspirations. In A. Zander and H. Medow (Eds.), *Group aspirations and group coping behavior.* Ann Arbor, MI: Institute for Social Research, University of Michigan, 1964.

Zander, A., & Newcomb, T., Jr. Group levels of aspiration in United Fund campaigns. *Journal of Personality and Social Psychology,* 1967, *6*, 157–62.

Zimbardo, P., & Ebbesen, E. G. *Influencing attitudes and changing behavior.* Reading, MA: Addison-Wesley, 1969.

Zimmer, R. J. Validating the Vroom and Yetton normative model of leader behavior in field sales force management and measuring the training effect of
Telos on leader behavior of district managers. Unpublished dissertation, Department of Business Administration, Virginia Polytechnic Institute and State
University, 1978.

Name Index

Subject Index

Eco-behaviorial science, 206
Emergent leadership: stages for, 104; reinforcement theories for, 127–28; idiosyn-
cracy credit theory in, 128; behavioral differences between leaders and nonleaders
in, 129–30; valence mode of, 130–32; as a
"Problem," 132; orientation stage in, 133–
34; conflict stage in, 134; patterns of,
135–38; acceptance of the leader in, 138;
methodology as tested in, 139–40; types of
acts in, 140; hypothesis of models in, 142–
44; preliminary results of problem-solving
in, 144–46; emphasis on, 252–53; mentioned, 240
"Espoused Theory," 4
Espoused theory data: Argyris responds to, 96
Ethology, 206
Evaluation, 3
Experience: leader, 9; measured by months
in service, 17; measures of, 19–20; and
stress, 21; real world, observations of,
29–32
Expertise, 231
External validity: question of, 68–69

Factor Analysis Studies: discussion of the,
176–79; mentioned, 169
"Fads, Fashion, and Folderol in Psychology,"
7
Favoritism: in conflicts, 237
Feedback loops: in Argyris's models, 95
Field research: areas of, 69–70
Field research approaches, 65
Field research trends: discussed, 74–75
Field studies: precision and clarity of man-
ipulations in, 70
Field validation, 66
Fiedler's Contingency Model: basic variables
of, 87; reviewed, 255; mentioned, 79
Follow-up Studies, 179
Formative Years in Business, 30

Goal clarification: of organizational leaders,
237–38
Goal Emphasis, 181
Goals: of organizations, 230
Goal setting, 166, 167, 174, 176, 183, 194
Group behavior: dimensions of, 108; in
Schriesheim et al. model, 152
Group cohesion: concept of, 149
Group cohesiveness: as subject of research
investigations, 111; review of, 115; effects
of, 115, 117
Group creativity: laboratory experiment on,
12–21
Group development: stages of, 112–13, 120,
133, 147

Group drive: defined by Stogdill, 110–11; re-
view of, 114–15; effects of, 115–17
Group goals: degree of conformity to, 154
Group leader: as a chosen one, 233
Group performance: studies on, 12; and
leader intelligence, 12; determinations of,
119–20
Group productivity: defined, 109–10; review
of, 114
"Groupthink": hypothesis, 151–52

House's path-goal model: reviewed, 255. *See
also* Path-goal approach; Path-goal theory
Human behavior: testing theory about, 68
Human information processing, 48

dividual development: comprehensive ap-
proach to, 26; image of the individual in,
234
Infantry squad leaders: study of, 14–16
Information processing: research on, 59–60
Initiating Structure: items in, 165; men-
tioned, 213
Integration: and coordination within organi-
zations, 228; and coordination, 236
Integrative model: diagram of, 121
Intelligence: leader, 9, 11, 12; utilization of,
17; and performance, 18–19; measures of,
19–20
Interaction: dyadic, 107–8; between leader
and subordinate, 202
Interaction facilitation: defined, 171; men-
tioned, 183, 194
Interaction process analysis, 227, 243
"Interfaces": description of, 26; existence of,
26
Inter-rater agreement: methods used to
compute, 194–95
Interrelationships: portrayal of, 154–55
Invention, 3
ISR Survey of Organizations, 169, 179

Kepner-Trego (K-T): TELOS program designed by, 39–45. *See also* TELOS program

Lab/Field: leadership study in area of, 6–8
Laboratory approaches, 65
Laboratory experimentation: assets in, 94;
mentioned, 66, 68
Laboratory research trends: discussed, 81
Laboratory studies: emphasis on, 256
Leader acceptance measures, 13
Leader behavior: history of research on,
75–78; as a dependent variable, 81–82; ef-
fect on subordinate behavior, 83; defined,
111–12; boundary conditions and limita-
tions in, 123; relationships with regard to,

Date Due

DEC 13 1983			